THE
AMERICAN
LOOK

THE
AMERICAN
LOOK

**FASHION, SPORTSWEAR AND THE
IMAGE OF WOMEN IN 1930s AND
1940s NEW YORK**

REBECCA ARNOLD

I.B. TAURIS

Published in 2009 by I.B.Tauris & Co Ltd
6 Salem Road, London W2 4BU
175 Fifth Avenue, New York NY 10010
www.ibtauris.com

In the United States of America and Canada distributed by Palgrave Macmillan, a division of St. Martin's Press,
175 Fifth Avenue, New York NY 10010

ISBN: 978 1 86064 763 5 (pb)
ISBN: 978 1 84511 896 9 (hb)

A full CIP record for this book is available from the British Library
A full CIP record is available from the Library of Congress

Library of Congress Catalog Card Number: available

Designed by: Syd Shelton Graphicsi.com

Printed and bound in the United States of America by Edwards Brothers, Inc.

IN MEMORY OF MY GRANDMOTHER, FLORENCE WHITING 1900–1977 AND DEDICATED WITH LOVE TO ADRIAN GARVEY

CONTENTS

ILLUSTRATIONS

ACKNOWLEDGEMENTS

As with any project of this length, many people have contributed to bringing this book to completion. I would like to thank Melvyn Stokes and Negley Harte my PhD supervisors in the History Department at University College, London, and my examiners, Tag Gronberg and Pat Kirkham, for their help and encouragement.

I have been very lucky to receive support from many friends and colleagues. At Central Saint Martins College of Art & Design, thanks to Jane Rapley, to Peter Close for removing obstacles, and for understanding the importance of history, to Alison Church, Annie Cooper, Karen Fletcher, Steve Hill, Mike Sossick, Renate Stauss and Marketa Uhlirova for their unflagging encouragement and kindness. Thanks also to all the Associate Lecturers who worked on B.A. (Hons) Fashion History and Theory, and especially to all the students between 2001 and 2006. Many thanks to Caroline Evans for her friendship and generosity, which extended to reading drafts, making sure I never lost focus and providing inspiration. I am grateful to the Arts and Humanities Research Committee for providing funding for the initial research, as part of the Fashion and Modernity project at Central Saint Martins, which led to my undertaking the original doctorate. My thanks to Jeremy Aynsley in the History of Design Department of the Royal College of Art. I am grateful for the enthusiasm of the staff of the Vogue Library in London, especially Janine Button, Simone Burnett, Brett Croft and last, but never least, Jooney Woodward. Thanks to the staff in the costume department at the Victoria and Albert Museum, particularly Susan North for her friendship and support, Suzanne Lussier, Sonnet Stanfill, and, at the Museum of Costume in Bath, Rosemary Harden and Elsie Barber.

In the United States the staff of the Costume Institute were exemplary in their professionalism and allowed me unrivalled access to their varied collections. For this my thanks to Harold Koda for his generosity and support, to Andrew Bolton for always looking after me when I visited New York, and to Jessa Krick, Beth Dincuff Charleston, Shannon Price–Bell, Elizabeth Bryan, Joyce Fung, Stephane Houy-Taylor, Jan Reeder, Lisa Faibish and, in the Irene Lewisohn Library Tatyana Pakhladzhyan and Rebecca Akan for whom nothing was too much trouble. Finally, Liz Larson, for being a great friend and for her incredible ability to find any reference. To Valerie Steele, Director of the Museum at the Fashion Institute of Technology, who supported this project from the start and helped me at every stage. Maria Connelli and Kim Hartswick for their hospitality. All the staff of the Museum at the Fashion Institute of Technology, especially Patricia Mears, Fred Dennis, Irving Solero and Clare Sauro and thanks to Joshua Waller, Maris Heller and John Corins in the Gladys Marcus Library. To the late Eleanor Lambert for talking to me about her career and for enabling me to catch a glimpse of the indomitable spirit of the women who shaped the New York fashion industry during the 1930s and 1940s. To Lenore Benson, of Fashion Group International, June Weir and Bernice Shafton, for sharing their memories of working in New York. To Ted Barber in the Anna-Maria and Stephen Kellen Archives Center for Parsons The New School for Design for introducing me to the work of Mildred Orrick. To the tutors and students I met on postgraduate courses at New York University, Parsons School of Design, the Fashion Institute of Technology and the Bard Graduate Center, especially Mary Donahue, who allowed me to read her doctoral thesis, and thanks to Nancy Diehl, Elizabeth Morano, and to Kohle Yohannan for his advice on researching Claire McCardell. To Phyllis Magidson in the costume department and Melanie Bowers in the photography department at the Museum of the City of New York. To the Smithsonian Institution for granting me a Pre-doctoral fellowship in 2004. Thanks to the staff of the Archives Center and the Library at the National Museum of American History, where I was based. To Michelle Delaney, Karen Harris, Suzanne McLaughlin, Dwayne Blocker Bowers, Carol Kregloh, Ellen Roney Hughes and Jane Rogers. To Priscilla Wood for her wisdom, expertise and friendship. I am indebted to Frank Goodyear at the National Portrait Gallery, and to Beverly Brannan for opening up the Toni Frissell Collection at the Library of Congress. To Randy Greenberg at the National Museum of Women in the Arts. To Kristina Haugland and Dilys Blum at the Museum of Art in Philadelphia, and to Heidi Campbell-Schoaf of the Frederick Historical Society's Collection in Maryland. For their help in gaining picture permissions, my thanks also to the Tate Gallery, the IOC, *The New York Times*, Best & Co Children's wear store, Brigitte Moral-Planté, Marjory L. Walker at the National Cotton Council, Rosamund Lehtinen at Michelin, Claire Fortune at Conde Nast, Alicia Colen at the Howard Greenberg Gallery and Elizabeth Shank at the Silverstein Gallery in New York. Thanks also to Neha Gandhi and Adam Bell at *Harper's Bazaar*, all material originally produced for *Harper's Bazaar* appears courtesy of the magazine.

My thanks to Stockholm University for granting me a Guest Professorship in the Centre for Fashion Studies in 2006/7, which allowed me the time to complete this project, and to the Erling-Persson Family Foundation for its support, and to Astrid Soderbergh-Widding and Louise Wallenberg for their encouragement of this project.

Philippa Brewster at I.B.Tauris for asking me what I most wanted to write about, a question that inspired this whole project and for her guidance when editing this book. I also owe a huge debt of gratitude to Ayesha Williams for taking on the task of gaining picture permissions for this book, and to Simon Lott for tying up the loose ends.

To my friends Marta Ajmar, Jamie Brassett, Christopher Breward, Victoria Kelley, Maya, Rani and the late Sanjaya Lall, Michael Newton, Roger Sabin and Rachel Worth, who were encouraging and always ready with sound advice. To my friends in New York, Amber Bennett, Andy Hoogenboom, Luise Stauss, and Yeohlee Teng, who made every trip enjoyable, and who understand why New York fashion matters. To Beatrice Behlen, for writing the best emails and making sure I maintained perspective. To Alison Toplis and Pamela Grimaud for sharing their wisdom and for reading the complete draft. Thanks to Simon Holland, Arlene Hui and the whole Hui family, for understanding the importance of taking breaks. To my family, especially Mutti, Dad, Jonathan and Simon, who were always there for me, and to Adrian Garvey, without whom this project would never have reached completion.

INTRODUCTION

In 1932, New York department store Lord & Taylor's Vice-President, Dorothy Shaver, initiated a series of window displays that focussed on specific New York designers' work. Each featured garments from the designer's current collection, with a photograph to promote the designer (see figures 1 and 4.2). Similar merchandising was then carried through the shop's interior and into the section that sold the clothes. Shaver used the term 'The American Designers' Movement' to describe what was to become an ongoing promotion of clothes by designers such as Clare Potter and Vera Maxwell, and positioned her campaign as part of a wider process to encourage awareness of American fashion design, independent of Paris' influence.

The windows encapsulated several developments in New York fashion at the time: they highlighted the growing importance of sportswear as an identifiably American form of dressing, appropriate to a wide range of women; they foregrounded individual designers (rather than manufacturers), both as the creators of the clothing and as an important promotional tool; and they crystallised the idea that American fashion related to a particular notion of easy-to-wear, modern clothing that stood apart from Paris' elite style. Sportswear, a category of casual but smart separates, dresses and coats, which encompassed resort, campus and career wear for young women, was ideal for the changes in economy brought about by the Depression, both in terms of what manufacturers wanted to produce and what consumers could afford to buy. Sportswear was identified by the wider fashion industry as America's most distinctive form of dress. It comprised three main sub-categories: active sportswear, to be worn, for example, to play tennis or golf; resort wear, which provided clothing to travel in and to wear for leisure and holidays; and town and country wear, most typically tweed suiting. As can be seen in figures 2 to 4, sportswear included clothing that was designed both for specific activities and for more general use. It was a form of dress that was to grow in significance during the eighteen-year period covered by this book. Under the impact of changes in the fashion industry, and in women's roles, because of the Depression and the Second World War, it shifted from being a specialised form of dress, to encompass clothing that was adaptable to a whole range of occasions and lifestyles. It was projected as a more egalitarian form of clothing, which addressed every woman, not just the elite, although the key market for much sportswear was white, middle-class women, including college girls, working women and housewives.

Jessica Daves noted how important the use of individual designers names was in shifting power towards them and away from manufacturers and retailers:

> This was recognition in public print of American fashion designers … this naming of names

1

1. Worsinger, Lord & Taylor interior display for Clare Potter 'American Designers' campaign, 1933. Museum of the City of New York, Print Archives

2. David Crystal advertisement, *Vogue*, 10 May 1930

3. Claire McCardell, cotton rayon butcher linen bra top and skirt from resort wear wardrobe, 1944. The Metropolitan Museum of Art, Gift of Claire McCardell, 1949. Photograph © 1998 The Metropolitan Museum of Art

4. Clare Potter, linen dress, 1937– 38. The Metropolitan Museum of Art, Gift of Janet Chatfield Taylor, 1962. Photograph © 1998 The Metropolitan Museum of Art

was opposed by stores for more than one reason. Anonymity as to the source was, merchants thought, good for business, except in the case of French copies. Anonymity made the store name more important, gave an impression of exclusivity, and permitted pricing to be an individual store decision. But in 1932 Dorothy Shaver … brushed these considerations aside and dropped her bombshell, with the idea of encouraging and improving the Depression-steeped industry: she advertised American designers by name boldly, importantly, proudly.[1]

Shaver's campaign marked an important moment in the status of America's homegrown fashion, as New York began to consolidate and promote its own designers and its own style. Lord & Taylor's window displays, created at the worst point of the Depression, exemplify the New York fashion industry's slowly evolving interest in exploiting its own strengths, rather than relying solely on Paris for fashion ideas and trends. Sportswear was to become central to this endeavour. Its design ethos and adaptable styles came to epitomise ideals both of American style and a particular strand of American femininity. This book will explore the ways that New York fashion sought to sell sportswear in terms of 'modern' ideals of femininity and how these related to wider notions of lifestyle, class, and Americanness. New York's role as a centre of fashion will be considered, as will sportswear's importance as a focus for ideas of Americanness. It will ask how and why sportswear was promoted as the definitive embodiment of American style within the realm of high fashion during the 1930s and 1940s, and how this related to shifts in the fashion industry as a result of the Depression and Second World War.

This book will, therefore, examine interconnecting themes in American women's visual identity, as seen in high fashion magazines such as *Vogue* and *Harper's Bazaar*, during key periods of flux: the Depression and the Second World War and the immediate aftermath of the war.[2] These magazines represent a key site in which ideas of high fashion were formulated, and therefore offer a crucial source of information on the way New York sportswear, a mass-produced, ready-to-wear form of clothing, was gradually integrated into the previously elite sphere of fashion. Since this book focuses on mid-range sportswear, targeted at middle-class women, *Vogue* and *Harper's Bazaar* will also provide important insights into the idealised view of appearance and etiquette that these magazines projected to their white, middle- and upper-middle class readers. While sportswear by Clare Potter, Carolyn Schnurer and their peers was aimed at middle-class women, it was mass-produced, and also inspired copies at cheaper price ranges. This meant that an ideal rooted in a perception of 'good' taste that was derived from the sportswear of the European leisured elite was made available, through editorial and advertising imagery, as well as through actual garments, to non-elite women. While the fashion media projected this as a positive example of America's democracy, it was equally symptomatic of a strong conformist strand within the nation's identity. As will be seen, there existed a long tradition of encouraging immigrants to adhere to an idea of Americanness that relied upon the white, middle-class attitude towards acceptability.

Since its inception, New York's clothing industry was promoted as the binary opposite of Parisian couture, and its appeal was predicated upon the idea of a rejection of couture's Old World artificiality and spectacle, in favour of America's New World democracy and practicality. Although, historically, sportswear was a form of clothing that developed in England, in the early twentieth century, French couturiers including Chanel, Jane Régny and Jean Patou adapted its reduced forms to modern clients' more active lifestyles. It was the United States, though, that really embraced and experimented with sportswear design and promotion. The Depression's onset meant that cheaper, ready-to-wear clothing took on a greater importance in America. It was more widely covered in fashion magazines and promoted more vigorously by department stores. Technological changes had made it easier to produce large quantities of clothing quickly and cheaply, but these new manufacturing methods required simple pattern pieces and a reduced number of pieces per garment. Sportswear designers such as Claire McCardell and Clare Potter were able to integrate this need for simplicity into their design ethos, to produce clothes that were stylish yet at the same time cheap to produce.

Mass-produced ready-to-wear was normally manufactured by type of garment, that is, there were those producers who specialised in coats or skirts or blouses. In retail terms, department stores were then merchandised in accordance with this, with sections devoted to different types of garment. In contrast, sportswear manufacturers tended to make-up a wider range of garments because the category itself embraced different types of garment and outfits for various activities. This difference extended into the retail environment since, by the mid-thirties, sportswear was often given its own section, sometimes a pre-semester college store, within the larger department store to promote whole wardrobes of casual wear together. This consolidated the way sportswear was presented within stores, as well as in window displays.

Sportswear advertising was also distinctive, since it frequently connected the garments being promoted not just to imagery of its youthful target market, but also to signifiers of national identity. In 1940 a *Christian Science Monitor* article on 'American clothes, designed by Americans for Americans', described American sportswear as 'the smartest, most practical and most beautiful designed anywhere in the world' and connected this to ideas of national identity:

> Sports clothes symbolize – to us – our declaration of fashion independence … The impetus which sent them [Americans] across the plains in covered wagons battling Indians and privations … will give virility and versatility to our fashion designing.[3]

This statement embodies several of the ideas that were already connected to America's fashion industry. These ideas were to become defining features in the way it was, and to an extent continues to be, written about. Advertisers, marketers and merchandisers had increasingly attached these ideas to American ready-to-wear since the 1930s, eager to sell Seventh Avenue-made clothes as the embodiment of patriotic ideals of national identity. As the United States went through a period of uncertainty, suffering the ongoing effects of the Depression and the Second World War, the fashion industry sought to 'sell' sportswear as an antidote to anxiety and chaos. Its simple lines and practical fabrics and styling, along with its reliance on familiar 'classic' garments, were projected as emblematic of the country's indomitable spirit and pragmatic and determined approach to life.

Sportswear was not the only type of clothing made by American designers and manufacturers. During the period covered by this book, there were also a number of successful American made-to-measure designers, such as Hattie Carnegie, Jo Copeland and Valentina. However, while sportswear was increasingly identified with Americanness, made-to-measure designers tended to work within a recognisably French-inspired idiom. The garments they created were more expensive, although some, such as Carnegie, also sold ready-made garments. They did not project public personae that were so closely allied with national identity, as was the case with sportswear designers. Although their work was sometimes included under the banner of the *American Look* discussed below, this had more to do with the fact that they lived and worked in New York than because their work expressed ideals of Americanness.

Other 'genres' of ready-to-wear included French-inspired 'copies' (including copies of couture sportswear), which were made up with varying degrees of accuracy to appeal to American taste, while maintaining the original couture garment's blueprint. Hollywood also inspired a specific genre of ready-to-wear, which was sometimes given its own boutique within a department store or sold in chain stores. Some designers who had already worked on film costumes, such as Adrian, created more expensive ready-to-wear ranges that drew upon the Hollywood connection for publicity. Both Adrian's designs, and original film costumes that the cheaper chain store clothes were derived from, may have been inspired in part by Parisian models. Film production and distribution ran to a completely different time-frame from fashion seasons and it would have been difficult for trends to synchronise, although inevitably there was some cross-over in influence, as, for example, the medieval references that were popular in high fashion and film in the late 1940s. Robert Gutafson has criticised the way that 'the supposed power and influence that Hollywood had on its audiences is often silently accepted in the study of the American cinema'.[4] His research confirmed what was widely acknowledged by fashion insiders at the time, who felt that while Hollywood, which aimed at the mass audience, might encourage and publicise particular fashions or body ideals, it did not, in general terms, set fashions.[5] Hollywood-marketed fashions, like much cheaper copies of French styles, were rarely shown in high fashion magazines.

The American market was so huge that it would have been unwise for designers to propose dramatic style changes that were unlikely to appeal to a mass audience. Even when American buyers went to Paris, they tended to purchase conservatively. As Elizabeth Hawes commented of the period when she was a sketcher in Paris before the 'Crash' of 1929: 'I was instructed to sketch Fords. A Ford is a dress which everyone buys'.[6] Buyers sought out variations on previous best-sellers and often ignored more daring designs, which suggested new directions and trends. Despite this, fashion promoters pushed the mystique of Parisian fashion and, intrinsic to this, the idea that consumers needed to refresh their wardrobes regularly in line with French dictates. Even though French fashion houses lost money because of copyists who stole their designs, America remained their most lucrative market, and, since manufacturers could generate sales through glamour-by-association with Paris, fashion remained the most convincing way to add attraction to mass-produced garments.

Sportswear, therefore, needed to be marketed to distinguish itself from French style and yet, at the same time, convince American women to buy. It was necessary for fashion promoters and merchandisers, to tap into sportswear's more 'fundamental values' to highlight its appeal, hence continued reference in advertising to its 'practicality' and 'durability'. American sportswear and therefore its designers were projected as everyday and approachable, in stark contrast to the image of couturiers, who were viewed as elite creators of works of art.

One problem for sportswear promoters was that they were more accustomed to using seductive notions of fashion and, in particular, Paris-born fashion to promote apparel and this ran counter to sportswear's, in many ways, anti-fashion ethos. The prevalence of fashion as a means to sell had increased during the Depression, as it seemed an effective way to add 'value' to consumer goods and encourage people to buy. Sportswear presented an awkward fit with promoters' and journalists' faith in fashion's power to sell. It might more accurately be described as clothes, since it does not really fulfill the criteria of the more traditional conception of fashion. For, while sportswear operated within the fashion system, styles evolved gradually, there were rarely any radical shifts from one season to the next and, until the early 1930s, designers were rarely individually named. Sound business sense mediated against drastic style changes. If something sold, it would be repeated in different colours and fabrics to maximise sales, as designer Margot Kops McKlintock advised in 1938: 'Good models revamped should remain best sellers for more than one season'.[7] However, sportswear collections were not completely unchanging, since, as noted above, fashionable components were incorporated into their design. Sportswear therefore, represented a balance between stasis and flux, fashion trends and seemingly unchanging 'classic' garments.

American sportswear was able to represent the attributes of an active lifestyle through its simple lines, and designers developed sets of basic garments that could form a capsule wardrobe for busy women who had to move easily from office, to party, to home, or who needed to be able to pack a small suitcase for a trip. The clothes appeared modern, as they solved women's need to look smart, attractive and streamlined in a number of different roles, often within the course of the same day. Interchangeable wardrobes developed by Claire McCardell and Vera Maxwell in the 1930s, have become a fashion staple; indeed Donna Karan built her success in the 1980s in part through her very similar 'Seven Easy Pieces' wardrobes, which were targeted at career women. However, in the middle of the twentieth century, they were new and innovative. This approach to design was encapsulated in the idea of the American Look in the 1930s and 1940s, a term which became an important rallying point for the promotion of New York sportswear and, which provides an interesting case study of the relationship between fashion design and promotion, and also wider ideas of cultural identity. The term American Look, although not in common use until Dorothy Shaver's 1945 promotional campaign, was distinctive by the end of the 1930s. The Look continued to be promoted as an American form, with production focussed in New York's Seventh Avenue. In the 1930s and 1940s its style was associated with career women, college girls and, increasingly, with busy housewives. What these women had in common was a need for relatively cheap clothes that were adaptable to active lifestyles. The kind of language that was attached to the Look in Shaver's promotions relates to women's changing role during the mid-century, and will be considered, alongside its alignment with other media of communication, for example newspapers and magazines, within each chronological chapter.

It was not just the clothes themselves that fashion promoters suggested could make women's lives easier. New York sportswear was distinguished visually from both Parisian and Hollywood-inspired styles. It was a deliberate refutation of studio-based fashion photography, which was coded to signify detachment from everyday life and to imply couture's, and thus the Paris elite's, rarefied style. Fashion photographers reinforced the idea that the American Look was more relaxed, through models' posture and environment. This included the use of natural light to provide the primary source of illumination, casual poses, and the 'snapshot' quality that blurred the boundaries between documentary and editorial photography. This representational style was crystallised in Martin Munkasci's work during the 1930s and will be described in this book as the *modern sportswear aesthetic*, one, indeed, that was recognisable enough by the mid-1930s to be appropriated to promote other products.

At the beginning of the twenty-first century, many of 1930s and 1940s sportswear's key features, such as simple, draped jersey separates and McCardell-inspired resort wear details, have been discernible in collections from major luxury brands such as Prada, as well as smaller high fashion labels including Mother of Pearl. New York designers such as Tommy Hilfiger, Donna Karan and Calvin Klein have used ideas of interchangeable separates, smart yet casual layers, and clear-cut colour combination throughout their careers. These elements have become ubiquitous, but were formulated in the middle of the twentieth century by Mildred Orrick, Claire McCardell, Vera Maxwell and others, whose ideas at that time were viewed as pioneering and innovative. For contemporary designers, these reference points provide an already easily understood set of meanings that attach to their brands and immediately place them as 'American', 'practical' and 'comfortable'. Thus, the ideas that gave character and appeal to earlier designers' work have been transferred through both stylistic detail within later New York designers' collections and the imagery that is generated to advertise and market each designers' brand. Since New York designers, then and now, aim to sell clothes that are at first glance simple and unremarkable, this imagery, and the text used with it, have become crucial to formulating an identity for a particular brand, and to encourage consumers to buy each season. Strategies that were developed by early fashion public relations pioneers such as Eleanor Lambert and by photographers such as Toni Frissell and Louise Dahl-Wolfe are still in operation today.

Frissell and Dahl-Wolfe reinforced the freshness of sportswear designers' work. They took models out of the studio, and removed the blank white backdrop that acts as a distancing device in fashion photographs.[8] The backdrop excludes context, and forces the viewer to inspect the clothes as separate entities, displaced from time and space and constructed as icons of fashion and style. A large proportion of American sportswear was placed within outdoor scenarios, whether urban or rural, which provided an invitation to the viewer (and potential consumer) to imagine the clothing within her own environment and experience. Although this environment evoked a fantasy ideal of American life whether the mythical West, the freedom of the open plain or the rustic 'simplicity' of farm-life, it was still closer to the average consumer than staged studio shots, and seemed more specifically to suggest possible purchase of these garments.

These scenarios are echoed in later American designers' promotional material. Donna Karan's advertising frequently uses New York streets as a backdrop, while Tommy Hilfiger has focused more on the American landscape to provide a sense of authenticity and accessibility to his brand. These settings help to direct the clothes at as wide a market as possible. The guilt attached to the purchase of designer labels is mediated by the implication that these clothes are a sensible choice, since they are portrayed as more durable and wearable, and they suggest inclusivity despite the exclusivity enforced by their cost. The relationship between business sense, design and dissemination of fashion information is crucial to understanding the dynamics of American fashion, and this book will combine discussion of shifts within the fashion industry during the middle of the twentieth century with analysis of the ways that merchandisers, department store directors, stylists and advertisers incorporated changes in technology, working practice and economics into their strategies to promote American fashion, and particularly sportswear, as a distinct force.

Discussions of American fashion have tended to focus on mid-century as a key period when New York sought to formulate a marketable identity for its apparel trades. There has been a slow but steady growth in writing about American sportswear over the last ten years. These texts provide important descriptions of primary resources that relate to sportswear, and suggest the importance of developing the analysis of this evidence further, situating it within its contemporary cultural and historical context.

This book will therefore build upon the work of previous authors in its use of surviving dress and archival material relating to key figures of the period. While it will cite the 1940s as a crucial period in the evolution of American style, it will analyse developments during the 1930s in more detail. This will show how promotional and design techniques evolved under the impact of the Depression, and were consolidated during the war. Assertions, such as those concerning the 'democracy' of the American Look, will be questioned and related to the complex ideals attached to New York sportswear. The importance of changes within the fashion industry and wider issues such as women's increasing professionalisation within fashion will also be considered. During the period under discussion, most sportswear designers were women, Tom Brigance being one of the few exceptions. Women were also important as department store executives, merchandisers, advertisers, buyers and stylists. As will be seen, this was partly because fashion had been seen historically as a 'women's' industry and offered women better prospects in terms of both promotions and wages. American style will be discussed in relation both to the contexts of the fashion industry and economic and social changes.

Images and surviving dress of the period are therefore viewed as vital pieces of primary evidence, rather than merely as illustrations. They will thus, like this study as a whole, map the ways that fashion simultaneously contributes to and takes from the contemporary discourses that comprise Americanness, as it is defined over the course of the book. Democracy was an important theme within this, especially since this was a period that saw the rise of fascism and communism in Europe, which challenged such an ideal. Other important themes are the dichotomy of urban and rural, city and countryside, which is intrinsic to American national identity. The seemingly conflicting impulses of individualism and conformity are equally significant, and these are explored in sportswear's design and representation. Fashion is also inherent to the discourse of gender and to American women's changing role over the period. Modernity is crucial to fashion's, and, in this case, sportswear's negotiation and aestheticisation of identity.

The idea of modernity is an important facet of the sportswear aesthetic and the identities it suggests. Peter Wagner asserted that 'modernity is about the increase of individualism and individuality'.[10] While this individualism may relate to people's experience of advertising and even of consuming sportswear and its related imagery, this is equally rooted in a conformist drive to fit into wider group identities. As Wagner states, this ambiguity is also at the heart of modernity and 'resides in the double imaginary signification of modernity as individual autonomy and its substantive or collective other'.[11] The experience of living in a modern metropolis is fragmentary and confused, with individuals at once alone and part of a crowd, sportswear responded to their ambiguous identity with designs that were simultaneously anonymous and protective, both from the elements and from women's fears of dressing inappropriately. Sportswear provided dress that was equally adaptable for the city, suburb and countryside and as active and leisurewear. Its modernity lay in a pragmatic design aesthetic that was formed by machine technology, shaped for mass-production and optimum wearability for a range of women from different social and cultural groups and of different body sizes. Sportswear seeks to incorporate modernity's ambiguity and paradox: it simultaneously appears to offer a resolution to contradiction, yet never fully succeeds, since it pulls between a number of apparent oppositions: elite and everyday, fashion and dress, leisured and active, city and country, old and new, avant-garde and conformist, authentic and artificial. Again, this irresolute resolution relates to modernity itself. This ambiguity and contradiction is intrinsic to the way sportswear is discussed within this study.

The methodologies of cultural history will be employed to examine the interrelationship between these broader thematic discourses and the specificity of New York's fashion industry. Since, as Miri Rubin noted, 'what… [cultural history] highlights and treats as fundamental to human interaction are the conditions of communication, the terms of representation, the interaction between structures of meaning – narratives, discourses – and the ways in which individuals and groups use them and thus express themselves'.[12] This approach will thus enable developments within sportswear's design and promotion to be examined in terms of the way the fashion industry created and disseminated cultural ideas and ideals relating to the body and the ways it could acceptably be adorned.

The book's timeframe reflects specific events in the fashion industry and the impact of major historical events on fashion's practices and its representation. It begins with the onset of the Depression in 1929, which had grave financial implications for manufacturers and retailers, as well as influencing the way fashion was acceptably represented and the kind of styles that were favoured. It ends in 1947, as the hardships of the war were being superseded by greater affluence, as exemplified by Christian Dior's Corolle line, the 'New Look' of autumn/winter 1947/48, which marked a shift back towards Paris couture as the fount of high fashion trends. 1947 is also important since the Costume Institute at the Metropolitan Museum in New York held an exhibition, 'The Woman of Fashion, Spring/Summer 1947', which purported to show the wardrobe of a fashionable American woman of the time. An examination of the clothing chosen and the accompanying catalogue will provide an illuminating final exploration of the nature and prevalence of sportswear within fashionable dress and ideals of femininity at the end of the 1940s.

Thus, an exploration of New York sportswear brings together an analysis of a number of important questions surrounding women's shifting status in American society in general and their growing professional involvement in fashion in particular. It requires an exploration of contradictory ideas of conformity and avant-garde identity; anonymity and notions of modern lifestyle; and seeks to question the role of sportswear in the cultural construction of gender, national and class identities. This book aims to achieve greater understanding of sportswear's place within fashion and design history, and its significance within mid-century American culture.

1   *Jessica Daves, Ready-Made Miracle: The Story of American Fashion for the Millions* (New York: G.P.Putnam's Sons, 1967), 53.

2   All magazines referred to are American editions unless otherwise stated.

3   Barbara E. Scott Fisher, 'American Styles Attain New Prestige', *The Christian Science Monitor*, 14 March 1940, F1.

4   Robert Gustafson, 'The Power of the Screen: The Influence of Edith Head's Film Designs on the Retail Fashion Market', in *The Velvet Light Trap*, no. 19 (1982), 8.

5   See, for example, *Vogue* editor Margaret Case's essay, 'Where do Fashions Come from and How do They Grow?' in Margaretta Stevenson, ed., *How the Fashion World Works: Fit Yourself for a Fashion Future, Addresses given at The Fashion Group's Training Courses by Fashion and Merchandising Experts* (New York and London: Harper and Brothers, 1938), 8.

6   Elizabeth Hawes, *Fashion is Spinach* (New York: Random House, 1938), 59. Sketchers were employed by New York department stores and manufacturers to sketch garments at the Parisian couture shows each season. These sketches could then be made up into models in America, without the need for the American manufacturer to purchase the original from the couturier. Hawes notes that a good sketcher could take down 15 sketches per show. In 1929 she worked for manufacturers Weinstock and Co., who paid her $450 for 300 sketches. She could then sell on the sketches to buyers who did not employ their own sketchers and make $500–$1000 every 4 months. She notes that it was possible at that time to live very well on $100 per month. Couturiers attempted to clamp down on this practice, but it was difficult to police who was allowed into the shows and into the salon to view models.

7   Margot Kops McKlintock, 'Designing in the Wholesale Field', in Stevenson, *How the Fashion World Works*, 13.

8   Jean Moral and Martin Munkacsi had pioneered this approach in their work for *Harper's Bazaar* in 1932 and 1933, which saw the model walking through city streets in Moral's case or running along a beach, dressed in simple sportswear in Munkacsi's, see figure 1.5.

9   See articles such as, Juliana Albrecht, Jane Farrell-Beck and Patricia Campbell Warner, 'Clothing as Barrier: American Women in the Olympics, 1900–1920', in *Dress*, vol. 24 (1997): 55–69 and Sandra Stansbery Buckland and Gwendolyn S. O'Neal, ' "We Publish Fashions Because They are News": The New York Times 1940 through 1945', in *Dress*, vol. 25 (1998): 33–41, and books and exhibition catalogues including: Richard Martin, *American Ingenuity: Sportswear 1930s–1970s* (New York: Metropolitan Museum of Art, 1998), Kohle Yohannan and Nancy Nolf, *Claire McCardell: Redefining Modernism* (New York: Harry N. Abrams, 1998) and Linda Welters and Patricia A. Cunningham, eds., *Twentieth-Century American Fashion* (Oxford and New York: Berg, 2005).

10 Peter Wagner, *A Sociology of Modernity: Liberty and Discipline* (London: Routledge, 1994), 6.

11 Wagner, *Sociology of Modernity*, 15.

12 Miri Rubin, 'What is Cultural History Now?' in David Cannadine, ed., *What is History Now?* (London: Palgrave Macmillan, 2002), 81.

CHAPTER ONE
NEW YORK AND THE EVOLUTION OF SPORTSWEAR 1929–39

NEW YORK CITY

The model strides confidently across the rain-soaked street. New York's skyscrapers and the urban landscape of cars and traffic lights provide a dramatic architectural backdrop to her approaching figure (figure 1.1). Dressed in a wide-collared raincoat to protect her from the elements, she is depicted as self-possessed and in control. The diagonal lines on her coat add to the sense of dynamism, and its over-sized metal buttons reflect the light and draw the eye upwards towards her face, which is framed by a jauntily tilted hat. Her gloves, galoshes and umbrella complete her outfit. Martin Munkacsi's photograph for the November 1934 edition of *Harper's Bazaar,* combined city and fashion in a unified image of soft greys that mirror the blurred tones of the rainy skies. The model seems at one with the city she inhabits, the epitome of the fashionable ideal of a New York woman in the 1930s, active, chic and modern. Her clothes follow the current fashionable lines, but do not inhibit her movement. Their graphic prints reference the symmetry of the windows that punctuate the buildings around her, adding a feeling of rhythm and drive to her body and the landscape behind her. The photograph is typical of many from fashion magazines of this period. New York City had become the key context in which New York sportswear fashions were shot. The meanings of each became entwined as clothing and architecture were projected as archetypes of national identity.

This chapter will examine New York City as an actual and a symbolic city. It was home to the fashion design and manufacturing industries, the fashion media, and the Fashion Group, which represented the industry's interests. It will begin by tracing the connections between fashion and the city of New York both in real and symbolic terms, it will then look at sportswear, the genre of dress that was designed and made in the city, and which, between 1929 and 1947, came to represent New York style. It will conclude with a discussion of the way that the city's fashion media disseminated information about sportswear, in particular how they visualised it through the formulation of a modern sportswear aesthetic. The chapter will therefore explore the gradual shift from active sportswear, designed for specific sports such as golf or tennis, towards a more general use of the term sportswear to encompass various types of smart casual clothing. This change occurred over the course of the 1930s, as active sportswear, resort wear and town and country wear all contributed to the formulation of a distinct kind of dress that was increasingly marketed as inherently American. Sportswear related to various ideas of national identity, including myths of rural America, and concepts of city and modernity, specifically in relation to New York. These were depicted within fashion imagery as intrinsic to Americanness

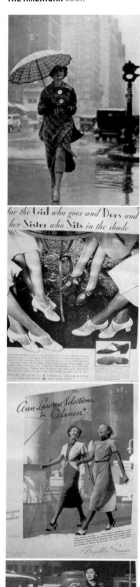

1.1. Martin Munkacsi, U.S. Rubber, John Wanamaker, *Harper's Bazaar*, November 1934.
      Photograph © JoanMunkacsi. Courtesy Howard Greenberg Gallery, NYC

1.2. United States Rubber Company advertisement, *Vogue*, May 1 1933. Courtesy of Michelin

1.3. Franklin Simon advertisement, *Vogue*, 15 December 1936

1.4. Mrs Franklin advertisement, *Vogue*, 15 March 1932

in the interwar period. They will be analysed with respect not just to the creation of clothing, but also to the way it was marketed and represented within high fashion magazines.

By the end of the 1930s, New York City and sportswear became increasingly interlinked, under the influence of wider forces of change, including the Depression and the rising number of women in the workplace. This economic and social environment accelerated concomitant shifts within the fashion industry, which was keen to promote home-grown designers and types of dress. As idea and reality, pictures like those in *Vogue*, and their equivalent within documentary photography, had shaped an 'urban identity' which William R. Taylor describes as central to an understanding of New York. He cites modernist photography, by Stieglitz and his contemporaries, as intrinsic to the evolution of this city identity between 1910 and 1930:

> It was the product of a process in which art came to the aid of sensibility, a process that began with the adumbration of visual images to represent how it felt to live in such utterly new surroundings – surroundings that the city-dweller found a kind of house of mirrors, in which perceptions and self-perceptions were crazily confounded, in which one could both see and see oneself from strange new angles. But it … [soon] became clear that more than visualization was involved in these new perceptions. The objects portrayed in the new photography – like the skyline view of the city – soon began to take on aesthetic values of their own. What began as orientation to a new setting ended as romance, although the line between documentary representation and flattering portrayal remained thin and elusive. In a matter of decades the city underwent a process of aesthetic transformation – from aesthetic *terra incognita* to the 'stylish' city of urban mythology.[1]

While documentary photographs tended to focus on the dynamism of New York architecture, frequently shown without any passers-by to clutter up its modernist lines, fashion imagery re-peopled the city. As described above, New York provided a means with which to contextualise clothing and to add the concept of the city to changing ideals of femininity and also, importantly, to add meaning to the simple designs of sportswear.

Michel de Certeau at the start of his essay, 'Walking in the City', described the experience of viewing the city from above, in his case from the World Trade Centre. At that height, he argues, it is the 'concept of the city' that supersedes the 'urban fact'.[2] This 'concept city' imbues the space with meaning and makes it 'believable' to the spectator: 'This is the way the concept city functions; a place of transformations and appropriations, the object of various kinds of interference but also a subject that is constantly enriched by new attributes, it is simultaneously the machinery and the hero of modernity'.[3]

As James Donald has noted, for Certeau the city panorama 'is the fantasy that has motivated planners and reformers in their desire to make the city an object of knowledge and so a governable space. They dream of encompassing the diversity, randomness and dynamism of urban life in a rational blueprint, a neat collection of statistics, and a clear set of social norms. Theirs is an idealised perspective, which aspires to render the city transparent'.[4] The town planners yearned for a rational city – 'a purified, hygienic space', which would make the 'labyrinthine reality' of the streets not just knowable, but would cleanse them of city grime.[5] This utopian vision corresponds with that of contemporary sportswear designers, such as Vera Maxwell and Clare Potter. They too sought to design clothing that was *of the city* in that it enabled its women to rise above the confusion of roles and spaces that they inhabited as they moved around New York's urban environment. While sportswear originated as a form of clothing for active sports, it soon evolved to encompass resort wear, town and country, and travel clothes, all of which enabled ease of movement. This can be seen literally, as women strode through both city and suburban town, and metaphorically, since their figures were rationalised in simple garments that erased difference and allowed women to negotiate a range of work and leisure spaces, while retaining the socially-required level of 'appropriateness'.

The aesthetic conceptualisation of New York made the city containable and knowable, at least when seen from the panoramic view at the top of a skyscraper. Its layout was clear from there and comprehensible, in a way that was impossible for those who walked the streets below, hemmed in by tall buildings and unable to see anything but the crowd that surrounded them. Although sportswear was conceived for 'non-city' spaces and denoted modes of being and lifestyles that were anti-urban, in New York it was increasingly used during periods of social and economic flux in response to women's more fluid and ambiguous role. It presented an apparent means with which confidently to negotiate Certeau's 'non-sites', through a system of dressing that was anonymous and ambiguous enough to slip between places and mediate the web of identities that the city-dweller had to adopt. Sportswear mimicked this sense of lack of place or identity, with its own placelessness, unlike earlier modes of dress. It was increasingly without a specific time of day or particular purpose.

As with the city itself, the sportswear wardrobe was an attempt to plan a logical resolution and to rationalise space and the body within an urban environment. Although sportswear began as a reflection of elite, leisured lifestyles, in the interwar period it increasingly came to represent the dynamism and flux of modernity and the city. It became emblematic of a modern lifestyle. Sportswear was simultaneously everyday and of the crowd, since it was mass-produced and inexpensive. Yet it also offered a utopian 'view from above', a category of clothing that rose above fast-moving fashion trends, complex decoration and cut, to create a façade of calm and control, and thus an urban identity that was rational and manageable. It seemed that sportswear could circumvent fashion's confusion of styles and codes.

Sportswear seemed to offer a lifestyle vision that celebrated the everyday – an everyday that was constantly changing as women moved from home to work to leisure. Although it produced an often contradictory response to the problems involved in constructing an urban identity, it suggested that these garments could paper over the contradictions of modern femininity that had to incorporate issues of class, gender, sexuality and ethnicity in order to allow women to function effectively as workers, wives, mothers and socialites. This vision was shaped by fashion images, which, as will be discussed, relied upon the discourses of the modern, present in the documentary photography that Taylor cited as central to the construction of the 'idea' of New York. City and sportswear were each conceptualised and promoted to interconnect with the burgeoning 'urban identity' that incorporated architecture, fashion and technology in relation to ideals of modernity and Americanness.

Indeed, the interrelationship between woman, technology and street life within the city was celebrated in fashion magazines as quintessential to New York's identity. On 1 January 1935, *Vogue* ran an article entitled 'The Aura of New York' by Princess Marthe Bibesco, who described her first impressions of the city in relation to an idea of femininity she saw as uniquely American:

> The air of New York lashes women, making them walk erect. The giant towers force them to lift their heads. The city emanates pride. It has produced a race of haughty creatures with high-held necks, small faces and slender and elongated legs. There is a way of walking here, a way of dressing and of being American which can be compared to nothing else.[6]

This positions New York as the progenitor of a particular sense of urban identity, demonstrated by a way of moving through the streets, and taking possession of surrounding space. It also suggests that New York has altered women's genetic make-up, shaped their faces and figures, rationalised the diversity of the immigrant population into a uniform race of tall, slender figures, in response to the forceful thrust of the architecture and the wind that blew through the cavernous streets. Bibesco was not alone in this view of American women as possessors of a particular body form that followed contemporary ideals of youth, athleticism and drive. In 1930, *Harper's Bazaar* quoted Daisy Fellowes' opinion that 'America has influenced Paris clothes enormously … Since the War I think all clothes have been designed for the American woman … you are so youthful that all the world wants to ape you'.[7] Whether she meant that the clothes were literally designed for Americans, since they formed so crucial a section of couture's clientele, or metaphorically, as this vision of American women as the embodiment of modern femininity was so common, is unclear. However, women, city and style were seen as combining to create an image perceived as particular to America, as epitomised by New York, which was developing a distinct identity for itself and its inhabitants in the inter-war period.

New York was 'both the epitome of America and utterly alien to it'.[8] It represented the forces of modernity in its dynamic architecture and busy streets, which seemed to embody an optimistic drive towards the future. However, it could also seem intimidating for those who lived outside the metropolis. While first documentary, and then fashion and fashion photography, formulated an idea of New York as emblem for America as a whole, the shift away from the countryside and towards city living created a widespread feeling of unease. The growth in city life and the common experience of mass culture caused anxieties, compounded by a loss of confidence after the First World War and concerns about, for example, changing lifestyles and belief systems.

New York was itself a cipher for fears of alien forces, yet transcended them, at least in part, through its embodiment of consumerism and pleasure, and fashion was an important element within these discourses. It provided a range of tempting products and enabled people to construct new identities that readied them for the new modern lifestyle of work and leisure. Taylor describes New York's celebration of the 'emerging commercial culture', and positions it as a 'city designed as a showcase, at once a stimulus and a gratification to the mass of consumers, whose identity was being redefined by a new concept: "the public"'.[9] The evolution of this mass identity predicated on consumption was, in Taylor's view, enmeshed in the idea of New York, which he describes as:

> A vast and efficient emporium for the handling of goods … Efficiency and visual seduction were the watchwords of the new order, which required the creation of countless service vocations – sales clerks, floorwalkers, buyers, copywriters, window display artists, doormen, busboys, bellhops, typewriters.[10]

Many of these occupations were closely linked to the fashion industry, and sportswear was to provide the clothing for many of the women who worked in the city. Inherent in its success was the 'efficiency and visual seduction' that Taylor relates to New York's image. These qualities were conveyed in the seamless presentation of clothing in department store windows and interior displays, in the skilled charm of its salespeople and in the promotional strategies behind editorial photographs and advertisements that smoothly combined city and sportswear. These suggested a city of growth and progress, rather than one gripped by the Depression.

Advertisements for example, for Mrs Franklin's Inc luxury knitted sportswear emphasised ease and versatility, qualities that Princess Bibesco associated with the city itself, where 'everything is smooth, easy, distinguished, perfectly adjusted'.[11] This seamless comfort was part of the machinery of the modern city: along with the service people listed above, it facilitated consumption of products and leisure and conveyed an air of trouble-free modern ease that militated against the chaos of traffic and crowds out on the streets.

Princess Bibesco would undoubtedly have experienced only certain, uptown zones of the city. She notes that men were downtown at work during the day, while women inhabit the more luxurious, leisured, uptown areas.[12] Indeed, Sophie Watson has asserted that 'urban development and planning have tended to reflect, and also reinforce, traditional assumptions about gender', not just through the separation of residential, work and shopping areas but through, for example, public transport, which was not always viewed as safe or convenient for women and children.[13] William R. Taylor also relates the city's zones to town planning and the coincidental fruition of a number of projects at once:

> The full spatial order of modern New York had emerged by the end of the 1920s, partly as a result of three dramatic and almost simultaneous changes in the city: the rapid development of luxury apartment housing on Park Avenue after the Grand Central rail tracks were placed underground; the equally rapid construction of office buildings in midtown, set off by the construction of Rockefeller Center; and the flowering of Broadway as a middle class theatrical mecca … The new connotation of Park Avenue as the home of the "socialite" (to use a 1920s neologism), was understood by everyone by the end of the decade.[14]

Vogue's 27 April–1929 edition underlined the importance of understanding the layout of the city. Its first editorial page contained a graphic representation of the area of the city that upmarket shoppers used. A neatly dressed woman was drawn atop the *Vogue* building on Lexington Avenue. She faced away from the viewer, towards the main site of New York consumerism: the stretches of Park, Madison and Fifth Avenues between 35th Street and Central Park. All the major stores are marked on the map and the editor, Edna Woolman Chase, writes that 'Mr Whalen in his traffic tower introduced, almost overnight, a whole new series of traffic laws that have changed the face of New York's streets. New Zones have been laid out, streets opened up, right and left turns regulated, and congestion relieved'.[15] These developments, combined with *Vogue*'s guide to New York shopping, enable the reader to take a 'straight and simple' route, so that 'even a stranger can not lose the way!'[16] It would therefore be possible for them to avoid the 'wrong' areas and focus their attention on the convenience and luxury of uptown shopping streets.

Vogue aimed to school its constituency in the city's 'correct' areas, not just the well-known stores, such as Bonwit Teller and Saks, but the smaller ones that would make readers feel like insiders, *au courant* with both fashions and districts acceptable to their aspirations. In March 1929, an article was published called, 'Little Shops Above the Fifties', which stated that 'to the woman who knows New York, the little shops on Madison Avenue and the side streets are a constant joy. Shopping in them is almost like shopping in Paris itself'.[17] Europe, specifically Paris, is cited as the centre of fashion, yet it is notable that New York can even incorporate the French capital's style within its own diversity. American clothing had been given more prominent coverage in *Vogue* and *Harper's Bazaar* since the late 1920s. This trend gained momentum in the 1930s under the impact of the Depression, and enabled New York fashion to assert its own visual identity.

New York's zones of course were not just defined by purpose and activity, but also by class and gender. Middle and upper-class white women inhabited a different city to those of other ethnicities or social and economic groups. This division was expressed on the pages of *Vogue*, where socialites were shown in fashion editorial shoots: at the races and other such events, and even in staged 'snapshots'. These showed society women relaxing in sportswear in the city and countryside.

The selective map of New York that *Vogue* promoted was articulated by Lois Gould, daughter of New York designer Jo Copeland, who recalled that:

> My mother's city had strict geographical rules. Park Avenue was where people lived; it ran up the East Coast like a starched French ribbon. Fifth Avenue was where you shopped or

had lunch at the Plaza. Central Park was a transverse that you tunneled across to where you had to go 'downtown' i.e. work. That she went every day to Seventh Avenue was scarcely acknowledged. She went to Number 498, 'the place', in a taxi, without looking out the window. For all practical purposes the city's northern frontier was 90th Street, unless one was on a train for some reason.[18]

Jo Copeland's regular journey 'downtown' to Seventh Avenue represented a geographical shift for middle-class women employed in the fashion design and manufacturing industry. Seventh Avenue had been the focus for the garment industry since the nineteenth century and the construction of new, fireproofed buildings designed to combine factory and showroom space in the 1920s consolidated the area's importance. Rents increased in the upper stretches of the Avenue and the mass production houses were usually focussed on Broadway.[19]

As Jessica Daves, *Vogue's* Editor-in-Chief from 1952– 62, pointed out: 'This new, bold concept of a group of buildings to house all the women's-garment manufacturers was entirely successful from 1925–30. Then came the Depression, dotted by Seventh Avenue bankruptcies from 1930 to 1941. But the Garment Center Capital survived and today [she was writing in 1967] houses the most important group of ready-to-wear manufacturers in the world'.[20] Daves goes on to stress the commercial imperatives which the developer had considered within the design of the twenties buildings: 'Helmsley-Spear … have developed the idea of limiting the occupancy of each building, especially in the case of inexpensive dresses, to certain price ranges, on the theory that the buyers of these dresses might do all their purchasing in the same building, without, as the real estate man said "crossing the street"'.[21] Each zone of the city was designed for the convenience and ease of its users, and thus promoted commercial transactions, whether wholesale, or further uptown, retail.

In 1938, New York's importance to fashion in America was stressed by Edna Slocum, a journalist at the influential trade paper, *Women's Wear Daily*, when she wrote about the eagerness of America's department stores and buyers for news of what was happening in the city's stores: 'they want to know about the fashion shows of New York stores, what fashions are chosen, how great the attendance, and what the response'.[22] New York's influence was reinforced by *Kansas City Star* fashion editor, Nell Snead, who advised other editors to 'go to Paris if you can, but by all means know the New York markets, for here clothes are made and distributed throughout the country'.[23]

In the late nineteenth century, New York had established its dominance in the manufacture of women's ready-to-wear. Although its share of the market dropped from 65 per cent of the womenswear market in 1904 to 57.3 per cent in 1925, it maintained its position as the fashion leader.[24] Garments that were easiest to mass-produce were shifted to the outlying boroughs of Brooklyn and Queens, but as Nancy L. Green states, 'the highest priced dress lines remained closest to the fashion core, but in 1945 only twenty-eight per cent of the cheapest dresses were still made in Manhattan'.[25]

While fashion garments were undoubtedly an important part of the industry's success, sportswear names such as Claire McCardell, Clare Potter and Tom Brigance also remained in Manhattan, along with cheaper lines such as Gotham Sportswear. As the 1930s wore on, sportswear became increasingly significant in both New York's, and by extension America's, search for a recognisable fashion identity that assimilated the period's social, economic and cultural shifts. Sportswear underwent a process akin to the one that New York had undergone earlier in the twentieth century, as 'real' and 'concept', clothing and image, were imbued with meanings to construct an appropriate 'urban identity' for modern women.

SPORTSWEAR

In *Harper's Bazaar's* April–1926 edition, Marjorie Howard commented that 'My strongest impression of New York dressing on my recent visit was that sports clothes have not yet taken as important a place in the town lives of well-dressed Americans as in those of their Parisian prototypes. I saw clothes collections in New York, designed for what is called a fashionable clientele, in which the sports type as made famous by Chanel, for example, was conspicuous by its absence'.[26] This was in contrast to Paris collections by Patou and sports clothes specialist Jane Régny. Sportswear (and to an extent menswear) had been adapted for women in the workplace at the end of the nineteenth century, when office workers adopted the shirtwaister. This type of dress, evolved from men's shirts, was a popular style for women in white-collar jobs. In the twentieth century, firms such as B. H. Wragge adapted the shirtwaister to current fashions, as did numerous sportswear designers in the 1930s and 1940s, including Tina Leser and Claire McCardell. Its simple form, basically a long shirt, sometimes cut to fit more closely to the body, was often in its twentieth century incarnations, belted to emphasise the waist. However, it was to take the impact of the Depression, and later the absence of Parisian influence from 1940, to consolidate sportswear's position as a multi-purpose form of dressing in New York. While sportswear was a popular clothing category already, it needed to be clearly associated with a wider range of activities and significantly, to be associated with the discourses of fashion and the modern, as it already was in Paris, to raise its status and crystallise its centrality to New York fashion and ideas of Americanness. This was apparent in advertisements from the late 1920s onwards, which strove to promote the idea that sportswear was not just appropriate for activities such as tennis, golf and fishing, but could easily be adapted to daywear.

This is made clear in figure 1.2, which shows a 1933 advertisement for shoes manufactured by the United States Rubber Company. From the headline 'For the Girl who Goes and Does and her Sister who Sits in the Shade', to the image, which shows four women's feet under a garden table, it is clear that they are intended to be worn for both 'passive' and 'active' pursuits. The shoes follow fashionable styles and, just as sports clothes were often promoted for their washable fabrics, the ease with which they can be cleaned is stressed as a selling point. The last line of the caption is also telling: 'Utterly modern, even in price'.[27] Cost was imperative in the early thirties to encourage consumers to judge their purchases valid at a time of economic crisis. The copywriter's use of the word 'modern' linked the product to desirable discourses of dynamism and currency, which were to become as crucial to sportswear's appeal as they already were to the idea of New York.

Sportswear was mass-produced (apart from the more exclusive ranges, such as Mrs Franklin Inc.), and aimed at different types of women, from college girls and office workers to housewives. For all these women, it offered the veneer of fashionable modern lifestyles, with its references to athleticism and activity. As leisure and work became a part of the wider range of women's lives, sportswear gradually became an appropriate form of dressing to reconcile varied activities. However, there were problems for fashion writers and advertisers in categorising such clothes. In *Vogue*'s 1 February 1932 issue, a fashion spread entitled: 'Paris takes to jersey for town and sports', the caption began: 'For sports and for that wide range of activities known as semi-sports, including everything from playing jacks to shopping'.[28] Terms such as 'passive sportswear', 'semi-sports' and, 'spectator sports' were used to try to address sportswear's ambiguous role.[29] These terms expressed wider tensions about women and sport, and the need to preserve elements of traditional 'passive' gender ideals of femininity even within clothing that simultaneously suggested activity and modernity. This was expressed in an Abercrombie and Fitch advertisement from spring 1929, which suggested that women can appear less threatening to men if they wear sportswear. Under the headline 'When a Woman can Wear Sport Clothes', the caption read: 'the masculine mind may and does admire the loveliness of a girl in eveningwear, but clothe the same girl properly in sports attire and see the different attitude of the worshipful man. To him she now seems to be a more friendly companionable creature, a more permanent part of his daily life and thoughts'.[30]

The advertisement implies that the 'everyday' nature of sportswear will insinuate its wearer into a man's everyday life in a way that eveningwear's glamour could not. Sports clothes' lack of overt sexuality, despite their close relationship to the body, and their connotations of practicality over glamour are used by Abercrombie and Fitch as selling points, which separate the sensible sports clothes wearer from the frivolity and artifice of fashion. However, the wearer's need for taste and discernment is stressed: 'There is a greater art in the wearing of sports clothes than in the wearing of silks, chiffons and velvet-and-lace. The art begins in choosing the right materials, in having them made by tailors who know sports clothes and sold to you by someone who has sports clothes instinct and understanding. In other words, everything the A & F label assures'.[31] Thus, brand and wearer are perceived through ideals of quality, subtlety and cut.

Another means of associating sports clothes with other pursuits came in the guise of resort and travel wear, a category that followed the seasons of wealthy, leisured women, who holidayed in resorts such as Palm Beach each year. Its styles incorporated influences from the Riviera where, as a 1938 guide to fashion sources stated: 'sun clothes, yachting clothes, and beach wear of beauty [originated] … it is frequented by American designers and store stylists who wish to copy these resort fashions'.[32] Other sources included Paris, for high fashion; London, especially for tweeds and sportswear; Swiss and Austrian Alpine resorts for winter resort wear; and Hollywood and California, viewed by the article's author as gradually gaining significance for sun wear.[33]

These clothes responded to improvements in air travel and luxury cruises to produce fashions for women to wear while they travelled and once they arrived. As with city clothes, the ambiguous nature of sportswear was ideal for the transitory spaces of airports and cruise ships. 1930s advertisements often showed models contrasted with the machinery of travel. However, the Depression meant that people travelled less. Despite this, models posed next to cars, in front of aeroplanes and onboard ship, since travel represented a potent symbol of modernity, progress and freedom. figure 1.3 shows an example from 1936 of two models striding across the deck of a cruise liner. They laugh happily, swinging their arms as they walk. They appear dynamic and in control, clad in simple, smart 'resort dresses … slim, figure molding, artful. Conjuring up visions of sun-drenched decks and southern skies'.[34] Their clothes enable them to dress respectably and stylishly without wearing high fashion garments that would ally them with a more decorative notion of femininity. Sportswear's relationship to active sport also suggested the type of holidays its wearers favoured, where pursuits such as swimming and sailing were as important as sunbathing to achieve fashionable tanned, sleek bodies.

Louise Dahl-Wolfe's photograph for *Harper's Bazaar* in February 1938 underscored the association of resort wear with relaxation as well as activity. A model shields her eyes from the sun, her red lipsticked-lips glowing on her suntanned face. Her hair is loose and blown by the breeze and her simple, cotton dress is splashed with lime green and purple flowers. The only other adornment to her figure is a shell ankle bracelet that emphasises her bare feet. She stands on a beach, the sea crystal blue beside her, palm fronds casting a shadow that reaches out to her toes. The image is of happiness and leisure, qualities that are overlaid onto the dress. The outfit would appeal equally to those who wanted to buy something to wear on holiday, and to those who were seduced by the sunny aspect of the picture, to buy a dress that would remind them of summer. There is an air of playfulness to the image; indeed, the dress is similar to cotton frocks worn by very young girls. Sportswear frequently drew on childrenswear for inspiration. This could take the form of simple designs for dresses, shorts or beach playsuits, or the choice of fabrics that were resilient and washable, such as cottons, and denims that were popular for children.

The idea of play had become increasingly important in the inter-war period. Martha Wolfenstein's 1958 essay based on her research into child-rearing over the previous thirty-eight years described trends in adult attitudes to play and coined the phrase 'fun morality' to summarise her conclusion that 'instead of feeling guilty for having too much fun, one is inclined to feel ashamed if one does not have enough. Boundaries formerly maintained between play and work break down. Amusements infiltrate into the sphere of work, while in play self-estimates of achievement become prominent'.[35] This idea was clearly linked to the emergence of mass leisure and entertainment, which in turn were provided with a visual identity through the various categories of sportswear already described. Wolfenstein noted that, in childcare, 'play, amusement, fun have become increasingly divested of puritanical associations of wickedness', and this shift in attitude spread to adults, who felt they too must have fun.[36]

There existed an uneasy relationship between work and leisure, which, for women, was more acute because they were still in the process of negotiating their position within the workplace, and trying to determine how their bodies could be displayed at work and at leisure, without compromising their respectability and femininity. *Vogue*'s 1937 article, 'We Want Uniforms', by Robert Littell, discussed men's fondness for 'uniform' dress, is useful to consider in relation to the growing significance of sportswear, which, although it offered differing styles, was united in over-arching design philosophy and aesthetic. Littell writes that men 'find relaxation in complete similarity … how pleasant to wake up secure in the knowledge that what we put on to-day we shall also put on tomorrow'.[37]

Chanel had already aimed to transpose such qualities to womenswear in her own dress since 1910, and in her design work since the twenties, which experimented with masculine tailoring and fabrics. In America, sportswear was able to incorporate elements of masculine uniformity and ease into its styles. Littell saw other further compensations in male attire: 'More important are the moral advantages. A uniform means release … a uniform means fraternity and good fellowship. For a man, there is dreadful isolation in wearing individual clothes, all the more dreadful because they usually turn out to look like the clothes worn by every one else'.[38] This erasure of individuality not only saved the wearer from fashion's caprices, but also enabled him to signal membership of a particular class, and demonstrated his awareness of socially-acceptable codes of taste and status display. The collective identity that menswear of the period displayed enabled men to integrate into the crowd, and thus function effectively in urban environments that could be confusing and chaotic. Menswear produced a body that was streamlined for work and leisure, through the quality of tailoring and fabric, with personal notes, such as ties, as a subtle indicator of character and individuality. For women, a similar approach to dressing could provide the same social camouflage and protection.

Masculine influences were not confined to tailoring as trousers slowly entered the female wardrobe. The style began with wide-leg pyjamas, worn at first for bed or for reclining at home. In 1931, *Vogue* noted in an article, 'Pyjamas – When are they Worn?' that 'the Bright Young People', otherwise called 'We Moderns', had adopted pyjama-style trousers and 'the convention, ruling for a time, that the pyjama's place is in the home is now dead and buried. A woman may and does wear pyjamas to quite formal dinners in her own house, to other people's dinners in town and country if you know them well and the younger and more iconoclastic members of the female sex even wear them to the theatre'.[39] It is notable that the shift towards trousers was linked to familiarity of surroundings and friends, so that the style could not be mistaken for a breach in etiquette, and that, as was usual, younger women led the change.

Women's appropriation of trousers was problematic, because of their symbolic representation of masculine control, and, although they became increasingly visible during the 1930s and the Second World War, they were not acceptable in more conservative circles or formal venues. It was not just social conventions that discouraged their adoption by all women. *Vogue's* regular 'Shop Hound' column noted with pleasure in February 1933 that 'the beach dress has the edge on the pyjama, this season; the pyjama is alright theoretically, but not always good anatomically'.[40]

Town and country wear was based on British men's tailoring traditions and its smart tweed suiting, although quite androgynous, was less problematic. Since they had originally been designed for English aristocratic sports such as fishing and shooting, its tweed skirt suits were therefore seen through the prism of class, taste and status. Beyond active sports, town and country wear was useful for travelling in, smart enough for the city, and its rich natural tones could be shown to advantage in colour photography, which was increasingly used by photographers including Louise Dahl-Wolfe and Robert Mack, in fashion magazines. It was a branch of sports clothing derived from Britain, and was understandably more straightforwardly associated with the city. This is expressed in figure 1.4, a Mrs Franklin advertisement from 1932, which shows a smartly-dressed model in plaid, fitted jacket, tailored black skirt and scarf-necked sweater striding through New York with her two dogs.[41] Sportswear was linked, firstly, to a wider range of work and social activities and, secondly, to a coherent idea of New

York fashion, and this involved shifts in style and attitude. Social and cultural concerns about women and active sports needed to be assuaged as part of sportswear's incorporation into women's wardrobes.

Town and country wear was, like active sportswear and resort wear, also promoted as the perfect way to ensure that a woman was appropriately dressed for all occasions. In 1929, *Vogue* advised that:

> The woman who lives in the suburbs has a different clothes problem from that of the woman who lives in town or the one who spends all her time in the country. Her wardrobe should be a compromise between those of the other two, and it will be most successful if it contains a variety of those costumes that come under the heading of "town-and-country clothes" and if she takes care to choose combinations that make each coat adaptable to a variety of occasions.[42]

The growth of the suburbs during the 1930s (and the escalation of this process after the war) meant that women needed different kinds of clothes to inhabit this environment and to travel back into the city, without feeling unfashionable.[43] While simple tweed suits were shown each season, as with other kinds of sportswear, they tended to follow the current fashionable silhouette, while they retained a pared-down design and reliance on interchangeable separates that could be integrated into women's wardrobes. Tradition was an important component of town and country wear's success and enabled American wearers to link themselves to a significant heritage of English aristocratic sportswear and, in consequence, to respectable ideas of 'good' taste.

London was renowned for its tailoring and Scotland for knitwear, each denoting authenticity and tradition, while French examples denoted high fashion and elite style. Chanel, Jean Patou and others made sportswear lines that were modern in their pared-down aesthetic, and which suggested athleticism. However, while they were created for women who led more active lives than those of previous generations, they were more frequently related to leisure and holidaying, than to active sports. European sportswear was, therefore, most effectively marketed and designed for wealthy customers. New York was, in consequence, able to distinguish itself from London and Paris, in its creation of sportswear at reasonable prices. It was well designed, and stylish enough to inhabit the pages of high fashion magazines, and to be sold in stores such as Lord & Taylor, which were known for their fashion–awareness.

Gradually, New York sportswear and named designers emerged from the shadow of London and Paris to produce a distinct fashion identity. However, it is important to note that this was not a steady progress. The Depression saw new initiatives to foreground homegrown fashions, but the allure of existing fashion labels and the power of London for town and country wear and Paris for high fashion was well entrenched. Both consumers familiar and comfortable with the status quo, and retailers and manufacturers, who had spent vast sums to build up the mystique of European fashion as an important selling tool, relied upon these ideas.

THE MODERN SPORTSWEAR
AESTHETIC I

In November 1929, *Vogue* ran an article 'The Revival of the Lady', which exposed tensions between traditional ideas of femininity and the emergence of a more forthright woman, who embraced modern urban lifestyles. It began with the claim that the Lady had 'nearly expired', and that, 'the bustling life of the day, so hard on elegant fragility, had much to do with it. But even more responsible was the new-found freedom of the Modern Woman, which had gone to the head of that energetic person and made her push to the wall any one less aggressive'.[44] Parisian couture is credited as an 'ardent supporter of the practical Modern Woman', although that season designers had created delicate, draped garments to construct a woman who 'has elegance, which is expensive, making it, after the way of the world, more desirable to him who pays ... a pleasant contrast to the hectic hurry of the Modern Woman'.[45] These conflicting visions of womanhood – one subservient to men, the other independent – were to continue as stereotypes of contemporary femininity throughout the 1930s. While the Modern Woman seemed to epitomise the present and lead the way towards a more emancipated future, the Lady's allure lay in her aspirational charm and non-threatening alliance to the status quo. Sportswear designers and promoters asserted the dominance of the Modern Woman, and sought to construct her as the binary opposite of the Lady, who was represented as an elitist anachronism, symbolised by Parisian couture, in contrast to the ideals of democracy and freedom assigned to sportswear and, increasingly, to New York sportswear in particular.

Sportswear originated in Europe and the Modern Woman was as evident there as in the United States. However, this seemed irrelevant to promoters, who were keen to ally both with ideas of Americanness. This was already evident in the modernist aesthetic of contemporary photography and cinema, as well as being fundamental to the way New York itself was perceived at home and abroad. The development of a modern aesthetic in American fashion photography can be seen as parallel to the development of a visual language to promote American sportswear. It is significant that Martin Munkacsi's famous photograph of a model running along a beach from *Harper's Bazaar* in December 1933 depicts sportswear (fig. 1.5). Jean Moral had photographed a model walking through the city for *Harper's Bazaar* a year earlier, and Munkacsi developed this style to encapsulate a new direction within fashion photography that drew upon documentary photography in its representation of a moment.[46] Hungarian by birth, Munkacsi's time in Berlin working for the Ullstein Press in the late 1920s

1.5. Martin Munkacsi, B. Altman, *Harper's Bazaar*, December 1933. © Joan Munkacsi. Courtesy Howard Greenberg Gallery, NYC

1.6. Jay Thorpe advertisement, *Vogue*, 1 January 1935

1.7. Dorothea Lange, Mother in California, 1937. FSA Collection, The Library of Congress

1.8. Sid Grossman, Coney Island, 1947–48. Photograph © Miriam Grossman Cohen. Courtesy Howard Greenberg Gallery, NYC

had provided a template for his later work in America.[47] He was inspired by 'The New Photography', as practised by, for example, László Moholy-Nagy and Albert Renger-Patzsch, who rejected the idea that photography should imitate art. Like them he instead embraced the camera's technology, and aimed to confront 'the realities of urban life and the complex new technologies that were both liberating and threatening'.[48] According to Nancy White and John Esten, Munkacsi's 'best fashion work shows the lessons of his Berlin period: effective close-ups, oblique angles, strong patterns, bold diagonal elements, vertical framing, ideas derived from progressive painting, and a sense of abstraction. To say nothing of spontaneity, style and handling of movement'.[49] These visual ideals were then applied to fashion photography, in images that were often set outdoors, rather than in the studio's artificial confines. While no less time and preparation went into this kind of fashion image, the result broke free from traditional fashion photographs that bore little relation to everyday life. They created a space within magazines for glimpses of the real, albeit seen through the prism of photographers' and fashion editors' idealisations of real lifestyles.

Carmel Snow, *Harper's Bazaar's* editor-in-chief from 1934 to 1957, wanted to revive the magazine through the appropriation of a European modernist aesthetic. She employed Russian exile Alexey Brodovitch to art direct and he developed a style that envisioned the magazine as a whole, with bold graphics and modern photography to give the layout a dynamic rhythm. As Andy Grundberg noted, it was '[Snow who] first saw that his [Munkacsi's] ability to capture action in a dynamic, spontaneous way could be used to express the new sense of American fashion: one of movement, excitement and casual flair'. This was married to Brodovitch's 'increasingly spare but always dynamic layouts … [which] played a role in the transformation of fashion from an essentially aristocratic enterprise devoted to clothes manufactured in Paris into a more broad-based (if no less narcissistic and hierarchical) preoccupation with personal and cultural "lifestyles"'.[50] *Harper's Bazaar* thus provided a more avant-garde fashion vision than its more conservative rival *Vogue*, which, under the art direction of Dr. Agha, retained a more sedate design aesthetic. Even in the pages of *Vogue*, though, this shift towards modern photography was visible in both editorial and advertising imagery and, as with *Harper's Bazaar*, this came through most strongly in sportswear photographs, where clothing design and modern representation fitted most smoothly together.

Munkacsi's influence can be seen in figure 1.6, an advertisement for department store Jay Thorpe's sportswear from January 1935.[51] Shot by Gray-O'Reilly at the Roney Plaza Sun Club's beach, three photographs depict the same model running along the beach, cycling and walking along the top of a breakwater. Her hair is tousled and windswept, she smiles at the camera, and is clad in basic sportswear pieces. In one, she wears pale culottes and striped top; in another, a 'homespun linen' playsuit comprised of wide-leg shorts and simple top with contrast buttons. In the final image she wears a 'three piece playsuit', in the season's fashionable ensemble of monogrammed blouse with button-through skirt undone to reveal matching shorts worn beneath. Her own ease of movement and lack of fussy styling is depicted in conjunction with her natural surroundings: the beach is dotted with seaweed and the sea swirls behind her.

Fashion photographs drew upon European modernism and the tenets of the photographers involved with the Farm Security Association [F.S.A.] in America. The F.S.A. commissioned a survey of living conditions across the country under the impact of the Depression. As exemplified in figure 1.7, Dorothea Lange's photograph of a young woman in California, the survey's stark aesthetic evoked people's suffering as they shifted from state to state in search of food and work. This connected to the documentary images of New York City produced by, for example, Berenice Abbott and translated into fashion imagery by Louise Dahl-Wolfe and Toni Frissell, who used the same stripped-down approach to foreground the figure in relation to the American landscape, albeit to very different ends.

Jenny Livingston has identified the period from 1936 to 1963 as key to photo-journalism's formulation and names sixteen photographers, including Louis Faurer, Helen Levitt and Sid Grossman, as central to its development. Small handheld cameras enabled the photographer to move easily and use available light to capture fleeting, candid moments, in a similar way to the F.S.A's photographers.[52] Under the tuition of well-known figures such as Alexey Brodovitch, who taught at the New School for Social Research, and under the influence of photographers Henri Cartier-Bresson and Walker Evans, they wanted 'to find a way of making photographs that would express a quick and charged *presentness*, and by so doing to move beyond what had already been done in their medium'.[54] This desire to capture the moment was expressed by Munkacsi's comment that 'all great photographs today are snapshots'.[55] Sid Grossman's photographs of Coney Island of the late 1940s epitomise Munkacsi's statement. Grossman strove to capture an instant, and figure 1.8 shows someone in baggy trousers seemingly flying through the air, caught mid-jump. The figure is photographed from below and looms over the viewer. The body is turned into a dark, twisting abstract form against the sky.

Edward Steichen pointed out an important difference between this kind of photo-journalism and fashion photography:

> One of the various advantages the technique of photography holds over the technique of painting is the lens to record a given instant. In the production of a fashion photograph, the given instant is not a normal happening – like the sunset, a landscape or a street scene – which may be photographed as the result of sensitive observation and patient waiting. The fashion photograph is more complex, as it is the picture of an instant made to order [on the day of the sitting] … What may casually seem to be hectic chaos is, in reality, an orderly, preconceived process of fitting the fashion material and the model to the picture. Keen, knowing editorial eyes calmly dominate the work. When a given subject begins to take shape, editorial eyes and camera eyes consult and coordinate the fashion idea with the photographic idea.[56]

Steichen exposed the constructed nature of fashion imagery, even when its aesthetic is derived from realist photography. Fashion magazines usually strove to maintain the seamless surface of their pages, which presented the reader with a fantasy world of text and image for her to consume. 'Realist' fashion photography became a recurrent feature in fashion magazines during the 1930s and 1940s. It was most often used to represent sportswear, which was closely allied to its outdoors aesthetic and snapshot ideals.

Sportswear was already used to sell a number of seemingly unrelated products, since its positive connotations added value to the brands involved. As Winifred D. Wandersee noted, advertising had grown enormously in the 1920s. She cites the total dollar value of advertising in 1918 as $1,468 million, a figure that rose to $3,426 million in 1929. The amount spent per capita on newspaper and magazine advertisements was $5.03 in 1919, which grew to a peak of $9.22 in 1929, before it reduced to $7.01 in 1931 under the impact of the Depression.[57] Despite the drop, marketing levels remained significant, its growth, in Wandersee's view:

> A response to a number of developments, including a communication gap between producers and consumers, the variety of new merchandise on the market, product differentiation, the widening market through improved transportation, and increased recognition by businessmen of the value of advertising as a means of building demand. Advertising increased quantatively, but it also changed qualitatively, playing upon the emotions, fears, and anxieties of Americans. That is, people's social insecurities made them susceptible to manipulation by advertisements that promised status and security through consumption.

Sportswear and its relationship to positive lifestyle values was one way in which advertisers could play upon the public's aspirational desires and fears.

Sportswear could therefore function in a number of ways within promotional material: to reassure viewers with its coherent, 'everyday' image; contradictorily as a subconscious link to the elite, leisured lifestyles from which it originated; to play upon viewers' desire for particular modern body ideals; and as a symbol of the active and educational values of sport itself and was used in advertising for companies including Coca Cola.

America and sportswear were closely related to ideas of modernity. Each developed an image that spoke of newness, progress and dynamism, while also representative of more ambiguous qualities. As the Depression made the public more anxious, so their need for a cohesive national identity to assuage the sense of imminent disaster grew, as did the New York fashion industry's need to project a coherent image that would encourage people to spend. This produced conditions that were conducive to the formulation of the modern sportswear aesthetic. The period's restlessness was part of this aesthetic, just as it was part of New York's identity. Collective and individual identities were intertwined, and 'presentness' became the most 'real' expression of identity. In the modern city, ambiguities, triumphs and disasters were magnified. If modernity, and sportswear as a clothing form closely allied to modernity's forms, provided a unifying vision of city and body, they could never completely erase the anxieties of the Depression and war period and differences in wealth, status and ethnicity, for example, that lurked beneath the surface. The modern sportswear aesthetic represented an idealised collective vision of Americanness which drew upon New York City as a centre of fashion, as well as of an emblem of modern design and the condition of modernity. This aesthetic also relied upon contemporary cultural ideals of, for example, the body and health and hygiene to construct its idealised vision. These discourses were equally important to the formation of American national identity and to the image of sportswear that New York City's fashion industry constructed.

1   William R. Taylor, *In Pursuit of Gotham: Culture and Commerce in New York* (New York and Oxford: Oxford University Press, 1992), 18.

2   Michel de Certeau, 'Walking in the City', in *The Practice of Everyday Living* (Berkeley and Los Angeles: University of California Press, 1988), 94.

3   Certeau, 'Walking in the City', 95.

4   James Donald, *Imagining the Modern City* (London: The Athlone Press, 1999), 14.

5   Donald, *Imagining the Modern City*, 14.

6   Princess Marthe Bibesco, ' The Aura of New York', *Vogue* 1 January 1935, 40.

7   Quoted in Kathleen Howard, No title, *Harper's Bazaar*, February 1930, 51.

8   Taylor, *In Pursuit of Gotham*, xvi.

9   Taylor, *In Pursuit of Gotham*, 35.

10 Taylor, *In Pursuit of Gotham*, 36.

11 Bibesco, *The Aura of New York*, 88.

12 Bibesco, *The Aura of New York*, 40.

13 Sophie Watson, 'City A/genders', in Gary Bridge and Sophie Watson, eds., *The Blackwell City Reader* (Oxford: Blackwell, 2002), 290.

14 William R.Taylor, 'The Launching of a Commercial Culture: New York City, 1860–1930', in John Hull Mollenkopf, ed., *Power, Culture and Place: Essays on New York City* (New York: Russell Sage Foundation, 1988), 112.

15 Edna Woolman Chase, '*Vogue*'s Eye View of the Mode, Zoning New York for the Shopper', *Vogue*, 27 April 1929, 57.

16 Chase, '*Vogue*'s Eye View of the Mode', 57.

17 'Little Shops Above the Fifties', *Vogue*, 30 March 1929, 73.

18 Lois Gould, *Mommy Dressing: A Love Story, After a Fashion* (New York: Doubleday, 1998), 82.

19 Jeanette A . Jarrow and Beatrice Judelle, *Inside the Fashion Business: Text and Readings* (New York: John Wiley and Sons, 1974), 112.

20 Daves, *The Ready-made Miracle*, 43.

21 Daves, *The Ready-made Miracle*, 44.

22 Edna Slocum, 'Writing Fashions For Trade Papers', in Stevenson, *How the Fashion World Works*, 155.

23 Nell Snead, 'Newspaper Fashion Reporting and Editing', in Stevenson, *How the Fashion World Works*, 158.

24 Nancy L.Green, 'Sweatshop Migrations: The Garment Industry Between Home and Shop', in David Ward and Olivier Zunz, eds., *The Landscape of Modernity: Essays on New York City, 1900–40* (New York: Russell Sage Foundation, 1992), 215.

25 Green, 'Sweatshop Migrations', in Ward and Zunz, *The Landscape of Modernity*, 215–16.

26 Marjorie Thompson, 'New Ideas from the Paris Openings', in *Harper's Bazar*, April 1926, 92. (The magazine's title did not change to *Harper's Bazaar* until October 1929).

27 Advertisement caption for United States Rubber Company, *Vogue*, 1 May 1933, 11.

28 Paris takes to Jersey for Town and Sports', *Vogue*, 1 February 1932, 39.

29 Advertisement caption for Philip Mangone, *Vogue*, 15 July 1934, 2.

30 Advertisement caption for Abercrombie and Fitch, *Vogue*, 16 March 1929, 15.

31 Advertisement caption for Abercrombie and Fitch, 15.

32 Elizabeth D. Adams, 'How to Look For and Use Fashion Sources', in Stevenson, ed., *How the Fashion World Works*, 2.

33 Adams, 'How to Look For and Use Fashion Sources', in Stevenson, ed., *How the Fashion World Works*, 2.

34 Advertisement caption for Franklin Simon's Ann Lawren Selections. This advertisement is also notable since it states that the clothes are 'Tailored by Townley', an early advertisement for the firm Claire McCardell designed for, although her name is not given. *Vogue*, 15 December 1936, 7.

35 Martha Wolfenstein, 'The Emergence of Fun Morality', in Eric Larrabee and Rolf Meyersohn, eds., *Mass Leisure* (Glencoe, Ill.: The Free Press, 1960, originally published in 1958), 86.

36 Wolfenstein, 'The Emergence of Fun Morality', in Larrabee and Meyersohn, *Mass Leisure*, 92.

37 Robert Littell, 'We Want Uniforms', *Vogue*, 1 January 1937, 47.

38 Littell, '*We Want Uniforms*', 47.

39 'Pyjamas – When are they Worn?' *Vogue,* 1 June 1931, 71.

40 'Shop Hound', *Vogue*, 15 February 1933, 68.

41 Advertisement caption for Mrs Franklin Inc., *Vogue*, 15 March 1932, 93.

42 'The Chic Suburbanite Goes to Town', *Vogue*, 7 December 1929, 106.

43 Louis H. Masotti and Jeffrey K. Hadden draw upon the United States Bureau of the Census figures to plot the steady growth of the suburbs. They state that population distribution rose as follows: in 1920, 28.9 per cent lived in central cities and 14.8 per cent in the suburbs; in 1930, 31 per cent in the central cities and 18 per cent in the suburbs; in 1940, 31.6 per cent in the central cities and 19.5 per cent in the suburbs and in 1950, 32.3 per cent in the central cities and 23.8 per cent in the suburbs. Louis H. Masotti and Jeffrey K. Hadden, eds., 'Introduction', in *Suburbia in Transition* (New York: A New York Times Book,1974), 7.

44 'The Revival of the Lady', *Vogue*, 9 November 1929, 97.

45 'The Revival of the Lady', 97.

46 See Martin Harrison, *Appearances: Fashion Photography Since 1945* (London: Jonathan Cape, 1991), 10.

47 Nancy White and John Esten, *Style in Motion: Munkacsi Photographs* '20s, '30s',40s (New York: Clarkson N. Potter, 1979), n. p.

48 White and Esten, *Style in Motion*, n.p.

49 White and Esten, *Style in Motion*, n.p.

50 Andy Grundberg, *Brodovitch: Masters of American Design, Documents of American Design* (New York: Harry N. Abrams, 1989), 66.

51 Grundberg, *Brodovitch*, 19.

52 Jenny Livingston, *The New York School, Photographs 1936–63* (New York: Stewart Tabori and Chang, 1992), 259.

53 Livingston, *The New York School*, 260.

54 Martin Munkacsi quoted in 'Think While You Shoot', *Harper's Bazaar* November 1935, 92, in White and Esten, *Style In Motion*, n. p.

55 Edward Steichen quoted in 'A Fashion Photograph', *Vogue,* 12 October 1929, 99.

56 Winifred D. Wandersee, *Women's Work and Family Values, 1920–1940* (Cambridge, Mass.: Harvard University Press, 1981), 16.

57 Wandersee, *Women's Work*, 16.

CHAPTER TWO
AMERICAN BODY CULTURE

BODY IMAGE/ BODY CULTURE

The 1930s saw a rise in the general popularity of sports for women, as both participants and spectators. As Lois Banner noted, 'aside from film stars, the most prominent women in the United States in the 1920s and 1930s were sportswomen'.[1] Figures such as Babe Didrikson, Gertrude Ederle and Helen Wills acted as role models for other women. 'In addition to these athletic stars', Banner continues, 'lesser-known, but nonetheless able women competed in almost every sport except football and boxing. Metropolitan tabloids promoted women's swimming matches. Commercial firms employing women sponsored competitive basketball and baseball teams'.[2] Such sporting activities naturally increased the degree to which women's bodies were displayed and scrutinised. Physical culture in the 1930s was epitomised by these active pursuits, but also included diet and hygiene regimes, as well as the growing cosmetics and beauty product industries. Allied to these goods aimed at modifying the body, was the growth of sportswear as the final element to create the modern, athletic ideal. As this chapter will show, American visual culture, from high art to popular art and from fashion magazines to Hollywood films, disseminated and popularised body culture, as well as ideas concerning the most culturally and socially acceptable body. Sportswear was imbued with many of the discourses so important to contemporary body culture and therefore body image. This chapter will consider the most significant of these in the crystallisation of the sports body as a fashionable ideal: discourses focussing on health and hygiene, and exercise and dance.

Discussions of body image and culture within contemporary media dwelt upon the means to achieve the 'right' body, as well as on accounts and representations of those seen to have achieved it. However, as the disciplines of psychiatry and psychology developed in America in the first decades of the century, underlying theories on the formulation of body image were also emerging. Paul Schilder was one of a number of Freudian-trained 'refugee analysts' to emigrate to America in the 1930s and, alongside younger Americans in the field, helped to consolidate and standardise teaching for professionals in the new training institutions founded during that decade.[3] Schilder wrote, in *The Image and Appearance of the Human Body: Studies in Constructive Energies of the Psyche*, that physiology, neuropathology and psychology needed to be combined in order to understand 'the building up of the spatial image which everybody has of himself'.[4] Schilder's study enhanced the concept of 'body schema', previously employed by psychologists, to define the idea of 'body image', which in his words meant 'the picture of the human body which we form in our mind, that is to say the way in which the body appears to ourselves … we are not dealing with a mere sensation or imagination. There is a self-appearance of the body. It indicates also that, although it has come through the senses, it is not mere perception. There are mental pictures and representations involved in it, but it is not mere representation'.[5]

Schilder took his examination of body image much further than just a discussion of appearance, to develop for example his work on World War I amputees who could still 'feel' their severed limbs. However, his book addressed issues such as imitation and beauty ideals that are important to an understanding of body image construction, and its relationship to body culture and its representation in 1930s mass media.

Barbara Morgan's photograph, 'Ekstasis-torso' of 1935, shown in figure 2.1, encapsulates the physical ideal that emerged in the early thirties as the etiolated, androgynous silhouette that was favoured in 1920s' fashions gradually developed rounder, more feminine curves. Shot from below, the body is shown as a column, cropped at the shoulders to remain an anonymous, idealised, classical figure that dominates the frame. The model's toned legs and slim waist are emphasised by her close-fitting knitted dress. Her body is that of a dancer or athlete, shaped through exercise. Her right leg is slightly bent, straining against the fabric's elasticity and adding a dynamic thrust to the diagonal slant of her figure against the pale backdrop.

1930s fashion images are dominated by such representations of a 'classical' body, its musculature an athletic, impenetrable shield that disguises fears of physical frailty. Tim Armstrong argues that this body gained particular meaning during the first decades of the twentieth century, because of greater mastery and exploration of the body through advancing scientific and cosmetic processes:

> Modernity, then, brings both a fragmentation and augmentation of the body in relation to technology, it offers the body as a lack, at the same time as it offers technological compensation. Increasingly, that compensation is offered as part of capitalism's fantasy of the complete body; in the mechanisms of advertising, cosmetics, cosmetic surgery and cinema; all prosthetic in the sense that they promise the perfection of the body.[6]

Fashion can be added to this list of means to 'perfect' the modern body and construct an image, real or photographic, expressing a disciplined and contained representation of beauty. This physical ideal itself promotes hygiene, exercise and control. Such discourses had been a growing concern in western countries since the health, hygiene and dress reform movements of the second half of the nineteenth century. In the 1930s, practices such as calisthenics and swimming

2.1.   Barbara Morgan, Ekstasis-torso, 1935. © Barbara Morgan, The Barbara Morgan Archive,
Courtesy Silverstein Photography. © Smithsonian Photographic Services

were harnessed to a variety of political and cultural agendas, from Soviet and Fascist mass demonstrations of social hegemony and, in the latter's case, racial superiority, to Olympic principles of sportsmanship.

'Care of the self', as Foucault characterised it, comprised just such regimes of diet and exercise as those mentioned above, regimens intended to construct a body that was culturally acceptable, in line with current ideals of health, status and respectability. The discipline necessary to conform to such strictures signified control and power of the physical self that emanated not just from individuals, but also from the wider culture and, therefore, Foucault maintains, 'this "cultivation of the self" can be briefly characterized by the fact that in this case the art of existence … is dominated by the principle that says one must "take care of oneself." It is this principle of the care of the self that establishes its necessity, presides over its development, and organizes its practice'.[7]

Foucault contends that 'care of the self' is therefore an 'imperative', a duty to be performed in order to shape the physical self to imply an orderly and well-structured life. Historically, these practices had been the elite's privilege, symbolic of their status and wealth, allowing them to spend time and money perfecting mind and body. However, by the 1930s, both mass-market and high fashion magazines promoted physical culture as attainable and, perhaps more importantly, desirable for everyone. Health, hygiene, diet and, by extension, body ideals evoked seemingly contradictory impulses of freedom and pleasure, discipline and control. The continued publication of diet regimes and exercise programmes in fashion magazines was in contrast to the representation of health and exercise in the context of fun and leisure time. *Life's* cover of 28 June 1937 demonstrated how magazines could combine ideas of athleticism and pleasure, in this case embodied by a smiling model standing in the surf. This playful mood was continued in a picture-led article inside the magazine that showed people of various ages swimming in the sea. However, discipline was equally significant in representation of and texts on health, and served to emphasise that, for a woman, physical culture was also a serious undertaking, necessary to create a body image acceptable not just to herself, but also one which corresponded with contemporary ideals.

As fashions became more revealing and corsetry gradually less restrictive, greater body surveillance was needed. In *Vogue's* 6 July 1929 edition, women are warned that 'many sports dresses are scant … and all are barren of concealing drapery. All of this may be very smart – or very dreadful. If one is young and slim, all or any of these revelations are safe. If one is definitely not-so-young and not-so-slim, all should be avoided'.[8] The article continues in this vein, emphasising the reader's need to take the:

Greatest care and attention … [since] even a slight flaw, a lack of grace, may make a woman's whole body seem ugly when one is made over conscious of it by too much abbreviation and fidelity to fashion.

Remember, too, that the scanty mode in its present extreme versions is the delight of the cheap little shop.[9]

Although *Vogue* disapproves of cheaper copies of fashionable clothing, this indicates the wide-ranging availability of such styles and, therefore, of the need to create the body required to wear them.

A *Harper's Bazaar* article entitled 'Cruise' of February 1933 again revealed the relationship between sportswear and greater body display, in this case linked to elite leisure pursuits and to developments in cruise ship design. The layout of new ships promoted contemporary physical culture ideals by encouraging passengers to view their time onboard not as a transitional period and a suspension of activities between destinations, but as a holiday in itself and, importantly, as an opportunity to swim, play deck games and sunbathe. The article described the scene onboard ship:

There are no such things as travel clothes any more. Within the last year or so, the sun-decks and sun-deck swimming pools of the very new ships have revolutionized the very meaning of travel. You used to wear city clothes, and sat on air-pillows and looked at the rail … Now you lie flat on your back on the sun-deck in a bathing suit and twirl your dark glasses at time.[10]

In the previous month's edition of *Harper's Bazaar* an article, 'Sun-burning Fashions', had detailed the extent to which fashionable swimming and sunbathing costumes were revealing women's natural bodies. Costumes had shrunk rapidly in size during the previous decade. By the later 1920s they were often similar to men's in shape and construction, comprising knitted body-fitting suits such as the one shown in figure 2.2. By 1933, far more emphasis was placed on gender and display of the feminine figure. As *Harper's Bazaar* described it: 'you will see some two-piece brassiere-suits with bare skin showing between'.[11]

Knitted jerseys displayed the body and new fibres were developed that made fabrics elastic and helped them to retain their shape without going saggy after repeated wear. Lastex, invented in 1932 to add stretch to fabric, was a widely-used example, which enabled manufacturers to produce even more body-conscious garments, that sculpted to the figure. The variety of swimsuit styles available and their relationship to fashion grew steadily over the decade.

The association between body image construction, in terms both of an individual's sense of their physical self and an idealised notion of physical perfection, has close connections to the culture of consumption. The slim body that developed in the 1920s and 1930s was promoted through the wider availability of magazine articles, photographs and cinematic images that served as models of behaviour and attitude. Susan Bordo cites the late nineteenth century bourgeois interest in diet as the precursor to this Western culture of slimness, which is pursued as an aesthetic ideal, as opposed to a moral or ascetic ideal, as it had been in earlier periods.[12] Further to this, Patricia Campbell Warner has shown how, in the first decades of the twentieth century, cinema and still photography influenced the spread of the uniformly slim body, and, in the 1930s, the sportswear that showed this body off to such effect. She cites a major reason for this as the fact that the camera lens gave 'the impression of [actors and actresses] being ten pounds heavier', encouraging those who worked in front of the camera to lose further weight.[13] There was also a moral imperative to mould the outer body as the physical manifestation of discipline and power over the self. The streamlined body that was ideally created was akin to the array of consumer goods advertised and displayed in stores and was itself the product of a consumer society, constructed through purchasing the 'right' food, exercise and sports classes, sportswear, undergarments, beauty products and even holidays and leisure pursuits. Advertisements and fashion editorials provided seductive templates of how, where and when to buy and/or wear these goods.

Schilder refers to the earlier work of French psychologist J.G. Tardé in his examination of the imitative reflexes involved in body image's formulation. He summarises Tardé's theory that 'a person who imitates somebody else in dressing and entertainment has previously taken over his feelings and desires. Imitation goes therefore, according to Tardé, from inside to outside'.[14] Thus, women had to take on, consciously and unconsciously, cultural ideals of body image, as put forward through the media, their education and their social circle, before they were ready to adopt sportswear and the more body sculpting styles of the 1930s. The proliferation of images heightened women's awareness of cultural desires, needs and expectations of their bodies and the way they should construct and 'care' for a culturally and socially acceptable body.

Fashion magazines represented a space in which new and emerging ideas of physical culture were displayed. Readers were in turn enticed by the seductive glamour of the glossy imagery, and chided into feeling they should adhere to the attitudes and behaviour patterns shown. Models, society women, sportswomen, college girls and actresses were used by *Vogue* and *Harper's Bazaar* to embody the fashionable ideals that women should aspire to. Schilder notes the importance of identification with other people in the construction of body and image, and the possibility for each individual to produce a composite image, drawn from a number of sources. These could potentially include peers and the media, since 'the identification takes place with persons whom we admire and with whom we are in love ... but the fact that identification is in the unconscious makes it possible to identify oneself with several persons at the same time'.[15]

Schilder's work suggests a complex reading of women's relationship to and 'use' of fashion imagery, in this case representations of sportswear and the meanings attached to it. This relationship is not a one-way process, with ideas passed from fashion magazines, with their primary focus on elite culture, to readers who passively adopt behaviour, beauty and physical ideals and desire for clothing and accessories, which are then diluted to fit their own social setting and economic means. From Schilder's study of the ways body image is formulated, it is clear that information is processed in neither a linear nor a vertical manner, rather it is constructed as a collage of feelings, experiences and images. He cites 'appersonization', in which people 'take parts of the bodies of others and incorporate [them] into our own body image' but also 'projection' in which our own body image is projected onto others.[16]

Fashion imagery is an important aspect in women's construction of this collage of, firstly, desires and, ultimately, actions, that go towards body image creation. Since fashion magazines constitute an almost exclusively feminine space, in which women can immerse themselves in a dreamscape of imagery, they have control of the way they read them, and can return to specific articles or images and look at them for as long as they like, in contrast to the fleeting (though influential) passage of a film. Magazines and fashion mimic the fluidity of body image as set out by Schilder, as:

> Body-images and their beauty are not rigid entities. We construct and reconstruct our own body-image as well as the body-images of others. In these perpetual processes we interchange parts of our images of others, or, in other words, there is a continual socialization of body-images.[17]

Fashion's seasonal changes and fashion magazines' monthly reinvention of beauty and body correspond to this sub-conscious process. They make visible the cultural and social pressures on women to conform to particular norms, while suggesting constant variations and alternatives. Sportswear was fashionable at all levels of the market during the 1930s and its increasing representation in fashion magazines as the Depression wore on made it a more prominent factor in shaping contemporary body ideals.

HEALTH AND HYGIENE

Hygiene was one of the many competing discourses that contributed to the collage of femininity discussed above. Dirt was no longer merely a domestic matter, but was something modern, urban and alien, to be dealt with by scientific methods. This is reinforced by an advertisement published in *Harper's Bazaar* in July 1930 for 'Ambrosia, the pore-deep cleanser'. Below a picture of a woman gazing up at a white-coated doctor, the tagline asked 'What is this "modern dirt" skin specialists warn against?'[18] The answer was provided in quotation marks that imply the 'doctor' is speaking directly to the magazine reader:

> Modern dirt is a grimy, greasy deposit very different from the light dusty dirt of earlier days. Motor exhausts, soft coal soot, oil from machines, have made it so.

> Modern dirt finds its way into the pores of the skin. Is kept there by its oily content, impervious to ordinary cleansing.[19]

Ambrosia is recommended to deal with this problem of modern living, its special combination of ingredients designed to cleanse deeply and bring 'renewed life to the skin'. A bottle of 'modern dirt', from: 'the filter of the New York Public Library', is shown above diagrams of this grime's penetration into the skin's pores to reinforce women's need to be extra vigilant about their skin's condition.

These concerns were echoed in the advertising and editorial content of the 1930s American fashion magazines. Modern living was identified as presenting particular problems in maintaining culturally and socially required levels of hygiene and, in response to this, contemporary consumer culture supplied an increasing range of products designed to combat these issues. This was despite the fact that, as Suellen Hoy comments, modern technology had simultaneously made many aspects of city life much cleaner:

> Paved streets and closed cars were the major elements in eliminating the layers of dirt and dust that had permeated so much of everyday life. Filthy, unsanitary working conditions also improved as machines took over back-breaking, sweaty jobs … inside the home, where electric lights and gas stoves began replacing kerosene lamps and coal stoves [living spaces were more sanitary].[20]

Hoy writes that this, combined with the rapid growth of the cosmetics industry, whose sales tripled between 1919 and 1929, had prompted the foundation of the Cleanliness Institute in

1927, a co-operative that included soap manufacturers, health officials, educators, publicists and women's club representatives.[21] The Institute sought to promote cleanliness as a necessity for all levels of society, with commercial advertising targeted at a wide range of consumers, supported by school and municipal-based campaigns to encourage cleanliness and, of course, to boost soap sales.

Modern lifestyles were active and, as revealing, body-skimming garments became more popular, fewer foundation garments were worn. This meant that underwear no longer protected clothing from the body by absorbing sweat before it reached outer layers of clothing. Women were therefore encouraged to police their bodies even more carefully to ensure that they were kept scrupulously clean and odour-free. Greater involvement in active pursuits meant that sportswear and sporting scenarios were often used in advertisements for underarm deodorants and sanitary pads, such as a 1930 advertisement for Kotex: 'The New Sanitary Pad which deodorizes', where two models were shown in sportswear carrying golf clubs. Hair removal was also seen as essential for women to appear acceptably feminine and 'clean' and models were often shown at the beach, where revealing swimming costumes exposed the body to greater scrutiny than in previous decades.

This kind of 'care of the self', with its focus on constant surveillance of and ritual cleaning of the body, was identified in *Vogue* 1 February 1939 as a particularly American preoccupation. In 'Bathing Beauty: An American Institution', the anonymous author comments that the time capsule recently buried at New York's World's Fair lacked one thing: 'a bath-tub, stream-lined, gleaming like a pearl and full to the brim with scented foam ... no picture of our lives and times is complete without a view of the Great American Bath'.[22] Bathing is suggested to be intrinsic not just to American life, but 'the clean look' is described as 'one of the essential elements of all American beauty'.[23] *Vogue* clearly regarded cleanliness as a prerequisite of American femininity. The point was continually reinforced within this and other magazines by pictures of immaculately groomed models, all of whom embodied a white, middle-class standard of beauty. Mary Lynn Stewart has written of the commercial imperative that encouraged French women to view hygiene as a prerequisite of acceptable femininity, but it was in America that this idea was really developed and turned into an explicit issue of national, as well as gender, identity.[24]

Women were guided to measure themselves against classicised representations of slim, white, modern bodies, which had emerged from layers of garments and decorative adornments. Richard Dyer has written of the way that Western culture represents whiteness as 'neutral', against which other ethnicities are judged. He links this in part to the development of lighting and film technology, as privileging whiteness. Contemporary technology, as applied to both still and moving pictures, combined with ancient ideas of beauty in favouring white skin, long limbs and firm muscles that allowed light to bounce off the body to create glowing images of modern goddesses. This is especially apparent in fine art, photography and cinema, where 'idealised white women are bathed in and permeated by light. It streams through them from above. In short, they glow'.[25] Black and white fashion photographs and colour photography, which became increasingly popular in 1930s fashion magazines, lit models to emphasise their pale skin and glossy hair.

Photographs linked physical ideals to cleaning regimes that 'prepared' the body to fit in with cultural norms. This homogenous appearance mediated against fears of 'otherness', particularly as embodied by recent immigrants. Martha Banta described the consolidation of this template in late nineteenth-century graphic art as demonstrative of 'who is and who is not perceived as being "American" amid the welter undergoing simplifications of the kind that denied immigrant and minority groups visual identification as "the best type"'.[26] Illustrations in popular and fashion magazines were dominated by representations of young, white women and this created the façade of a collective feminine identity that appealed to middle and upper-class sensibilities, irrespective of the diverse ethnic and cultural make-up, not to say class identities, that actually existed in America.

Magazines' idealisation of whiteness had clear links to concerns about physical hygiene and its relationship to outer appearance. Hoy notes that cleanliness had been established as a key element of Americanness, within the middle and upper classes, by the turn of the twentieth century. This was at least in part a 'confrontation with racial and cultural outsiders ... [which] transformed cleanliness from a public health concern into a moral and patriotic one'.[27] Hoy details the lessons given to recent immigrants to ensure that they knew how to keep themselves in line with American standards of cleanliness. Immigrants were pressured to undergo a process of 'Americanization' before they even arrived in the United States, as relatives sent letters recommending that travellers should leave behind their own clothes, as they would be unacceptable in the New World. Barbara Schreier discussed the problematic demands placed on immigrants to assimilate quickly, and effectively 'become' American. She elaborates upon this through her study of Jewish women who entered America between 1880 and 1920, and who had to learn to dress and comport themselves to imitate American ideals of femininity to avoid being labelled a 'greenhorn'. For these women, Schreier notes, 'a change of clothes as the first part of their journey had centrally to do with the need, and the opportunity, to enter the mainstream of a new social life. Their appearance and self-image were inextricably linked, and both were in constant renewal'.[28] Immigrant identity comprised a continual negotiation between appearance codes established as 'American' and their native culture's ideals and traditions.

It was not just physical cleanliness that was advocated during the 1930s; developments in fabric and washing machine technology meant that clothing could be kept clean more easily and cheaply than ever before. The Sanforization process was invented in 1933. This meant that textiles were shrunk completely and permanently when they were manufactured, which allowed them to be washed with ease, a quality that was particularly significant to sportswear. Sanforized cottons and silks were advertised widely, often with explanations of their unique properties. Soap manufacturers soon made links with various, usually sportswear, firms to promote their products in conjunction with an endorsement from a well-known store or clothing maker. In June 1934, *Vogue* published an advertisement for 'Ivory Flakes' washing powder that was linked to the Sportswear Guild. Photographs of outfits by eighteen leading New York manufacturers, including Townley Frocks, who employed Claire McCardell, were featured above the tagline, 'The Sportswear Guild, America's Leading Creators of Sport Clothes Advise Pure Ivory Flakes for these smart washable fashions'.[29] Such promotions were mutually beneficial and extended ideas of cleanliness from articles on physical hygiene to keeping clothing acceptably clean.

Fashion magazines called easy-to-wash garments 'tubbables', a widely used phrase in advertising and editorial copy during the 1930s. Indeed, in its 1 July 1933 edition, *Vogue* published a lengthy article on 'Tubbable Fashions' that explained in great detail how to wash different fabrics and clothing.[30] It included advice for hand-washing, as well as using washing machines for 'a lady who plans to instruct her maid, or even roll up her own sleeves and get down to business'.[31] Since the onset of the Depression, many domestic servants had had to be dismissed and more women had to do their own housework and laundry. Electric washing machines had been developed for domestic use in the 1920s and their design was gradually made more streamlined and appealing. Advertisements for washing machines glamorised them as a means to achieve 'health and happiness'.[32] However, they were still not widely used and commercial laundries were at their height in the 1920s. Coin-operated 'Laundromats' only came into operation in the late 1930s, serving 'as a transition between the commercial laundry and the home washing machine by teaching women to use equipment [that] would be affordable to middle-class families after World War Two'.[33]

During the 1930s, fashion magazines connected this focus on personal cleanliness to issues of health and beauty. In 'Modern Hygiene: A Twentieth Century Survey', *Vogue* articulated this connection:

> 'Beauty is based on health'. This is the war-cry of the present generation, heard echoing on every side. The smart woman, whose appearance is a triumph of artifice, builds from a foundation of sound physique. And, as health is vitally important to her, so is the fundamental attribute of cleanliness. She is clean – immaculately, fastidiously clean, from every detail of her clothing to every detail of her body.[34]

Cleanliness was the first step to 'look' healthy, something that was to become increasingly important as the decade wore on.

Healthiness was a quality that had to be cultivated in terms of both lifestyle and outer appearance. Tanning had become fashionable in French Riviera resorts in the mid 1920s, promoted by fashionable figures such as Coco Chanel, and had lost its proletarian connotations of outdoor work. Sun tans were connected to elite leisure and wealth, since they symbolised holidays, sailing and swimming, all of which were highly fashionable pursuits that entailed exposing the body to the sun in new, brief swim– and sun-bathing costumes. Indeed, *Vogue* even produced a daring cover illustration for its 1 June 1934 edition that showed a topless sunbather lying on a towel at the beach.

It was necessary to buy the right tanning lotions and make-up to achieve a 'natural' look. Developments in cosmetic technology meant that make-up was closer to (white) skin tones than ever before and the mask-like quality of 1920s make-up, which had played up artificiality, was eclipsed by the idea of 'natural' beauty products.[35] Lighter skins dominated fashion magazines, and popular make-up brands did not cater for ethnic minority complexions. This was despite their recognition that, as Anne Harris of Dorothy Gray cosmetics pointed out to a Fashion Group meeting in the early 1930s, 'in America you often see Scandinavian skin joined with Italian hair and eyes. Sometimes you see an English skin made exotic by Russian, Jewish or Dutch blood'.[36] However, olive was the darkest colour provided by mass-market ranges.

Diet was another important signifier of women's fashionable healthy lifestyle. In February 1938, *Vogue* reported that 'in New York, women are taking the calcium usually prescribed in pre-baby diets as part of their beauty regime'.[37] Vitamins and minerals were promoted, as were diet plans, which were regularly included in fashion magazines. While it was not fashionable to be 'too' thin, a slim body was aimed for through detailed charts of what, when and how much to eat. These sometimes comprised straightforward lists of food to eat over the course of a week, or were combined with a complete regime of beauty parlour and spa treatments. They glamorised the process of losing weight and honing the body to meet current ideals in exclusive salons, where professionals would devote themselves to individual clients and special food and health drinks were served. However, these emblems of wealth and luxury were underpinned by demands that women should deprive themselves of certain foods.

In September 1933, dieting was characterised in *Harper's Bazaar* as an American fashion, which had irritated French restaurateurs forced to cater to tourists' eating habits. The slender body that was aimed for was perceived as healthy, and also, youthful. Although fashions for the 'mature' woman were featured throughout the period, youth was favoured and this was seen as an especially American ideal. Fashion magazines constructed an image of femininity predicated upon this ideal of youthful, healthy, hygienic living, and women were persuaded that they should follow advertisers' and editors' advice in order not just to appear fashionable, but also to be acceptably 'American'.

EXERCISE AND DANCE

Lined up with military precision, a row of models stand to attention for the camera. Anton Bruehl's photograph for *Vogue*, 1 June 1936, drew on Busby Berkeley's chorus girl aesthetic of replication and glamour to create a seemingly infinite queue of groomed models. They wore identical cartwheel, straw hats, their brims pulled up at the front to show off the models' bright smiles. Bruehl's repeated use of the same costumes, grouped in threes, confuses the eye. At first, it is hard to tell whether they are mirror images, a photographic trick or, as is actually the case, different models wearing the same bathing suits. Their swimsuits recall dancers' rehearsal clothes, popularised by backstage musicals, including *Broadway Melody* of 1929, and produced by department stores such as Best and Co., which, in January 1930, placed an advertisement in *Vogue* with the tagline, 'Dance, Exercise, Or Follow Your Favourite Sport to Keep Thin'. The advertisement showed a similar array of 'rehearsal togs' outfits that combined influences from underwear, swimsuits and dance clothes.[38]

The models' uniformity is complete: despite different hair colours, their faces and bodies appear the same. They combine American conformist ideals of long-legged slimness with references to machine-age production lines. The models' status is ambiguous: they promote the latest consumer goods and in the process become more and more like products themselves, lined up for inspection and (visual) consumption. As Lucy Fischer noted of Busby Berkeley's compositions of chorus girls: 'he lines them up behind one another until their multiplicity is subsumed in an image of apparent unity'.[39] Fashion magazines created an equally homogenous image of femininity through both multiple images of similar models and repeated use of the same models, or similar model 'types', in each edition. This optical illusion was a trope through which the notion of replication as a positive attribute was reinforced, as image after image suggested to readers that it was desirable for them to become a part of this endless mirroring of a uniform feminine ideal.

In 1929, Elizabeth B. Hurlock wrote in *The Psychology of Dress: An Analysis of Fashion and Its Motives* that 'foreign visitors are astonished by this [American] uniformity. English and French women pride themselves on their individualism, and to be different is far more desirable to them than to be like others. The truth is, the American man or woman is a product of a nation which boasts of standardization'.[40] She links this uniformity to America's ready-made industry, which enabled women at most income levels to wear fashionable clothing of similar styles. However, it was not just clothing that promoted conformity: women's bodies, as represented in fashion magazines and by models in photographs and fashion shows held in salons and stores, also represented a uniform vision of modern femininity.

In part, as discussed above, this was produced by diets but it was also the result of exercise. Exercise regimes were increasingly featured in fashion magazines and were seen as important for health, fitness for sports and modern lifestyles, as well as to sculpt and slim women's bodies. If women were unwilling or unable to devote themselves to exercise regimes, alternatives were offered, which, as always, involved further purchases. Corsets and other shaping foundation garments were often featured in the same articles as exercise programmes. Women were encouraged to see both as necessary components in re-forming their bodies. Modern technology offered a more radical route to 'health and beauty'. An advertisement from 1929, for example, claims that 'dieting or back-breaking exercise [are] no longer necessary! For an ingenious new device, the Battle Creek Health Builder, enables you to keep gloriously healthy – pleasingly slender – *without any effort on your part*'.[41] However, promotions for such devices were rare and invariably appeared towards the back of the magazine. While they represented appealingly swift ways to gain a slim body, fashion magazines implicitly disapproved of short cuts, and preferred to instil virtues of discipline, control and perseverance in their readers. Exercise developed women's figures, and was a part of a cultural shift towards viewing movement as a quintessentially modern aspect of (feminine) identity. The snapshot style of photography promoted a sense of dynamism in the 'moment' captured within the frame, and exercise and dance extended this representation of constant motion.

Body image and physical movement is copied from those around us and, potentially, from visual representations. Paul Schilder used the example of small children who would unconsciously replicate the way others in their classroom moved, and his studies further showed that 'there exist, however, real imitation actions which are due to the fact that the visual presentation of a similar movement of another is apt to evoke the representation of a similar movement of one's own body, which, like all other motor representations, tends to realize itself immediately in movements'.[42] The way exercise, gesture and movement were represented in 1930s fashion magazines was more allied to natural motion than the studied poses of earlier decades, especially when sportswear's casual lines were displayed. The 'real' settings that were used, such as city streets and beaches, combined with this to encourage readers to emulate the models shown and train their own bodies to conform to the shape and movement depicted.

Cinema enabled audiences to watch moving bodies in the comforting, escapist environment of a darkened movie theatre. Actors' and actresses' use of exaggerated gesture in publicity stills, as well as on film, provided role models for their fans and encouraged further scrutiny of performers' bodies, posture and movements. Films often included elaborate 'fashion show' sequences, designed to show off clothing and bodies, such as the colour sequence of a made-to-order fashion show in the otherwise black and white film, *The Women* (1939).[43]

Stars such as Fred Astaire and Ginger Rogers provided aspirational ideals of fluid movement, which were heightened by the bias cut of Rogers' gowns and the feathers and sequins used to garnish her dresses and shimmer under the lights as she danced. Bernard Newman designed the dress Rogers wore in the 'Let's Face the Music and Dance' sequence in *Follow the Fleet* (1936).[44] The dress is made of silk, embroidered with self-coloured glass beads and has a faux fox fur collar. The fabric is pale blue, dyed to produce a diaphanous glow around Rogers' figure as she moved and to emphasise the beads' shine, as it would show up on black and white film. The series of images in figure 2.3 from 1936, show Astaire and Rogers dancing to this song and demonstrate how film could heighten the effect of fabric on the moving body. Freeze frame imagery like this enabled the viewer to perceive each movement and gesture, and was replicated in fashion photography that showed models performing popular dance moves.

It was not just popular and social dance that altered perceptions of how the body could move. Developments in modern dance since the turn of the century had striven for 'modern' ways to move and express emotion through gesture and movement. As with 1930s fashion, this frequently combined interest in the newly revealed natural figure with reverence for classical precedents. Representations, as well as performances themselves, popularised classical-inspired dance classes, and related high-art practice to photographic and cinematic depictions of moving bodies. In figure 2.4 shows Isadora Duncan's fluid gestures and the wispy, classicised clothing that revealed her body and denoted her modernity: she is free from restrictive Victorian ideals of domesticated femininity.

In the early twentieth century, avant-garde dance suggested new possibilities of movement. It conceptualised modern bodies, which were clad in costume that emphasised suppleness born of gymnastics' rhythmic exercises and posited greater exposure of women's 'natural' silhouette. Duncan's performances were patronised by the international elite, but the ideal she embodied also had resonance amongst a wide range of young women, who sought to explore the possibilities of women's gradual shift from private to public space through the more mundane world of work.

2.2.   Jantzen swimsuit. National Museum of American History, Smithsonian Institution.
        Photograph © Smithsonian Photographic Services

2.3.   Unidentified artist, Fred Astaire and Ginger Rogers, 1936. Photograph © National Portrait Gallery, Smithsonian Institution

2.4.   Arnold Genthe, Isadora Duncan, c.1916. Photograph © National Portrait Gallery, Smithsonian Institution

Estelle Hamburger was one such young woman, starting at R.H. Macy's & Co in 1916, and going on to become one of the most important advertising executives in the New York fashion industry. She was ambitious and enthusiastic, keen to develop a new form of promotion for department stores that focussed on style and fashionability rather than price and quality. She wanted to write copy that spoke directly to the consumer in language she might use herself, and which enticed people to buy through words that showed an intimate knowledge of garments and accessories.

In 1917 Hamburger saw an advertisement in Macy's in-house magazine *Sparks*, which stated that the department store would provide a teacher to run a course on any subject that eight or more staff were interested in. As she later recalled: 'At this time my sole interest outside of Macy's was the dancing of Isadora Duncan … Could it be possible that Macy's meant to provide a teacher of aesthetic dance?'[45]

The classes enabled Macy's youthful employees to experiment with future movements, and new ideals of body and dress. While the more timid amongst them only removed their shoes, more daring girls danced barefoot in undershirts and bloomers, impassioned by the teacher's plea that 'we want to be free'.[46] Hamburger described their tutor's dramatic first class:

> Mlle Delova entered and looked at the faces of her pupils. Then she did what no words could have done. She threw off her cloak and stood before us in pale green chiffon drapery. She pulled the hairpins out of her flaming hair and let it fall to her waist. She slipped off her sandals and her feet were bare. She floated over to an old phonograph with a mouth like a mammoth morning glory and put on a cylindrical record of Mendelssohn's 'Spring Song'. She tossed a silver balloon into the air, and … wafted her lovely body through space in pursuit … Her red hair swirled about her head like fire. The green drapery was alive, winding and unwinding about her bare white limbs. Her body arched and curved…She captured [the balloon] and held it above her head, poised like a figure on a Greek figure vase.[47]

For Hamburger this was escape: dance provided the means to aspire to a body and freedom of expression that was yet to become fully acceptable for New York's young working women. An identity was formulating through the medium of dance that encapsulated modernity's sense of flux and fluidity. Natural and machine movement combined to produce utopian ideals of a future body free from material constraints. As dance critic John Martin said in 1911, 'Miss Isadora Duncan … is directly responsible for a train of barefoot dancers who have spread themselves, like a craze over two continents'.[48] This craze was still apparent in fashion magazines of the late 'twenties and early 'thirties. In its 16 February 1929 issue, *Vogue* discussed the beauty of dancers' bodies and their graceful movements, which could be emulated by other women. Readers were advised that 'we can choose a dance movement here and there that we can adapt to our own particular routine of daily exercise, thus injecting novelty and impetus into the search for personal beauty'.[49] Photographs of an American-born dancer, Miss Georgia Graves, who performed at the Folies-Bergère in Paris, illustrated the article. Dressed in fluid Grecian-inspired dresses, she is shown in various poses, balancing a translucent balloon in her hands. The text coaches women to emulate her movements, which are 'always large and soft ... look at a figure on a Greek vase or frieze and try to emulate it'.[50]

Young working women's lives in New York in the first half of the twentieth century provided models for a modern, productive, public existence for women; dancers, actresses and fashion models embodied their future subjectivities. These women, already of dubious reputation because of their public professions, were the first to embrace the freedom of movement that avant-garde dance and innovative fashion suggested, and which Hamburger anticipated when, although still corseted, literally and metaphorically in her everyday life, she said of her aesthetic dance classes: 'with my eyes closed I was Isadora Duncan'.[51]

A photograph in the Musée de la Mode et du Costume de la Ville, Palais Galliera's collection of Madeleine Vionnet's mannequins, shot during a Biarritz catwalk show of the mid-1930s, echoed the rhythmic repetitions of Duncan's dance movements. With their immaculate blonde hair and almost identical, monochrome gowns, they could be a freeze-framed animation of a single woman walking across the platform. Isadora Duncan trained her pupils with 'movement processes common to everybody in the round of ordinary experience – walking, running, skipping, leaping and the like', and mannequins' exaggeratedly fluid progression in the defilé also worked upon the impact of re-emphasised natural motion.[52] Mannequins' gestures and poses, designed to enhance the swirls of fabric and curve of seams, provided another example of heightened body-consciousness. This was expressed as ideals of femininity, upon which women were encouraged to project their fantasies of selfhood and construct their future body.

While Vionnet's innovative construction techniques were available only to wealthy women clients, who were daring enough to pioneer the exposed modern body, it was not just Parisian couturiers who experimented with clothing forms that would echo evolving active lifestyles. The Musée de la Mode et du Textile's 1999 exhibition, *Garde-robes: Intimatés Dévoilees, de Cléo de Mérode à...* included aristocrat Mme. Françoise de Saxcé's wardrobe of the twenties and thirties.[53] This included elite designs from couturier lines such as Lanvin Sport, Maggy Rouff and Patou integrated with New York department store sportswear, in this case in the form of a mid-brown playsuit of 1939 from B.Altman & Co., which, with its workwear aesthetic and, for the period, unisex style, harks back to Futurist designs for utopian uniforms. In their work of the late 'thirties and 'forties, several New York sportswear designers, including Claire McCardell and Mildred Orrick, looked in particular to Madeleine Vionnet for inspiration, which they then combined with references as diverse as, for example, American history and yoga positions.

Martha Graham, in her dance performances of the 'thirties and 'forties, addressed issues of individual and collective identity, through references to historical and contemporary ideas of Americanness. Mark Franko wrote of modernist dance of the period:

> If personal affect could be eliminated from dance, bodily movement would obtain an autonomous significance: It would appear aesthetically absolute in its physical self-delineation. Although apparently in conflict with the fact that modern dance was created and performed in many instances by strong-willed and charismatic individuals, modernist impersonality could nevertheless draw on personal charisma to project its vision of universal subjectivity.[54]

Franko's evaluation of Graham's work as dependent upon 'American space' seems equally applicable to sportswear of the period, particularly Claire McCardell's combination of prairie style and modernist restraint. Both Graham and McCardell's work connected to ideas of modernity in their incorporation of ambiguity, particularly ideas of individual and collective identity. Each recognised these issues as inherent to Americanness, and, in McCardell's case, to sportswear as an emblem of this contradictoriness.

Martha Graham's body, movement and gesture became a medium through which to comment upon cultured and so-called primitive elements of American identity. Her toned figure, captured in figure 2.5, a photograph of 1937 by Barbara Morgan, twists on the floor, one leg bent forward over the other, her arms curved under her turned head. Her pale skirt drapes to emphasise the shape her legs make, while her top clings to her narrow torso, her face illuminated by a monochromatic striped collar. She sought to contain subjectivity and draw upon the 'staccato' beat of machinery to articulate modern identity's paradox and fluidity.[55] Graham commented that, in modern dance, 'an impassioned dynamic technic [sic] was needed and gradually appeared. Dance accompaniment and costume were stripped to essentials'.[56] Dancers provided women with ideals of beauty that were founded upon a disciplined, toned body, formed through

2.5. Barbara Morgan, Martha Graham, 1937.
      Photograph © Barbara Morgan, The Barbara Morgan Archive, Courtesy Silverstein Photography

exercise and movement. Fashion magazines disseminated information about modern dance, with reviews of shows and features on well-known dancers which provided detailed accounts of their grace and elegant movements, as well as integrating dance into articles on exercise and 'good' posture. In combination with the emphasis on an idealised vision of American physical beauty, and stress placed on its link to health and hygiene, these magazines constructed a multi-faceted ideal for women to emulate, either through consumption of a range of products, from bath oils to figure-fitting clothes, or by modifying their bodies from within through diet and exercise. The resulting image belied the amount of effort taken to create and maintain it, as it was founded on an aesthetic of 'natural' and 'unadorned' beauty.

SPORTS BODY

This aesthetic was embodied by a number of different groups of women, who were depicted in fashion magazines, and in some cases other less elite media, as aspirational role models for their readers. Fashion models were the most pervasive group. Many of them represented an established ideal that related to aristocratic notions of beauty, which were themselves tied to Parisian couture's status as the apex of fashionability. It was a style of representation that, as figure 2.6 shows, had a long art historical lineage that drew on the untouchable status of sitters in portraits by society artists, such as John Singer Sargent.

American photographers including Louise Dahl-Wolfe were still inspired by this style, as seen in figure 2.7. However, as has already been shown, the growing popularity of sportswear as fashionable casual clothing, and the more relaxed attitude to dressing that it represented, led to models being styled and photographed to encapsulate ideas of health, cleanliness, toned athleticism, and, therefore, Americanness. figure 2.8, a Martin Munkasci photograph from *Harper's Bazaar*, August 1938, shows how models were often shown in pale sportswear clothes that played with a limited tonal range. This was made possible by continuing advances in Kodachrome colour photography techniques that showed off fashionable beige, grey and greige shades to the full. The models' department store dresses, by Altman, Best and Co. and Bonwit Teller, echo their skin tones and pale gold hair. This produces a subtle composition of neutrals that is alleviated only by the bright blue sky and their dark brown and forest green accessories, which stand out against the sand dune they sit on, while maintaining the focus on natural colours.

During the 1930s, magazines increasingly blurred the distinction between editorial shoots and their society pages, which contained 'real' snapshots of women from the international elite. Although fashion magazines, undoubtedly purveyed fantasies of luxury and unattainable beauty, they simultaneously included a 'counter-discourse' that constructed imagery which was designed to be read as reality. In the 1930s, this style of article was mimicked in fashion spreads that gave not just the names of the women shown, but also listed the clothes they were wearing. These images had an ambiguous status within the magazines, as captions did not state to what extent the magazine staged them, or how much they were just opportunistic snapshots.

This direct invitation to emulate their clothes validated society women's status as fashion role models: their garments, accessories, hair, style of beauty and body images are explicitly offered as templates. The fact that these are 'real', albeit very wealthy, women is another device that adds

2.6.   John Singer Sargent, Ena and Betty Wertheimer, 1901. © London, Tate Britain 2007

2.7.   Louise Dahl-Wolfe, *Harper's Bazaar*, February 1938. © Courtesy of the Museum at the Fashion Institute of Technology, New York. Photograph by Louise Dahl Wolfe

2.8.   Martin Munkacsi, B. Altman, Best & Co. and Bonwit Teller, *Harper's Bazaar*, August 1938. © Joan Munkacsi. Courtesy Howard Greenberg Gallery, NYC

weight to their fashion and lifestyle choices, and it is significant that society women occupied a continued, prominent position within fashion magazines. Although many would have worn Parisian couture sportswear, their images fed into the discourse of realist fashion photography used to show American sportswear. Articles integrated pictures of society women into regular columns on shops and current fabric trends, which helped to create a complex of ideas around sportswear itself and the ideal physique to wear it, as embodied in this case by society women.

It was not just fashion magazines that used women from the upper echelons of society as role models for body and posture. Sara K. Schneider described the trend towards greater realism in shop mannequins in Paris during the 1920s. This related to greater potential animation of the figures through the use of more malleable materials such as rubberine, and manufacturers' provision of alternative limbs that enabled a range of poses, as well as allowing mannequins to hold props such as tennis rackets.[57] The quest for realism became focussed in the mannequins' faces and:

> Once attention was given to the face, personality became associated with the mannequins – a personality that would transcend changes of body pose, or attitude. This led to the sense of a character that persisted throughout different poses, attitudes and activities and was reinforced by the display principle of *repetition*, in which viewers have an opportunity to perceive the same face in different positions in space.[58]

In the 1930s, American designers rejected mannequins made by French manufacturers, which were not thought to look like American women. American mannequin makers began to use real women as models for their own creations, to create mannequins that related to idealised versions of female consumers, rather than art objects. Lester Gaba was one celebrated proponent of this approach. His 'Gaba' girls, shown in specialist store Dewees' 1933 window, mimicked the fashionable posture of New York socialites such as Barbara Hutton, with their slightly hunched shoulders and pigeon toes. Mannequins repeated the fashionable contemporary idea of a 'standard' body size, since they were produced to reflect 'average' physical proportions. Thus, they added to a general sense of the cohesion and unity of American femininity in the 1930s that extended the realist imagery of fashion magazines into store windows. Mannequins, incorporated into various 'scenes' by display artists, became a part of city street life, a static replication of the women who passed by the windows, and a visual prompt for window-shoppers, whose own images would be reflected in the glass of the window panes. The window shopper was doubled in a ghostly window reflection, in contrast to the uncanny corporality of the mannequins. Like the mirrors frequently used in gymnasiums and fashion spreads, this endless reflection and replication of feminine bodies blurred distinctions between image, mannequin, fashion model and real women. Consumers, like magazine readers, therefore, constantly viewed their own bodies in relation to templates created by the fashion industry. These templates were all part of the way femininity was formulated, as set out by Schilder. They acted as points of identification for women, who could then incorporate elements into their own identity formation.

Sports events such as the Olympics gave further exposure to the toned sports body and encouraged wider participation in organised sports. The relationship between sportswear, the body and performance had been discussed in relation to American women as early as 1905, when Flora McDonald Thompson commented that a French girl would even play tennis differently: 'never by any accident does she rumple her hair, disturb the poise of her hat, or appear overheated, but by a system of movements all her own – pretty, precise, withal skilful, she scores not badly, and even in defeat achieves a perfect triumph of her sex, so gentle is her presence, so pleasing is the picture she makes'.[59] The author reinforces the opposition set up between Parisienne women, as chic, feminine and more concerned to preserve their appearance than to win a game; and American women, who, by implication, do not follow this approach.

Thompson's idea that more traditional ideals of femininity, principally those of being well-groomed, decorative and non-competitive, were still desirable was an attitude that sportswomen had regularly to confront. In a 1936 article for *Vogue*, Paul Gallico outlined in great detail the sports that it was and was not acceptable for women to take part in. Only low-impact sports that involved as little visible exertion as possible were permissible. Squash, tennis, track and field events were all prohibited 'and any other sport in which women stick out places when they play, wear funny clothes, get out of breath, or perspire.[60] His desire for women to repress physical representations of their active participation, indeed, to contain their bodies completely, led him to advocate 'prettier' occupations such as flying and fishing. His article sits uneasily within the context of the magazine and is perhaps a result of *Vanity Fair's* incorporation into *Vogue* in March 1936. American women faced contradictory expectations and attitudes, even if college-educated and 'emancipated'.

Since the nineteenth century, there had been concern that women's involvement in sport would make their bodies masculine and bend their characters towards male ideals of control and perseverance. However, the rise of female physical education programmes at colleges at the end of the century, their widening roles during the First World War, and women's participation in the Olympics of 1920 and 1922 led to greater prominence of women in sport.[61] This greater visibility had other consequences. As women became sports personalities, they were used to add extra value to sportswear. Susan Ware reinforces the commercial potential of sportswomen's bodies, observing that 'during the 1930s, advertisers were discovering that the female body was a marketable commodity. Since athletes usually had attractive bodies … they were prime candidates for mass exposure. New sports clothing, such as lighter, looser tennis dresses and even the introduction of tennis shorts by Alice Marble in 1937, revealed more of the woman's body'.[62]

Further capital could be made from sportswomen's celebrity as shown by Amelia Earhart's clothing range, which was advertised in *Vogue* during the mid-1930s. In its 1 June 1934 edition, Earhart is shown at leisure in figure 2.9 for an editorial feature about her, 'Made for Motion'. She is described as, 'an acknowledged designer of clothes for women who love the open air on land or sea, and who insist on outfits that are simple, sturdy, and – above all- chic'.[63] Her range thus embodies the qualities of Earhart herself, and combines the important selling points of both practicality and fashion, as shown in the photographs of Earhart in relaxed, English-inspired tweed and flannel suits, wearable for town and country. Editorial features such as this were an important way to promote clothing, since they inferred that a magazine not only showed advertisements for a particular manufacturers' range, but that its fashion editors chose to show them on their fashion pages too. Earhart's products are linked to ideas of technology and progress, her skirt is fastened by 'Jiffy-Joins', 'a trick arrangement for easy fastening', and buttons and buckles derive directly from aviation: '[they are] mechanical gadgets … amusingly transformed from bits of aircraft equipment'.[64]

Sport enabled individual women to achieve great success and express themselves physically. Women, such as Earhart, could be said to be 'living out' the promise of feminism, since, although the women's movement itself was fragmented and lacked coherence during the 1930s, sport and in a different way the fashion industry, represented spheres in which women could gain greater independence and have fulfilling careers.[65] Earhart's own modernity, as an aviator and liberated woman, is overlaid onto the sportswear she is used to sell. John R. Tunis highlighted this general point in 1929: 'Sport has emancipated women's fashions … few who praise the clothes of the modern woman realize the debt the feminine sex the world over owes to sport'.[66] Tunis implies that these developments are associated with the rise of American designers of sportswear: 'up to a few years ago, at any rate, all such costumes were designed by a few *couturiers* in the well-known city of Paris, whose idea of a good afternoon's sport was to sit behind a *bock* or a *vermouth cassis* on the *terrasse* of a café'.[67]

His patent distaste for couturiers' perceived idleness restates stereotypes of Paris as 'Old World decadence', while American sports women are favourably positioned in opposition to this as active proponents of functional, rational clothing.

Susan K. Cahn described the way language was designed 'to alert readers to the sexual attractiveness – and, possibly, the erotic power of modern female athletes'.[68] Their sexual appeal was exploited in magazine coverage, in advertising link-ups and in cinema, both in newsreels and film vehicles for sports stars, as Cahn noted:

> These athletes did much more than establish women's place in sport. They helped fashion a new ideal of womanhood by modelling an athletic, energetic femininity with an undertone of explicit, joyful sexuality … they seemed to possess a self-awareness as 'modern' women pioneering not only athletic achievements but new styles of femininity.[69]

Such references related sports women to the realm of entertainment and female performance that included chorus girls, beauty queens and film stars, who were also reliant upon their bodies for their success.[70] Cinema's spectacularisation of the female form led various sports stars, including Sonja Henie and Esther Williams, to extend their careers into movie acting. Their success propelled women and sport further into the sphere of mass entertainment and leisure, which had begun to be consolidated during the 1920s.[71] Women made up a small but significant part of the American teams sent to the Olympics during the 1930s. Media coverage of athletes Mildred 'Babe' Didrikson, Helene Madison and other sports stars focussed not only on their achievements, but on imagery of their toned bodies in action as is apparent in figure 2.10.

As has been discussed, this new femininity was widely represented in fashion magazines, which favoured 'real' examples of the sports body: the sports star was the most heightened form of this ideal; the society woman of fashion was an elite version that combined sporting activities with attention to beauty-focussed health regimes; and models, particularly when shown through the prism of the modern sportswear aesthetic, presented an idealised form of this physique. It was a body primed for new sportswear styles and developed in parallel with the rise in sporty casualwear.

Indeed, fashion magazines drew direct comparisons between these groups. In 1929, *Harper's Bazaar* described the impact of sportswomen on fashion through their advocacy of 'common sense in dress', and commented that 'the galaxy of girl athletes we see each year ... is more like a display of mannequins at a fashion parade than a group of sports women engaging in the most strenuous competition open to the modern girl'.[72]

The same body ideal was thus replicated and repeated by various groups of women, mirrored in various types of media and constructed as both 'real' and 'fantasy' in its representation. The group that was most influential in bringing the sports body to high fashion magazines and therefore in promoting American sportswear was college girls. They bridged definitions, since their experience was closer to most women than that of fashion models, film stars or society women, and their favourite easy style and youthful, healthy demeanour held great appeal.

Figure 2.11, a photograph from *Vogue* in 1939, shows how sportswear's simple forms, in this case striped jersey and full skirt, took on a fresh, youthful air in the hands of college girls eager to set new fashions and define their own style. The skirt is daringly short and worn with knee-high socks. The photographer, Toni Frissell, shot the model from below, her figure filling the frame, outlined against the clear sky. The participation of college girls in a variety of sports is symbolised by her baseball glove and crouched position: she is primed, ready for action. Her body is lean and athletic; her clothes allow her to move freely and the outdoor location, as so often in images of college girls, reinforces ideas of healthiness and naturalism.

Late summer and autumn editions of fashion magazines focussed attention on college girls, as consumers, role models and trend-setters. August issues were often devoted entirely to college girls and combined specially targeted advertisements with editorial fashion stories and content dictated by real college girls. *Harper's Bazaar,* which had featured college girls since 1934, and had an annual 'college girl panel', which comprised students chosen through an essay competition and invited to edit the magazine. College girls were used as models and asked to write copy, which sat alongside images of models dressed and posed on campus sites to replicate their style. Department stores and industry collectives such as the Fashion Group also exploited college girls' influence. College girls' usefulness as a focus group helped to increase the commercial potential of sportswear, as well as a wide range of products that included date dresses, luggage and sports equipment.

College girls enjoyed widened access to higher education in the first thirty years of the twentieth century, but they had to negotiate the masculine-dominated environment of academia. As David O. Levine noted, college numbers increased after the First World War, with double the number of students by 1940 as there had been in 1915. However, the proportion of women within this

2.9.   Anton Bruehl, Amelia Earhart, *Vogue*, 1 June 1934. Originally published in
       Vogue. © Condé Nast Archive / CORBIS

2.10. Helene Madison, start of one hundred metres freestyle race, Los Angeles
       Olympics, 1932. © I.O.C. / Olympic Museum Collections

2.11. Toni Frissell, Bonwit Teller, *Vogue*, 15 August 1939. © Toni Frissell
       Collection, The Library of Congress

figure dropped from half to forty per cent within the same period, and 'education with a material rather than a cultural motive was accepted only for men. Even if educated, the woman belonged in the home'.[73]

Sports and exercise programmes were integral to women's education, their bodies a focus for improvement and this promoted the idealised 'sports body' within colleges. Margaret A. Lowe described how college represented a space in which young women could 'try out' new identities and, with the rise in mass-market fashion in the inter-war period, fashion became an increasingly important part of campus life.[74] Changes in popular culture and increasingly daring representations of women in magazines and cinema seeped into campus life and sexualised the image of college girl's bodies. As Lowe comments, during the 1930s, under the influence of psychological ideas from professionals such as Paul Schilder, 'the notion that individuals both create and assimilate a body image [gained ground]'.[75] College provided a transitional space at a crucial time in young women's social development, in which this could take place.[76]

The body image bestowed with the most cultural, social and fashionable 'value' was the sports body, imbued as it was with American ideals of youth, health and dynamism. It was spoken of in patriotic terms in fashion magazines, as a 1935 *Harper's Bazaar* article on college girls, from shows:

> Her contribution to fashion is as American as Coca-Cola, baseball and hitch-hiking … the sweater girl's uniform developed not from designers in Paris nor promotion in America; it sprang direct from her own love of the practical; from her passion to live with the comfort and health of a child.[77]

This body image, and the attitude it embodied, was replicated in campuses across America. Campus dress codes portrayed subtle variations from college to college. It was this insider knowledge that fashion magazines and department stores craved, eager to demonstrate currency and credibility that was imbued with greater authority since it came directly from girls who were already studying at the colleges.

College clothing presented a microcosm of wider American attitudes to body, gender, identity and dress. Campuses generated their own fashions, mimicking the seasonal progress of the industry itself. College girls' need to construct an acceptable body image and identity was in part a result of the intensively regulated environment of American colleges. This balance between individual and group identity was as inherent to the condition of modernity, and integral to sportswear, as it was to the ideal of the sports body. Women were encouraged to view their body image as a construction, to be assimilated, as Schilder described, from templates, in this case from fashion and advertising imagery based on dancers, athletes and actresses; groomed through women's consumption of beauty and health products; and disciplined through exercise, cleanliness and diet regimens. Body culture in the 1930s occupied an ambiguous space, as it crossed between real and fantasy images and examples to convey a physical ideal that was gradually projected as distinctively American, partly genetic and partly formed through active American lifestyles. The disparity between myth and reality was commented on in *Mademoiselle*'s September 1937 edition:

> America is said to be breeding a race of Amazons – we women growing apparently bigger, taller and more athletic every year. But facts are irrefutably to the contrary. Analysis of insurance statistics reveals that more than 52 per cent of a good cross section of the female population measures five feet four or under. Avaunt, therefore, Amazons, and let us consider the normal, shorter *us*.[78]

In spite of these statistics, and the growth of junior and misses ranges that catered to not just younger, but also shorter women, the Amazonian myth of American women persisted in high fashion magazines. The image created was a white, middle-class ideal that required adherence to strict rules of posture, gesture and deportment, despite its relationship, both real and visual, to ideas of freedom and modernity. It was a body that was ready for action and thus ready for the growing market of sportswear that became increasingly significant during the economic restraints of the Great Depression.

1   Lois Banner, *American Beauty: A Social History through Two Centuries of the American Idea, Ideal, and Image of the Beautiful Woman* (New York: Alfred A. Knopf, 1983), 276.

2   Banner, *American Beauty*, 276.

3   Edward Shorter, *A History of Psychiatry: From the Era of the Asylum to the Age of Prozac* (New York, Brisbane, Toronto: John Wiley and Sons, 1997), 168.

4   Paul Schilder, *The Image and Appearance of the Human Body: Studies in Constructive Energies of the Psyche* (New York: International Universities Press Inc., 1970), 7.

5   Schilder, *The Image and Appearance of the Human Body*, 11.

6   Tim Armstrong, *Modernism, Technology and the Body: A Cultural Study* (Cambridge and New York: Cambridge University Press, 1998), 3.

7   Michel Foucault, *The History of Sexuality: Volume Three, Care of the Self* (London: Penguin, 1990), 43–44.

8   '*Vogue's* Eye-View of the Mode', *Vogue*, 6 July 1929, 35.

9   '*Vogue*'s Eye-View of the Mode', 35.

10 'Cruise', *Harper's Bazaar*, February 1933, 27.

11 'Sunburning Fashions', *Harper's Bazaar*, January 1933, 21.

12 Susan Bordo, *Unbearable Weight: Feminism, Western Culture, and the Body* (Berkeley and London: University of California Press, 1993), 185.

13 Campbell, 'The Americanization of Fashion', in Welters and Cunningham, *Twentieth–Century American Fashion*, 81.

14 Schilder, *The Image and Appearance of the Human Body*, 243.

15 Schilder, *The Image and Appearance of the Human Body*, 251.

16 Schilder, *The Image and Appearance of the Human Body*, 299–302.

17 Schilder, *The Image and Appearance of the Human Body*, 169.

18 Advertisement caption for Ambrosia Cleanser, *Harper's Bazaar*, July 1930, 119.

19 Advertisement caption for Ambrosia Cleanser, 119.

20 Suellen Hoy, *Chasing Dirt: the American Pursuit of Cleanliness* (New York and Oxford: Oxford University Press, 1995), 123.

21 Hoy, *Chasing Dirt*, 123.

22 'Bathing Beauty: An American Institution', *Vogue,* 1 February 1939, 95.

23 'Bathing Beauty: An American Institution', 95.

24 Mary Lynn Stewart, *For Health and Beauty: Physical Culture for French Women, 1880s–1930s* (Baltimore and London: The Johns Hopkins University Press, 2001), 197.

25 Richard Dyer, *White* (London and New York: Routledge, 1997), 122.

26 Martha Banta, *Imaging American Women: Ideas and Ideals in Cultural History* (New York: Columbia University Press, 1987), 93.

27 Hoy, *Chasing Dirt*, 87.

28 Barbara A. Schreier, *Becoming American Women: Clothing and the Jewish Immigrant Experience, 1880–1920* (Chicago: Chicago Historical Society, 1994), 4–5.

29 Advertisement caption for the Sportswear Guild, *Vogue*, 1 June 1934, 117.

30 See 'Tubbable Fashions', *Vogue*, 1 July 1933, 37 and 66.

31 'Tubbable Fashions', 37.

32 Ellen Lupton, *Mechanical Brides: Women and Machines From Home to Office* (New York: Cooper Hewitt National Museum of Design, Smithsonian Institution and Princeton Architectural Press, 1993), 15

33 Lupton, *Mechanical Brides*, 16.

34 'Modern Hygiene: A Twentieth Century Survey', *Vogue*, 13 October 1930, 81.

35 Kate de Castelbajac, *The Face of the Century: One Hundred Years of Make Up and Style* (New York: Rizzoli, 1995), 61.

36 Anne Harris, speaking to The Fashion Group, undated, c.1931–32, The Fashion Group Archive, File 5, Box 72, New York Public Library.

37 'True Confessions: An Exposé of Beauty Practised by Lovely Women in Three Capitals', *Vogue*, 15 February 1938, 95.

38 Advertisement caption for Best & Co., *Vogue*, January 1930, 3.

39 Lucy Fischer, 'The Image of Woman as Image: The Optical Politics of Dames', in *Film Quarterly*, vol. XXX, no. 1 (Fall 1976): 4. Adrian Garvey kindly drew this article to my attention.

40 Elizabeth B. Hurlock, *The Psychology of Dress: An Analysis of Fashion and Its Motives* (New York: The Ronald Press Company, 1929), 41.

41 Advertisement caption for Battle Creek Health Builder, *Vogue*, 9 July 1929, 111.

42 Schilder, *The Image and Appearance of the Human Body*, 244.

43 See Charlotte Herzog, '"Powder Puff" Promotion: The Fashion Show-in-the-Film', in Jane Gaines and Charlotte Herzog, eds., *Fabrications: Costume and the Female Body* (New York and London: Routledge, 1990), 134–159 for discussion of the use of fashion shows in film.

44 2001.0025.01, Division of Sport, Leisure and Entertainment: Popular Entertainment, National Museum of American History, Smithsonian Institution, Washington, D. C.

45 Estelle Hamburger, *It's A Woman's Business* (New York: The Vanguard Press, 1939), 40–41.

46 Hamburger, *It's A Woman's Business*, 42.

47 Hamburger, *It's A Woman's Business*, 41–2.

48 John Martin, 'Isadora Duncan & Basic Dance, An Outline for Dancers', in Paul Magriel, ed., *Isadora Duncan* (New York: Henry Holt & Co), 1947, 21

49 Francesca Van der Kley, 'The Bubble of Beauty' *Vogue*, 16 February, 1929, 62

50 Van der Kley, 'The Bubble of Beauty', 110.

51 Hamburger, *It's a Woman's Business*, 43.

52 Martin, 'Isadora Duncan and Basic Dance', in Magriel, *Isadora Duncan*, 14.

53 Musée de la Mode et du Textile, *Garde-robes: Intimates Dévoilees, de Cléo de Mèrode à…*(Paris: Union Centrale des Arts Décoratifs, Musée de la Mode et du Textile, 1999), 215

54 Mark Franko, *Dancing Modernism/Performing Politics* (Indianapolis: Indiana University Press, 1995), xi.

55 Franko, Dancing *Modernism/Performing Politics*, 51.

56 Martha Graham quoted in Merle Armitage, ed., *Martha Graham* (Los Angeles, California: Lynton R. Kistler, 1937), 86.

57 Sara K. Schneider, *Vital Mummies: Performance Design for the Show-Window Mannequin* (New Haven and London: Yale University Press, 1995), 71–73.

58 Schneider, *Vital Mummies*, 72.

59 Flora McDonald Thompson, 'Autumn Days in Paris', *Harper's Bazaar*, October 1905, 933.

60 Paul Gallico, 'Women Should Look Beautiful, But do they in Most Sports?' *Vogue,* 15 June 1936, 54.

61 Stephanie L.Twin, 'Women and Sport', in Donald Spivey, ed., *Sport in America: New Historical Perspectives* Westport, Conn.: Greenwood Press, 1985), 199–205.

62 Susan Ware, *Holding Their Own: American Women in the 1930s* (Boston: Twayne, 1982), 174.

63 'Made for Motion', *Vogue*, 1 June 1934, 90.

64 'Made for Motion', 90.

65 Twin notes a 'feminist perspective' among professional women, including sportswomen, who were at college before suffrage was gained in 1920. Twin, 'Women and Sport', 209.

66 John R. Tunis, 'Pour le Sport, How Tennis Helped the Modern Diana in Shortening her Skirts', *Harper's Bazaar*, July 1929, 74.

67 Tunis, 'Pour le Sport', 74.

68 Susan K. Cahn, *Coming On Strong: Gender and Sexuality in Twentieth Century Women's Sport* (Cambridge, Mass. and London: Harvard University Press, 1994), 47.

69 Cahn, *Coming On Strong*, 47.

70 Cahn, *Coming On Strong*, 206–7.

71 Michael Kammen, *American Culture, American Tastes: Social Change and the Twentieth Century* (New York: Basic Books, 1999), 16–17.

72 No title, *Harper's Bazar*, July 1929, 113.

73 David O. Levine, *The American College and the Culture of Aspiration, 1915–1940* (Ithaca and London: Cornell University Press, 1986), 126.

74 Margaret A. Lowe, *Looking Good: College Women and Body Image, 1875–1930* (Baltimore and London: Johns Hopkins University Press, 2003), 102.

75 Lowe, *Looking Good,* 156.

76 Lowe, *Looking Good*, 156.

77 'The Smile of America', *Harper's Bazaar*, August 1935, 39.

78 'Maid –to-Measure', *Mademoiselle*, September 1937, 43.

3.1. Barbara Lee advertisement, *Vogue*, 21 December 1929

3.2. Bloomingdale's advertisement, *Harper's Bazaar*, June 1935

CHAPTER THREE
SPORTSWEAR AND THE NEW YORK FASHION INDUSTRY DURING THE DEPRESSION

EFFECTS OF THE DEPRESSION

Perched neatly on a chair, her torso twisted towards the accompanying text, the carefully drawn mannequin who promotes quality fashion house Barbara Lee bridges two eras (fig. 3.1). In fashion terms, her close-fitting cloche and lowered waistline are traces left from the androgynous styles of the 1920s, while the added drapery of her cowl neckline looks towards the more fluid silhouette of the 1930s. The copy advertises Barbara Lee as 'A Tested Recipe for American Chic ... Take a Paris staff and an American office'. This tentative suggestion of America's claim to fashionability was gradually to become more assertive as the economic impact of the Depression encouraged America's, and in particular New York's, ability to generate fashion.[1]

The design and buying process described in this advertisement presented an idealisation of the design process of many New York manufacturers and fashion houses of the 1920s: 'with cables flying across the water between them [Paris and New York] ... add manufacturers eager to submit styles for the prestige of the Barbara Lee label ... with expert stylists constantly stirring the market for models – changing, eliminating, suggesting'.[2] However, as sales declined during the Depression, consequently decreasing the funds to maintain Paris offices, the New York fashion industry began to look for ways to promote its own production in terms that stated American values and creativity, independent of Paris's influence. While, as this advertisement shows, New York's need to adapt French style to the tastes and figures of American women was already recognised in fashion advertising and editorials, it would take time for the city's fashion industry to develop a systematic and coherent means of marketing itself as a convincing fashion capital.

This chapter will examine the impact of the Depression on the industry and the reasons why ideas of Americanness became an important motif in the text and imagery of the 1930s, together with the ways in which sportswear came to represent the epitome of American design. It will analyse the visual prompts connected to ideas of modernity and the city and to emerging body ideals, in relation to the way women were represented as producers, disseminators and consumers of fashion. This will be considered in relation to the growth in numbers of women entering the work place, and the important role sportswear played as an element of their working wardrobe, providing clothes worn for comfort and acceptability both in and out of the office.

This chapter will end with a discussion of the Fashion Group's establishment at the beginning of this period. The Group itself constitutes a case study of the professionalisation of women within the New York fashion industry. Its practices and discussions will act as an example of the ways in which the industry was, by the 1930s, considered as a coherent whole, from education to design and manufacturing, and including merchandising and promotion. Significantly, these issues were debated in Fashion Group meetings and publications in relation to the contemporary political, economic and cultural context. This suggests that the way practitioners at the time formulated their ideas, for example, for merchandising, was a response not only to fashion's impetus, but also to wider issues.

In 1928, Paul Nystrom, Professor of Marketing at Columbia University, wrote that:

> Fashion is one of the greatest forces in present-day life. It pervades every field and reaches every class. Fashion leads business and determines its direction. It has always been a factor in human life but never more forceful, never more influential and never wider in scope than in the last decade and it gives every indication of growing still more important.[3]

During the economic boom of the 1920s, fashion had become a value which, when added to a variety of products, from clothing to cars to furniture, increased their promotional and retail potential. As Estelle Hamburger noted, '[by 1925] Fashion had arrived as a force in fashion retail advertising'.[4] From her job in the advertising department at Bonwit Teller, she chronicled the power of buyers and stylists, who asserted fashion's pre-eminence, over need, quality and price, in the promotion and presentation of goods: 'not one of us who battled bosses and buyers and pounded typewriters in advertising departments … could have known that we were nurturing … the ever-changing power that helped to build a great and brilliant industry – the Fashion Business'.[5] If the 1920s saw the fashion industry come to maturity, then the Depression era saw it refocus and attempt to tighten its processes to address the straightened economic situation. Since the 1920s, the idea of fashion had been used to sell not only high quality but also mass-produced goods. Manufacturers and retailers frequently sought to link their goods to Paris as a guarantee of a garment or accessory's alignment with current trends and as a signifier of glamour.[6] While this practice continued in the 1930s, fashion alone could no longer be relied upon to ensure sales.

The Depression forced the industry to question its practices, and seek more effective ways to sell. Anthony J. Badger noted in his 1993 account of the Depression that:

> When in 1929 Americans ceased to consume at previous rates, inventories grew, man-ufacturers reassessed their futures, and declining confidence started the economy on a downward spiral. As businessmen started to cut back, they created the very conditions they

feared. The downward spiral was speeded up by particular structural weaknesses in both the United States and the international economy.[7]

Despite or perhaps because of the Depression, ready-to-wear grew in importance and volume over the course of the 1930s. Under the pressures of Depression conditions, all segments of the fashion industry had to target goods and their promotion more carefully. Although, as *Fortune* magazine noted in June 1930, fashion was 'the country's fourth largest industry', it had to adjust its practices to defend itself against declining sales, as the economy deteriorated in the first two years of the decade.[8]

Nystrom proposed a detailed and focussed account of the ways businesses could improve merchandising to increase turnover. This greater professionalisation of the industry was a feature of Depression-era writing on fashion and was apparent to Nystrom at the time: 'Business opportunity in the future will depend upon business acumen, careful planning, and close contact with consumer requirements to a degree heretofore unknown'.[9]

Retail sales slumped as the Depression deepened and many manufacturers and department stores made unsuccessful attempts to stave off bankruptcy. The economy was at its worst from July 1931 to September 1932, a period which saw widespread strikes in the garment trade: 20,737 workers from the Industrial Union were involved in 1,978 shop strikes in New York, with twenty-nine further strikes from the Cloakworkers union and thirty involving the Dress Workers.[10] An agreement between the dress and cloakworkers and the International Ladies Garment Workers Union expired in 1932, and although a minimum wage of $1.10 per hour was agreed by the New York dress trade, many firms negotiated deals individually, which led to wage cuts.[11]

The problems deepened as the Depression continued and manufacturers who had had an unsuccessful collection were forced to shut down at the end of the fashion season, causing further unemployment. The beginning of the New Deal after President Franklin D. Roosevelt's inauguration in March 1933 attempted to alleviate the situation, but production and turnover continued to shrink. The National Industrial Recovery Act, signed in 1933 as part of the 'One Hundred Days' measures, set up the National Recovery Administration which worked with various industries to establish codes of conduct and, essentially, to price-fix. However, Jack Hardy saw it as implementing only short term improvements: 'For several months after the adoption of the N.R.A codes, and the new labour agreements which followed, many workers found their wages substantially increased and their hours reduced to the legal maximums. Then came a breakdown in standards. By the summer of 1934 all of these illusions were shattered'.[12]

Retail was in similar disarray. Various strategies were used, including shop refits and aggressive price slashing, but retailers and manufacturers had to be careful not to lose customer confidence in the process. William H. Dooley wrote of this problematic balance in 1934:

> Merchants in order to 'move' their stock have 'liquidation sales' and lower price to cost and sometimes below cost. There are real bargains in the first liquidation sales. But as time goes on, the public desire lower prices and the standard manufacturer cannot lower the price and standard quality. Hence a group of sub-standard manufacturers start producing wearing apparel, not up to a standard, but at a lower price. This means wearing apparel of lower quality. While one may save some pennies on the lower price wearing apparel, it is not economical from the standpoint of service and satisfaction, fit and durability.[13]

High fashion magazines echoed this warning in editorial pieces, which continually counselled readers against buying cheap clothes that would not last. *Vogue* and *Harper's Bazaar* both included recommendations on how to save money. *Vogue* gave more copious advice for its readers. Its first direct mention of the Depression had come in summer 1932.[14] Then, in its 1 August edition, it directed readers away from cheap clothing, commenting how 'when the depression first came upon us we all went a little wild. Impelled by a worthy urge to retrench, we discovered the cheap racks of clothing and thought we had discovered Paradise'.[15] This idea was expanded upon throughout the Depression. For example, in its opening '*Vogue's*-eye View' section for 15 November 1936, the editor stressed women's need for 'more taste than money'.[16] The article was split into two columns: 'True Economies' and 'False Economies'. The first entry reads 'Pay more; buy less', and this advice reverberated through magazines of the time. Cynically, it was at least in part an expression of high fashion magazines' elite attitude, which often looked askance at anything cheap or mass-produced. However, *Vogue* was especially adaptable during the Depression, integrating a small, but growing number of New York-produced mass-market sportswear lines into its pages, while maintaining its middle and upper middle-class ethos with its focus on items that were considered 'good' taste and quality.

Two other entries in the 'True Economies' column demonstrate this: one states, 'Be true to one basic colour all season, so all goes with all', and another encourages women to 'copy the men. Go to good tailors for your suits. Collect classics. Build up a reserve fund of clothes you can fall back on at any time'.[17] These elements – colour coordination, simple, masculine–inspired pieces, and 'classics' – were to become integral to New York's distinct fashion style in the following decade. While Chanel had already established menswear as a key source for her own dress as well as her couture designs in France, it was New York sportswear that combined these elements to create interchangeable wardrobes that could be expanded and updated with new colour ways for garments and new styles each season. Figure 3.2 is an early example from a 1935 advertisement for Bloomingdale's 'Mix Well and Wear' wardrobe that demonstrated the potential for sportswear manufacturers to develop affordable selections of separates that would enable customers to create various outfits.

In February 1938, *Vogue* reiterated the link between this fashionable ideal and American–produced clothing. In its 'Fashions America Does Best' spread, three kinds of outfits are described as 'America's own – that we design better, wear better, make better than anyone else'.[18] These were: play-clothes, knitted clothes and prints. All three were prominent in sportswear collections and demonstrate the ubiquitous nature of the sportswear aesthetic within American mass-produced clothing by the end of the decade. While Paris–inspired and made-to-order lines were still dominant in *Harper's Bazaar, Vogue* recognised that if American fashion was to survive the Depression, then it needed to develop its own sense of identity. 'Fashions America Does Best' appeared in *Vogue's* first annual 'Americana' issue in February 1938. These editions, together with other magazine and department store promotions of American design, represented a consolidated attempt to promote American design and to formulate a distinct and viable alternative to Paris and London, even if, as Sandra Stansbery Buckland notes, the first 'Americana' edition did not give credits for any named American designers.[19] However, these measures, implemented by the New York fashion industry to combat the economic downturn, were to carry the New York industry through not just the Depression, but also the later war years.

In September 1932, *The New York Times* had published an article, 'A New Americanism is Emerging', that documented what its author, Anne O'Hare McCormack, perceived to be an increasingly patriotic mood that had grown up in response to the uncertainties of the Depression and President Herbert Hoover's lack of decisive action:

[Politicians] call it nationalism, but in that they are mistaken. It is what might be named Americanism, but only because it expresses a new synthesis of all those forces, ideas, race strains, mechanized folkways, social patterns, international relations, that have shaped this post-war, post-boom, post-millennial America. Up to now Americanism has been a method, a pioneering process, an industrial technique, what the Russians mean when they

'Americanize', what Europe thinks of when it speaks of Americanization. We have had no conscious ideology, no settled tradition, a spectacular surface but no known depth; no gauge, that is to say, of the extent to which our technique was a method of the mind, the instrument of a civilization deep-rooted and precious enough to be defended.[20]

This mood was present within the fashion industry, where ideals of American style and femininity gradually evolved in a more coherent form than ever before. As the article makes clear, this was an identity formulated *in extremis*, a result of national self-reflection in the face of chaos and uncertainty. Although, in the case of fashion, this was not a steady or co-ordinated process, with efforts strongest during the most severe passages of the Depression, it was the most consistent and thoroughgoing attempt to 'Americanize' New York fashion so far. Aspects of the entire cycle of the fashion industry, in conjunction with contemporary economic and social pressures, provided the environment for more successful home-grown fashions. This was evident in a number of areas: technological advances in manufacturing, fabric design and even washing machines, and strict union rules on labour, combined with growing educational provision for the industry and more sophisticated retail and promotional techniques, as well as an increasing focus on individual designers at both made-to-measure and ready-made fashion houses.

There had been a few champions before the 1930s of a distinctively American approach to fashion, but it was the exigencies of the Depression that gave this idea resonance and popular credibility for the first time. The first mention of the divide between American and French fashion in a major American newspaper was on 18 November 1883 when T. C. Crawford claimed, in his 'Topics of the Week' column for the *Washington Post*, that 'it is well known by experienced travellers that many fashions sent from Paris to America would not be tolerated here. Indeed there is a separate line of merchandise prepared for our market'.[21] *The New York Times*, in contrast, first mentioned American designers in 1897 in its description of the second annual benefit show of dolls dressed in contemporary fashions, which that year hoped to promote the idea of a 'school for American design', because of 'the prejudice which exists in favour of those of foreign design and make. In this way … American designers and dressmakers fail to obtain the recognition they deserve for what now is considered almost exclusively a European art'.[22]

The push for recognition of American design continued into the twentieth century: the *Ladies Home Journal* published an 'American Fashion' edition on 15 October 1910 and enterprising individuals such as manufacturer Phil S. Gill also promoted Americanism, with proud 'Made in U.S.A.' advertisements. The biggest push came from *Women's Wear Daily* writer Morris de Camp

Crawford in the mid–1910s. He was an enthusiastic proponent of American fashion and wrote numerous articles on the industry, as well as endorsing Native American crafts, both in their own right and as a source for contemporary American designers.[23] During the Depression, such ideals were compounded by America's isolationist trade policies, which, with the Hawley-Smoot Tariff of 1930, signalled the United States' protectionist stance, and by fears of quota tariffs, which the French government threatened on the importation of goods in 1932, which forced the New York industry to consider its own inspirations.[24]

In the 1930s, American fashion's emerging aesthetic had to incorporate existing ideals of femininity. As purveyed by high fashion magazines, these were conservative, with emphasis placed upon respectable notions of 'good' taste. This conventional gender construction was seen by some as offering an appropriate balm for the uncertainties of the period. Women were, from their early teens, guided to view femininity as something artificial, to be constructed through grooming and adornment, and to be scrupulously vigilant of respectable notions of acceptable taste. While older women may have been allowed slightly greater scope, *Vogue's* didactic approach in 'The Sub-debutante, With an Income Limited to Chic' of July 1931, is unequivocal: 'before you begin to concentrate on anything else, make yourself realize that yours is the task of dressing down not up. If you wear so much as one bead too many, you will be acidly criticized by your contemporaries; whereas while you are simply dressed, not one tongue will wag against you'.[25]

Such vigilant adherence to dress codes was translated into a hegemonic ideal of femininity that favoured signifiers of white, middle-class taste. Simplicity was thus favoured for conservative reasons, as well as for its relationship to the current modern aesthetic. There was also a commercial imperative for the more basic designs which were so prominent in New York sportswear. Emerging technology favoured simpler pattern pieces, and this imperative coincided with Frederick Winslow Taylor's ideas on scientific management. These had been published in a number of texts since the 1890s, and were brought together in 1911 in his book, *The Principles of Scientific Management*. Taylor, his biographer notes, 'perceived the interrelated character of the new management systems and the need for disciplined, comprehensive change if the manufacturer and the industrial sector were to attain the optimum results'.[26] He advocated a thorough overhaul of workplace management, since, 'maximum prosperity can exist only as the result of maximum productivity'.[27] To achieve this he encouraged employers to undertake a study of every aspect of production in order to promote the ideal of fast, well-organised labour practices. This included a detailed examination of employees' movements and the time taken for each element of a task, in order to produce a machine-like efficiency. His 'time and motion' studies, would produce an 'enormous saving of time and therefore increase in output which it is possible to effect through eliminating unnecessary motions and substituting fast for slow and inefficient motions'.[28] Thus, technology and body could become symbiotic, each tuned to move quickly, without loss of time or energy. The elimination of waste that Taylor recommended occurred at both a literal and representational level. Business practice was organised to limit waste and streamline production, and sportswear lent itself to this spare approach, since its design stripped away extraneous detail. Models wearing sportswear were then represented in advertising and editorial as rationalised figures, machine-like in their apparent efficiency of line.

As Jack Hardy noted, greater mechanisation and the scientific organisation of manufacturers led to a reduction in the number of workers needed, and a decline in skilled jobs, as work was contracted out to piece-workers who handled simple, individual components. New electric knives meant that larger than ever quantities of fabric could be cut simultaneously.[29] Hardy commented that 'manufacturing efficiency has gone up to the point where Fordized specialization and automatic flow of work have made modern clothing shops very similar to army units, each under the command of a foreman or sub-foreman'.[30] Sportswear, despite its connotations of leisure, expressed this discipline within its design and mass-produced machine aesthetic. This ideal was then transposed on to the wearer's body, through her clothing, and ideally, through exercise and diet's discipline. As more women entered the workplace because of financial problems and male unemployment, this ideal was extended in fashion representation onto the figure of woman as worker. The fashion industry had always employed a large number of women and, during the Depression, those at the top of the industry began to organise themselves to further American fashion. New job titles, such as stylist, which had emerged during the 1920s, became more professional, as businesses sought to eliminate waste and fashion magazines and books began to represent the American career woman as an ideal and to give constructive advice to young women who aspired to work in the fashion industry itself.

CAREER WOMEN

Apparently caught on camera as she runs out of her New York home or office, the model in Martin Munkacsi's 1938 shot for *Harper's Bazaar,* is the embodiment of the modern career woman (fig. 3.3). Busy and purposeful, her body is caught in action as she rushes through the city. Munkasci's photograph uses New York as a backdrop to the career woman's life: the 'Woman of Fashion' is no longer the sole occupant of elite fashion magazine pages. Her leisured figure, draped in elegant poses in glamorous studio settings, has been joined by the Depression-era working-woman. This model is depicted as active and dynamic, her clothes are cut to move with her figure. Her outfit epitomises the efficient ensembles made by sportswear manufacturers and smart department stores, in this case a neat pleated skirt, white Peter Pan collar blouse, dark blazer and beret from Saks. Her figure and garments are streamlined, and can in many ways be seen as representing the Taylorist ideal of efficiency transposed onto the female body. Her clothes are designed to be made quickly, wasting the least time and labour possible, they are sold in carefully merchandised displays, crafted to lead the consumer to make quick choices, eliminating the need for fittings. Their simple styles make them easy to wear and care for and the snapshot style of photography used to depict them reinforces the idea of speed, immediacy and constant movement. At every stage therefore, from conception to representation, the career woman's clothing resonates with the processes of modern business practice. The modern career woman was represented not just through clothing, but by her grooming routine, her posture, and the way she moved.

Despite the fact that the numbers of career women grew during the hardships of the period, the career woman herself was still a minority figure. Yet she was shown in fashion magazines as a positive role model, a woman who took an active part in contemporary life. Her image was allied to that of the college girl: she was an older, more sophisticated version of the latter, but she retained the college girl's verve and dynamism. Each constructed image was used to encourage women to consume an identity ready-made for their particular lifestyle, and each entered the realm of high fashion as the Depression set in. Magazines and retailers found themselves obliged to look to new archetypes and shifting ideas of fashion and style for modern women. Although many women did not actually lose their jobs, they were forced to make financial sacrifices, or to rethink the direction of their careers.

This is borne out by both Estelle Hamburger, in her account of her career progress during the Depression, and by Elizabeth Hawes, who wrote of the number of American women who were

3.3.   Martin Munkacsi, Saks Fifth Avenue, *Harper's Bazaar*, June 1938. Photograph © Joan
       Munkacsi. Courtesy Howard Greenberg Gallery, NYC

3.4.   Bergdorf Goodman advertisement, *Vogue*, 15 September 1933

3.5.   Vera Maxwell suit, 1937. The Metropolitan Museum of Art, gift of Miss Vera Maxwell,
       1945. Photograph © The Metropolitan Museum of Art 2007

sent home from Paris-based jobs in the early 1930s.[31]

Despite this sense of uncertainty, the number of women in the workforce steadily grew. The figure had risen by 4.3 per cent between 1920 and 1930, to become 24.3 per cent of the overall workforce; and, between 1930 and 1940, the figure grew by 4.5 per cent so that women by the end of the decade made up 25.4 per cent of the entire workforce. The New Deal did little to address women's issues in particular, and prejudice existed, particularly concerning the fact that more married women were entering the workplace.[32] As Winifred D. Wandersee has noted, despite these problems 'the women who overcame the economic handicaps and discriminatory policies of the Depression to remain in the workforce … provided a pattern of combining work and family roles that was to predominate in the post World War Two years'.[33]

Women's entrance into the workplace had ambivalent effects: while real progress was made, women still had to find a means to integrate femininity into a traditionally masculine sphere. Sharon Hartman Strom wrote of women's advances within the office, while she recognised the often unspoken 'rules' of administrative employment: 'By 1930 … the gender and class hierarchy of the office was securely in place. Both working-class and middle-class women were present in large numbers'.[34] However, women's position in the office had to be balanced by an acute awareness of the visual identity they constructed and 'the display of the female body in the office proved to be problematical for employers and workers alike. As a result, all women office workers were continually presented with the struggle of how to look and what to wear. Supervisors and women workers found hair and dress styles to be contested terrain'.[35]

High fashion magazines began to write positively about women who worked and promoted an ideal career woman, who incorporated existing ideals of fashion and grooming within a style that signified modernity and progress. A 1934 *Vogue* article, 'Beauty and Four Women', shows how, during the Depression, the career woman, or in this case 'business' woman, was integrated into the established format of its grooming pages. Together with the woman on a 'Limited Income', she has by now become a staple 'type', who sits alongside more familiar *Vogue* archetypes: the 'Leisured Lady', and the 'Globe Trotter'. The article chronicles each woman's day, and shows how a thorough beauty regime can, and should, be integrated into her lifestyle. The need to maintain the cosmetic standards of the 'Leisured Lady', who has the most social status, is made clear in this description: 'Mrs. Business Woman refuses to look as if she worked from nine to five daily (which she does) and has achieved her serene beauty through brilliant use of her spare time'.[36] She must do this through well-informed consumption of the right products and beauty services and, as stated, a strictly disciplined use of time. When her day is detailed, it begins with 'works at the office with concentration and efficiency from 9:30 to 12:30. 12.30 to 2: Has her hair done at Charles Bock's because she believes that a smart coiffure is one element of her success. While her hair dries, she has a manicure ... [and] has a simple but good lunch sent in on a tray'.[37] This new icon is therefore under pressure simultaneously to work hard, and to construct and maintain the correct image.

There were clear commercial imperatives in the inclusion of the career women, as magazines needed to maximise their readership by acknowledging the reality that a significant number of middle-class women did now have to work. Indeed, greater awareness of the realities of many women's lives was called for in the wider industry. At a Fashion Group meeting of April 1936 on the subject of 'better timing of fashions in accord with consumer demand', Mrs Ariel Dingwall, adviser in dramatics at Hunter College, provided a consumer's view when 'she urged stores and designers to stress suitability of styles to the working woman, rather than emphasize ultra-feminine trends'.[38] However, discussion of the career woman within the elite context of fashion magazines marked a subtle shift in ideas of femininity. It represented the evolution of the working woman's visual identity within a high fashion, middle-class milieu and contributed to her construction of a viable body image within the usually male-dominated workplace.

The 'career woman' was part of a modern ideal of femininity propounded in high fashion magazines during the 1930s. It had gradually emerged since women first began to enter white-collar jobs in the second half of the nineteenth century. Previously, activity had been represented mainly as part of an otherwise leisured lifestyle, and any exertion that was mentioned was a matter of choice: exercise, sports and travel were activities that befitted a woman with social status. Paid work was associated with the working class, or as something disreputable that actresses and dancers did. While women within the entertainment world could be included within fashion magazines because of the glamour and fashion associated with their profession, women who had to earn a living were only rarely represented within the fashion pages. This was ironic, since fashion magazines were predominantly staffed by successful career women. Fashion production and fashion consumption were, in most instances, kept separate in order to maintain fashion's façade of effortlessness. However, during the 1930s, fashion became one of the ways in which women could perform this emergent identity as dynamic and productive, literally by having a high-level career in fashion and metaphorically through visual consumption of the ideal in fashion imagery.

Vogue discussed the different, often contradictory ideas of acceptable womanhood that the career woman had to encompass in March 1930, in an article entitled 'The Toiling Lily':

> Like Janus, the modern woman who sought a career has two faces, both charming. One, a combination of fashionable beauty and Byzantine Madonna, is turned towards what used to be called a woman's life: home, society, and those frivolities which are essentially woman's. The other, a brave and clever face, looks out with wisdom and eagerness at the world of work. Toiler and spinner, she nevertheless retains the graces of the lily. In a world full of change, nothing reflects the angles of the modern trend more than she.[39]

Fashion magazines provided a variety of role models for women who had successful careers. Exemplars included arts and entertainment stars, such as Carole Lombard; sportswomen and aviators, such as Helen Wills and Amelia Earhart; and businesswomen from the fashion world, such as Hattie Carnegie and Dorothy Shaver. In April 1930, *Vogue* even included an article, 'The Times, the Job and the Girl' by Eleanor Roosevelt, which advocated a 'vocational bureau' to provide work experience and networking opportunities for young girls, who need to be made aware of the possibilities available to them.[40]

Despite such encouragement, at the end of the decade, many women still aimed for marriage rather than a career. *Mademoiselle* magazine, set up to target young college and career girls in 1935, was concerned to learn that only 7 per cent of their college readers polled for their July 1938 'Careers Number' felt marriage and a career were possible. This was despite the fact that, according to the 1931 census, eleven million women, that is one in three of those aged fifteen to forty-four, were employed. This prompted the magazine editorial to state that while it was normal to aim to get married: 'We believe that marriage and a career are compatible; more, we believe that every woman, married or single, should be educated for a career when and if necessity or inclination warrants it'.[41]

Within the fashion industry, it was becoming easier for girls to find information on careers and role models to aspire to. There was a gradual rise in practical courses, both at longer-established institutions, such as Parsons School of Design, and at newer ones, such as that set up by renowned fashion advisor Tobé Coller Davis and her sister, magazine editor Julia Coburn, in New York. There were also short courses and 'how to' books published by the Fashion Group itself. The fashion industry was not only training potential women executives, it was representing them in an idealised way in advertising and editorials, and making explicit connections between career women, America, and the city. Figure 3.4 depicts an advertisement for 'an original design by Bergdorf Goodman' from September 1933, which encapsulates the confident, well-groomed archetype of business success. The model looks directly towards the camera, one perfectly arched eyebrow visible beneath her severely angled hat. She is shot from the side, the top half of her body turns to the front, and one arm clasps a streamlined clutch bag behind her back, the other reaches across her legs. She is seated, yet her pose gives her figure a dynamic edge. Her demeanour matches the copy: 'The Well-dressed President'. Her upmarket department store dress gives her authority. It denotes luxury (the fabric is a rich, tactile Lyons cross-barred velvet), while at the same time adhering to a well-established American work wear style: the shirtwaister. Bergdorf Goodman's version adds slight fullness at the shoulders, a neat collar, and a contrasting white bow tie at the neck. Worn with pale gloves and a plumed hat, it balances the traditional feminine elements necessary to make it acceptable as womenswear with the need to project a smart, serious air. The accompanying text reinforces this, while also claiming such style as 'American': 'smart American women meet many occasions never met by smart French women … as presiding officers, political speakers, important business executives. Bergdorf Goodman original designs offer suitable clothes of a rich and rather severe formality'.[42]

This combination of femininity and 'formality' made sportswear collections a popular option. Lines were simple and feminine, yet lacked overt decoration or distracting details, and therefore posited equivalence with men's ubiquitous business suit. Sportswear designers drew upon British town and country wear tailoring, as well as smart, functional dresses and separates that were easy to adapt to different social and work environments. This genre of fashion was able to accommodate various aspects of contemporary women's lifestyles, since it addressed leisure, work, and home. An element of sportswear's appeal in this context was undoubtedly that its uncomplicated designs did not immediately draw attention to the wearer, as more trend-based fashion frequently did. This enabled wearers to remain anonymous yet appropriate. The subtle, sometimes innovative aspects of the designs were discernible only upon closer inspection.

Vera Maxwell was among the earliest New York sportswear designers to be recognised by her own name, rather than by that of the manufacturer or department store for whom she worked. Figure 3.5 shows a 1937 ensemble, which is just the kind of sleek, well-fitted skirt suit popular in the second half of the decade.[43] Made from soft taupe wool, the three-quarter length, narrow-cut jacket would mould to the wearer's figure, giving a streamlined appearance. All extraneous elements are eliminated: the neckline is collarless, with only a triple line of self-colour stitching to define its shape and mask the seams, a motif echoed either side of right and left seams on the front of the jacket. Discreet, horizontal pockets are placed just below the waistline and the shoulders are slightly padded to add stature to the wearer. The pattern pieces are bias cut to give a better fit and also to create another subtle decorative feature, since the diagonal grain creates a contrasting design with the rib of the fabric. The back of the jacket is equally restrained: cut in three sections, the seams are once again disguised by the triple line of stitching detail and a deep slit, running from waist to hem to allow ease of movement, is covered by a flap of fabric. The jacket comes with a matching skirt, which is again narrow cut, with a slight 'A' line to the hem. It fastens with a zip and two poppers on the left front with darts at the waistline to fit to the figure. The label reads: 'Vera Maxwell Original', a mark of Maxwell's own success as it was still rare for a designer's name to be used.

Such restrained styles were symptomatic of women's need to construct an image of authority and discretion within both office and city street, in order to conform to social and cultural expectations of femininity. The resulting garments should not be seen merely as a rejection of elaborate decoration and status display. They are a more subtle way for women to demonstrate their financial, social, and cultural standing. In common with men's tailoring, Maxwell's suit represents a form of 'inconspicuous consumption', a type of dress that, because of its discreet good quality, is most easily read by others of the same status, who are equally attuned to its subtle signifiers, such as the triple seamed stitching to hide the seams and bias cut silhouette.[44] Sportswear of this kind was contradictory: it was both simple and complicated, its design stripped to the minimum in terms of cut and decoration, but also intended to incorporate a variety of elements, from femininity to functionality, necessary for the career woman's burgeoning identity in the 1930s.

Vera Maxwell said of her role in developing the kind of clothing available to middle-class women:

> We were the first designers I guess to do clothes wholesale for the middle class … Not a rich woman but a well to do woman … And when I went out, I saw how many women would try things on, and almost all my designing had something to do with the ease of a woman buying it quickly, so she doesn't have to have hems turning up.[45]

During the inter-war period, middle-class women took on a wider range of roles outside the domestic sphere and this greater activity, whether for sports, social or work reasons, required a more flexible visual identity. Sportswear was able to incorporate these apparently contradictory roles, since Maxwell and her peers designed it to be wearable in both formal and informal situations. Garments could be worn in different combinations, and with an assortment of accessories to adapt to women's varied requirements. Etiquette books advised women on how to achieve this balance. Margaretta Byers' 1938 book, *Designing Women: The Art, Technique and Cost of Being Beautiful,* began by stating:

> A woman who wishes to feed her ego and to move with ease and social security in a chosen sphere of society starts by dressing the part. Her best bet is to dress impeccably and correctly, yet with that arrogant casualness which permits her to turn attention to conversation and conduct.

> Her costume, if advisedly chosen, conspires to help relegate it to the subconscious. Therein lies the test for good clothes: the wearer must believe so whole-heartedly in the smartness and suitability of her costume that she can forget about it. But the beholder must be kept constantly aware of how lovely the wearer looks.[46]

The image projected by middle-class women therefore needed to appear effortless and, importantly, had to indicate that such a woman was so knowledgeable about 'correct' dress codes that they were second nature to her. It was necessary to have adopted (or to have been born into) a set of accepted class values in order to 'pass' as a member of middle-class society. Women could best achieve this by having enough confidence in their status and taste to present an image of 'arrogant casualness', wearing simple, smart clothes that projected social standing subtly, rather than through, for example, flamboyant displays of wealth.

There were added pressures for middle-class career women, who needed to balance these ideals of femininity with the 'masculine' values of the work place. Byers had advice for the 'Executive' and proposed a wardrobe that largely comprised black and grey dresses and suits, occasionally enlivened by brighter colour accessories. She was clearly perplexed by the problem of how a woman might dress appropriately for a professional career:

> All women in business, and for that matter, men too, know they have to dress the part of the successful people who have amassed fortunes and are merely working for their health. However, the problem of clothes strikes no one quite so hard as the woman executive … you who meet the same clients over and over and impress them with your affluence, your taste, your knowledge of fashion etiquette are on the spot … Yet if you don't dress superlatively, someone else will get your job.[47]

These issues were compounded, Byers felt, by the lack of an equivalent of the French 'compromise' dress, which could be worn to go to dinner 'formally or informally', and executive women needed something that would allow them to 'look businesslike in the office and unbusinesslike at lunch or tea all in the same costume, for you never have time to change'.[48] However, in reality, designers such as Vera Maxwell, Claire McCardell, and Clare Potter were already making such adaptable ensembles, which, especially in the following decade, were seen as intrinsically American, and expressive of American women's lifestyles. Perhaps the most famous example of this type of clothing is the so-called monastic dress, designed by Claire McCardell in 1938. This was a style that slipped easily over the head, hung from the shoulders, and which could easily be dressed up or down with accessories. This dress's popularity in 1938 demonstrated how keen women were for simple clothing solutions.

While career women needed this kind of easy-to-buy and easy-to-wear clothing, they also needed to project an image of control, which stemmed, at least in part, from adhering to current notions of respectability. Sportswear's consumers occupied a culture that sought conformity to mainstream ideals. For women confidently to occupy the variety of public and private roles that were increasingly demanded during the Depression, it was often more politic to appear the same, rather than to assert difference.

While conformity was a strong element in women's search for acceptable ideals of femininity, it would be wrong to view this reductively. Fashion and sportswear are not simple categories that can be stereotyped as either positive or negative in terms of women's role in this period or in terms of the idea(l)s of femininity that they constructed. In some instances conformity was represented, but this was sometimes a means to negotiate higher education or the workplace, and therefore to advance women's status. Also, many women involved in the fashion industry sought to challenge male dominance, and, while they did not necessarily identify themselves as feminists, could be viewed as part of a feminist project to further women's position within society. Pat Kirkham and Lynne Walker wrote about the situation of women designers:

> Although contemporary conceptions of appropriate occupations for women and men were central to women's access to particular types of design, the conditions and parameters within which women worked were fluid and changed over time. The concepts of 'women's work' and 'women designer' were redefined and extended. Women were active participants in the construction of new meanings about themselves – challenging, resisting, and negotiating restrictive ideologies about 'suitable' activities.[49]

The fashion industry had always provided women with a variety of occupations: originally at home and, as work became more industrialised in the nineteenth century, in office and factory as well as retail outlets. Fashion was one of the few areas of work where women had the opportunity to hold positions of power and influence and, potentially, to become financially independent.[50] At the end of the 1920s, successful women from various areas of New York's fashion industry began to discuss ways in which they could consolidate their influence and pool their knowledge.

THE FASHION GROUP

In May 1932, Edna Woolman Chase, editor-in-chief of *Vogue*, wrote an article, 'The Business of Fashion', which detailed what she saw as the most important issues to concern women working in the industry. The strapline read: 'At this time, when practically every young woman has a job or is looking for one, *Vogue* believes its readers will be interested in this speech given by Mrs Chase at the Metropolitan Museum in cooperation with the Fashion Group'.[51] In the worst year of the Depression thus far, Chase was keen to encourage women to regard the fashion industry as a promising career prospect, while not assuming that they would automatically be good at fashion because of their sex. She advocated careful research and an eagerness to learn and admonished readers not to be 'afraid of being too difficult to please. Ready acceptance is the path of mediocrity. Cultivate an ability to criticize ably and constructively. People may not love you for it, but they are bound to respect you if your opinions are sound'.[52] Chase wanted this rigorous and professional approach to be taken by individual women and by organisations, since 'that is what I should like to see this Fashion Group become – a body of well-equipped, able critics of the mode in all its phases'.[53]

The Fashion Group set out to professionalise women's role within the fashion industry and to assert the importance of fashion within the wider social, cultural, and economic sphere. It comprised a collective of executive women from a wide cross-section of the New York fashion world. In recognition of women's growing significance at high levels of the industry, the Group aimed to represent and promote executive women's interests, as well as those of the American fashion world. Potential members had to be proposed and backed by five existing members and had to have worked at executive level for three years in order to qualify. Edna Woolman Chase had originally mooted the idea for the group in 1928, but the first official meeting was not held until three years later, as discussions to create the group as an adjunct of the National Retail Dry Goods Association [N.R.D.G.A.] were superseded by the idea for a separate and distinct association. Estelle Hamburger, one of its early members, commented:

> The Fashion Group had made its commitment to become a forum, a stage and a force for American fashion … It was not a women's movement, but a movement of women who held jobs for which they had been chosen by men, mainly because women would be likely to know more than men about women's clothes.[54]

The founder members wanted fashion, and women's role as creators and disseminators of fashion ideas, to be given greater validity. To this end the Group instigated monthly luncheon meetings at which not just fashion, but also wider cultural, social, and economic trends were discussed and leading experts from various business, artistic and political backgrounds were invited to speak on current issues. As the Group grew, strands were added that focussed on specific areas of interest, including cosmetics and home furnishings.

Speeches and discussions were collected together in monthly bulletins that were sent out to members and interested parties across America and, subsequently, branches were set up in other cities, for example in Los Angeles. From early on, the Group saw part of its role as educational: it held short courses on different aspects of the industry, with proceeds donated to the Fashion Institute of Technology's library, and it published books that provided advice and career tips from its members.

The Fashion Group included many of the most powerful women in the New York fashion industry, including Eleanor Lambert, who handled publicity for fashion designers from 1934, Dorothy Shaver, who was made a vice-president of Lord & Taylor in 1931 after sixteen years at the store, Carmel Snow, editor at *Harper's Bazaar* from 1932, and designer Claire McCardell, who began her career at Townley, Inc. in 1931. The Group's importance as a forum for discussion of issues and ideas that mattered to the New York fashion industry is indisputable. Its meetings reflected the industry's concerns, from its reactions to the ongoing Depression in the 1930s to repeated debates on how best to merchandise clothing in department stores.

Its first formal meeting, in January 1931, was addressed by Kenneth Collins, Vice-President of Macy's, who discussed the role of taste in selling goods and the public's growing awareness of artistic elements in design, garnered through department store displays and the growth in art classes run by women's clubs, as much as through visits to the Metropolitan Museum.[55] His use of a combination of factual information on sales figures, the role of merchandising and the need for better-trained staff to aid sales, with comment on the impact of wider cultural trends, was typical of the Group's meetings. Their monthly luncheons would normally include three speakers on a related theme and drew upon professionals from a broad spectrum of disciplines. During the Depression, these included reports from Paris by visiting couturiers, such as Elsa Schiaparelli in February 1933, alongside reports on the latest trends from American fashion journalists who had just returned from France. The Group invited members of the N.R.D.G.A. to speak to them about their latest surveys and reports, and in June 1933, held a meeting about sweatshop labour that brought together union and government representatives. Alongside these industry-focussed topics were debates on the impact of popular culture on fashion, in terms of trends, retail and merchandising possibilities, such as a meeting in March 1933 with Elizabeth Hawes, Adelia Bird, the fashion editor of Photoplay, and Miss Katsch who ran the Cinema Shop at Macy's, and one the following month on the potential of radio advertising for fashion retailers.

Bankers, architects, advertising executives, even comedians, gave speeches to the Group, which seemed eager to glean information on social, cultural, and economic trends that might affect the fashion industry. Kenneth Collins proved a stalwart supporter, originally brought in to discuss aspects of the business and participate in workshops held to give members guidance on how to increase sales despite the financial downturns of the decade. While other male speakers, from the records kept of their talks, seem awkward in the presence of so many powerful women, Collins was keen to celebrate their contribution and significance. When he spoke at the Group's tenth anniversary meeting at the Hotel Astor in 1941, he noted that such an association would have been impossible when he started his career in 1926, since the industry was still dominated by men and Macy's had only one female merchandising manager. As he looked back over the 1930s, he reflected upon the rise in women executives and speculated that when the period came to be 'written up' in one hundred years time, 'this emancipation of women, this new and more important status of one half of the inhabitants of the globe, will be considered the one significant fact of our times'. Collins saw women's growing role in the public sphere as representative of a deep shift in attitudes that fundamentally altered female status, since 'after all, the scars of war inevitably heal and governments rise and fall, and economic systems come into being, and educational systems are things that have their day, but this will persist … I don't think men will ever again be able to contemptuously refer to the weaker sex and talk about the things that women cannot do'.[56] Collins positioned the Fashion Group within this context and it is important to note that the period he is referring to in this speech is often seen as a time of fragmentation and stagnation within the wider American feminist movement. While the Group did not identify itself with feminism, its members, individually and collectively, 'acted out' feminist tenets of female advancement, education, career development and training, and also functioned as a carefully-organised forum to explore current business practices to enable female (and male) professionals to perform as effectively as possible within their own areas of the industry. As Collins noted, the Group comprised women who held powerful positions and who could affect the way large businesses operated. This was a 'group of women who were doing things and not just looking on', and he connected this to the Group's establishment 'at a time when it sort of crystallized the shift in this country from an era of buying to an era of selling'.[57]

This shift from stores focussing on their buying skills to emphasising tactics for selling goods was a recurrent topic for the Group, as members considered various techniques to increase sales and tailor products to the customer. In the nineteenth century production is often described as masculine, and consumption as feminine. In the twenties and thirties, this binary opposition is mediated by the additional truism that since women are the primary consumers in most households, they will also be particularly adept at selling, whether in advertising, retailing and merchandising. They were therefore employed to choose the right range of goods for a store as a buyer or to present merchandise effectively as a stylist. Women from all of these areas were represented in the Group's membership. The other career titles were more established, but stylist was the most recent addition and best epitomises the way that department store presidents and advertising executives increasingly turned to women during the boom years of the 1920s, when, under increasing pressure to use fashion as a sales tool on all commodities, it was felt that fashionable women would provide the necessary insights on how to sell products to consumers.

Paul Nystrom's description of the function of styling from 1932 demonstrates how it blurred distinctions between production and retail. Stylists could work on aspects of a commodity within both the manufacturing and the retail process. Their input could, for example, alter the line, colour, or decoration of an object, add to the way it was packaged and labelled or, within a department store, might contribute to the way it was placed amongst other objects within the store and the environment in which it was displayed.[58] Despite the possibility that stylists would add cultural and artistic value to a product, they could not guarantee its success, and, especially when the economy took a downward turn, the store executives could blame them for lack of sales and for over-spending. Stylists had been hired, at least in part, because they were deemed to have an understanding of fashion by virtue of their sex. When the Depression set in, they could equally be criticised for lack of any further specific qualifications. Nystrom and others noted that the debutantes, college graduates, and other women who had been employed as stylists because of their own personal style, could not always transfer this good taste onto the commodities they styled, and that 'many if not most of these new-placed stylists failed to produce adequate tangible results'.[59]

This very lack of a tangible product was part of the problem concerning industry perceptions of stylists. They were hired to add extra 'stylishness' to something that already existed and even their job title was hard to define. The job's ambiguity reflected that of women in the fashion industry in general: they were required to utilise skills that were perceived as feminine, yet simultaneously their work was open to criticism because it appeared to tap into an inherent instinct rather than any 'real' skills. Elizabeth Hawes gave a blunt summary of this new career as 'a bastard art' and one that was unsettling to those already employed in the industry as it seemed to question the buyer or merchandiser's judgement: 'No buyer wanted her [the stylist]. She was just another salary to the merchandising man. If the buyer couldn't supply what the store thought the public wanted, having an attractive girl at hand with large ideas on what was smart didn't solve the problem'.[60] Some stylists, however, did create a viable and successful career path. Estelle Hamburger gives a different view of the relationship between the stylist and other members of the fashion team, in this case at Stern's. Her discussion of collaborations with Tobé Coller Davis, who had become successful enough by 1927 to set up her own fashion advisory service, shows that stylists could also face resistance because they suggested new approaches that conflicted with long-established patterns of buying and merchandising.[61] Hamburger, who was equally keen to test new methods and to encourage better understanding of all aspects of fashion to create more successful and imaginative advertising campaigns, describes how she and Tobé would have to persuade buyers and salespeople from each department to focus on new fashions to raise the store's prestige and move away from what and how they had sold before.[62]

Tobé and Hamburger were amongst the first members of the Group and their own prominent careers, provided templates for aspiring fashion professionals. The Group was able, along with educational provision such as that provided by the Tobé-Coburn School for Fashion Careers, to help to professionalise newly evolved jobs such as styling and to ensure their continued relevance and validity, through its meetings and through the training schemes it ran. Many of its members gave regular public talks that helped to nurture wider understanding of the varied careers available within fashion, and the advice given was gathered together into books such as Margaretta Stevenson's 1938 work, *How the Fashion World Works: Fit Yourself for a Fashion Future*.

In the 1930s the Group represented women from the New York fashion industry which, as well as consolidating women's role in the fashion business, reinforced the City as the source of fashion information for the nation as a whole. Its 'Fashion Futures' shows, which began in 1935, gave an annual review of leading styles that was attended by industry professionals from around the country. These shows attracted, amongst others, department store buyers and journalists who were keen to have early information on coming trends. The Group's activities drew regular attention from the press, from within the industry, in national publications such as *Women's*

Wear Daily as well as from New York newspapers, and, when a particularly important story was linked to the organisation, especially during the Second World War, from newspapers in other cities.

Other organisations were set up during the 1930s to foreground particular issues, such as the Fashion Originators Guild established in 1931 to fight against design copyists and the Dress Creators' League founded the same year for similar purposes. However, these did not have the wide aims that distinguished the Fashion Group and did not therefore reflect the industry's range of concerns under the Depression's financial constraints as the Fashion Group did. Although fashion insiders realised the Group's significance and how powerful the leading members were, many speakers who were asked to attend meetings were unclear why fashion people would want to hear talks on seemingly unconnected subjects such as psychology or finances. However, the members appear to be acutely aware of their need to comprehend how to make their own business practices more effective and efficient through a deeper understanding of consumer impulses and desires, especially when there was less money in circulation.

At a business lunch chaired by Dorothy Shaver in January 1938, the Group was able to report progress in some of the areas it had covered in its 1933 meeting, discussed above. Ruth Kerr, the outgoing treasurer, reported the Group's 'coming of age' financially in 1936, so a financial plan was established. Membership now stood at well over eight hundred; subscriptions fees raised $10,600, and Fashion Training Courses raised $950. Outgoing president Winifred Ovitte reported a steady annual increase in members, expanded training programmes and a Placement Bureau that had found jobs for 'hundreds' of members.[63]

The Group's aim to contribute to the professionalisation of women's role in the industry was achieved despite the complexities of gender within fashion. Women had always been employed in large numbers in the fashion trades and it was one of the few major international industries where women could attain power and status, as attested by the women who came together to form the Fashion Group itself. However, most manufacturers were male, as were many executives at department and specialty stores and magazine publishers, so women had to negotiate the space they inhabited and consolidate their professional status. Allied to this delicate balance of gender and power was the fact that, despite the size and economic importance of the industry, it was often dismissed for the very reason that it was perceived to be run by women for other women and was therefore too trivial to warrant serious consideration.

This is amply demonstrated in an article from *Fortune* magazine in June 1930, the headline of which summarises this condescending attitude: 'Cloak And Suit ...The Country's Fourth Largest Industry Is At The Mercy Of Two Forces – Labor And A Woman's Vanity. Together, They Keep It Without Leadership And Without Stability'.[64] Although fashion had entered many areas of production, apparel, accessories, and cosmetics were deemed a feminine concern and there-fore worthy of contempt, even though men bought clothing and accessories too, and had to present a carefully groomed appearance to be taken seriously in business. *Fortune's* headline demonstrates how women, along with labour, were viewed as problematic to patriarchal capitalism. Women's status was ambiguous, as fashion knowledge was perceived as part of their nature, rather than a skill to be admired, and they 'only' had other women to compete with.

In another article of 1935, *Fortune* deploys loaded language to emphasise the lack of any 'real' achievement by women in the fashion world:

> The exclusion of businesswomen [from *Fortune's* list] who carry on their business in these lush pastures is not merely arbitrary. The basic, brass-tack proof of feminine success in industry is feminine success in those industries historically dominated by men. There are two reasons. The first is simply that the industries historically dominated by men are vital industries – manufacturing, banking, railroads, and the like.[65]

Fortune does not usually take such a judgemental view of how the entrepreneurs it covered made their money; the magazine also conveniently omits to mention the number of men involved in 'non-vital' industries, something that is borne out by what the article goes on to state:

> The second [reason] is that feminine success in the exploitation of women proves nothing but the fact that women are by nature feminine ... The difference is not merely that women meet less male competition in their own acreage. The difference is that success in style designing or in the sale of cosmetics or in the publicizing of women's wear implies little or nothing as to those activities in which womanhood is not a natural advantage. Elizabeth Arden is not a potential Henry Ford. She is Elizabeth Arden. It is a career in itself but it is not a career in industry.

> Elizabeth Arden and her kind, in other words, are not professional women. They are women by profession.[66]

Such discriminatory statements make the Fashion Group's achievements even more significant, both in terms of its collective works and those of its individual members. *Fortune* not only ignores the fact that Arden was in competition not just with other women, but with male entrepreneurs such as Max Factor and Charles Revson, but more importantly the fact that all women are not born with an inclination towards fashion. It also demonstrates by its very exclusions just how hard it was for women to be taken seriously both inside a 'feminine' industry and in the wider business world.

The Fashion Group provided a forum in which women could find ways to assert their status and enhance their business practices. While more women entered the workplace during the Depression they still had to negotiate a difficult route to acceptance: concurrently demonstrating their professionalism and reinforcing their skill, while remaining within restrictive codes of acceptable femininity. This extended beyond behaviour and conduct at work to mean that women were encouraged to construct a visual identity that would enable them simultaneously to become Taylorist, machine-like bodies, streamlined to work and move efficiently, and yet individual enough to distinguish themselves and demonstrate cultural and economic capital through their choice of attire.

As the 1930s wore on, the image that fashion magazines formulated expressed this contradictory ideal through dynamic images of women in tailored sportswear garments. These incorporated the ambiguity of modernity and suggested a means for women to adapt to the 'masculine' requirements of modern capitalism. It was an image that was portrayed in fashion media as intrinsically American, part of a way of life that was specific to the New World. It enabled middle-class women, whom it was assumed would lead a far more leisured existence in Europe, to move between 'male' production and 'female' consumption and to inhabit a space in between the two. Women executives constructed the means to disseminate fashion, through processes such as designing, buying, retail, styling, and merchandising. These methods of choosing fashions that were thought particularly to appeal to American women and of communicating this appeal effectively were refined under the impact of the decade's straitened means. Just as groups of women, such as executives and college girls, gained increasing visibility within the pages of fashion magazines, so fashion insiders, most of whom were women, began to push for greater promotion of individual fashion designers. This was prompted by growing confidence in American fashion's ability to define itself as distinct from Paris, partly because of genuine economic need to find new sources of fashion ideas and partly because a number of designers were creating sportswear that crystallised ideas about women's contemporary lifestyles and which was ideal for current methods of production. Leading members of the Fashion Group from Carmel Snow to Dorothy Shaver and Eleanor Lambert, were instrumental in constructing the ways in which American fashion and American women were to be represented and the ideas that were to become attached to New York sportswear.

1   Advertisement caption for Barbara Lee, *Vogue*, 21 December 1929, 7.

2   Advertisement caption for Barbara Lee, 7.

3   Paul H. Nystrom, *Economics of Fashion* (New York: Ronald Press Company, 1928), iii.

4   Hamburger, *It's A Woman's Business*, 170.

5   Hamburger, *It's A Woman's Business,* 170–71.

6   Paul Nystrom, *Fashion Merchandising* (New York: The Ronald Press, 1932), 4.

7   Anthony J. Badger, *The New Deal: The Depression Years, 1933–40* (New York: Hill and Wang, 1993), 30.

8   'Cloak and Suit', *Fortune,* June 1930, 92.

9   Nystrom, *Fashion Merchandising*, iv.

10 Jack Hardy, *The Clothing Workers* (London: Martin Lawrence, c. 1936), 57.

11 Hardy, *The Clothing Workers,* 169.

12 Hardy, *The Clothing Workers*, 181.

13 William H. Dooley, *Economics of Clothing and Textile: The Science of the Clothing and Textile Business* (Boston and New York: D.C. Heath and Co., 1934), 113.

14 'Follies of 1932', *Vogue*, 1 August, 1932, 43.

15 'Follies of 1932', 43.

16 '*Vogue's*-eye View of More Taste than Money', *Vogue*, 15 November, 1936, 49.

17 '*Vogue's*-eye View of More Taste than Money', 49.

18 'Fashions America Does Best', *Vogue*, 1 February 1938, 114.

19 Buckland, 'Promoting American Designers', in Welters and Cunningham, *Twentieth-Century American Fashion*, 105.

20 Anne O'Hare McCormack, 'A New Americanism is Emerging', *The New York Times*, 4 September 1932, SM1.

21 T.C.Crawford, 'Topics of the Week', *Washington Post*, 18 November 1883, 4.

22 'Society', *The New York Times*, 14 March 1897, 10.

23 See, for example, his discussion of American fashion and its proponents in Morris de Camp Crawford, *The Ways of Fashion* (New York: G. P. Putnam's Sons, 1941), 89–128.

24 See B. J. Perkins, 'Ask Hoover's Aid in French Import Curb', *Women's Wear Daily*, 31 March 1932, 1.

25 'The Sub-debutante, With an Income Limited to Chic', *Vogue*, 15 July 1931, 64.

26 Daniel Nelson, *Frederick W. Taylor and the Rise of Scientific Management* (Wisconsin: University of Wisconsin Press, 1980), 199.

27 Frederick W. Taylor, *The Principles of Scientific Management* (New York and London: Harper and Brothers, 1913, first published in 1911), 12.

28 Taylor, *The Principles of Scientific Management*, 24.

29 Hardy, *The Clothing Workers*, 10, 195.

30 Hardy, *The Clothing Workers*, 200.

31 Hamburger, *It's a Woman's Business* and Hawes, *Fashion is Spinach*.

32 Valerie K. Oppenheimer, *The Female Labor Force in the United States: Demographic and Economic Factors Governing its Growth and Changing Composition* (Berkeley: Institute of International Studies, University of California, 1970), 3, quoted in Ware, *Holding Their Own*, 22.

33 Wandersee, *Women's Work*, 102.

34 Sharon Hartman Strom, *Beyond the Typewriter: Gender, Class and the Origins of Modern American Office Work, 1900–1930* (Urbana and Chicago: University of Illinois Press, 1992), 367.

35 Strom, *Beyond the Typewriter*, 370.

36 'Beauty and Four Women', *Vogue*, 15 September 1934, 78.

37 'Beauty and Four Women', 79.

38 'Suggest Fashion Timing', *The New York Times*, 30 April 1936, 28.

39 'The Toiling Lily', *Vogue*, 1 March 1930, 55.

40 Eleanor Roosevelt, 'The Times, the Job and the Girl', *Vogue*, 26 April 1930, 45, 102.

41 'The Last Word … On Careers', *Mademoiselle*, July 1938, 19.

42 Bergdorf Goodman advertisement caption in *Vogue*, 15 September 1933, 3.

43 45.56.2a–b, Costume Institute at the Metropolitan Museum of Art, New York.

44 See Rebecca Arnold, 'Luxury and Restraint: Minimalism in 1990s Fashion', in Ian Griffiths and Nicola White, eds., *The Fashion Business* (Oxford: Berg, 2000), 167–82.

45 Vera Maxwell interviewed by Mildred Finger, for the Oral History Project of the Fashion Institute of Technology, no. TT139.073 v.54 (21 September and 11 October 1983), 15. Gladys Marcus Library, Special Collections, Fashion Institute of Technology, New York.

46 Margaretta Byers, *Designing Women: The Art, Technique and Cost of Being Beautiful* (New York: Simon and Schuster, 1938), vii.

47 Byers, *Designing Women*, 193.

48 Byers, *Designing Women*, 193–94.

49 Pat Kirkham and Lynne Walker, 'Women Designers in the USA, 1900–2000: Diversity and Difference', in Pat Kirkham, ed., *Women Designers in the USA, 1900–2000: Diversity and Difference* (New Haven and London: Yale University Press, 2000), 62.

50 See Wendy Gamber, *The Female Economy: Millinery and Dressmaking Trades, 1860–1930* (Urbana and Chicago: University of Illinois Press, 1997).

51 Edna Woolman Chase, 'The Business of Fashion', *Vogue*, 1 May 1932, 41.

52 Chase, 'The Business of Fashion', 107.

53 Chase, 'The Business of Fashion', 107.

54 Estelle Hamburger, 'The First Fifty Years', *in The Fashion Group, 1930–1980* (New York: Fashion Group, 1980), n. p.

55 Kenneth Collins speaking to The Fashion Group, c. January 1931, The Fashion Group Archive, File 1, Box 72, Series X, New York Public Library.

56 Kenneth Collins speaking to The Fashion Group, 10 February 1941, The Fashion Group Archive, File 10, Box 73, Series X, New York Public Library.

57 Kenneth Collins speaking to The Fashion Group, 10 February 1941.

58 Nystrom, *Fashion Merchandising*, 42.

59 Nystrom, *Fashion Merchandising*, 63.

60 Elizabeth Hawes, *Fashion is Spinach*, 93.

61 The Tobé Report is still published today and is a leading provider of trend information to the fashion industry.

62 Hamburger, *It's a Woman's Business*, 212–25.

63 Fashion Group Meeting, 26 September 1933.

64 'Cloak And Suit…The Country's Fourth Largest Industry Is At The Mercy Of Two Forces – Labor And A Woman's Vanity. Together, They Keep It Without Leadership And Without Stability', *Fortune*, June 1930, 92 –100.

65 'Women in Business: III', *Fortune*, September 1935, 81.

66 'Women in Business: III', *Fortune*, September 1935, 81.

CHAPTER FOUR
SPORTSWEAR'S PROMOTION
DURING THE 1930S

NEW YORK DEPARTMENT STORES

The onset of the Great Depression forced department store executives to think and act creatively to maintain their status as arbiters of fashion and style, despite job cuts and drops in sales. Sales and price-cutting were problematic, since they could suggest that a store was in difficulty. Stores needed to project a strong identity and use a merchandising policy that would reassure its customers that any changes necessitated by the Great Depression were strategic and planned, rather than ad hoc responses to a chaotic business environment. This was important for stores' future success, despite the fact that, as David E. Kyvig writes, all Americans did not equally experience either the prosperity of the 1920s economic boom, or the subsequent hardships of the financial crash, but:

> By 1932 an estimated 28 per cent of the nation's households, containing 34 million people, did not have a single employed wage earner. By 1933 Americans overall had 54 per cent as much income as in 1929. The immensity of the Great Depression caused virtually every American to feel personally vulnerable.[1]

As a consequence, stores had to aim to restore their customers' confidence that consumption could continue to provide them with a route to escape the hardships (real or threatened) of their day to day lives, as well as a stable way to construct a sense of self in a period of uncertainty. Changes in interior design, advertising or displays, needed to be incorporated into the store's existing identity, rather than running counter to it. These shifting expectations and desires were also part of the environment that promoted sportswear to a wider audience and broadened its appeal beyond active sports and spectator wear. This chapter will examine the ways that stores and magazines portrayed and advertised sportswear as fashionable dress during the Great Depression. It will explore the ways that these promotional tactics irrevocably linked sportswear to ideals of Americanness, which were to be fully exploited during the Second World War. The growing importance of sportswear will then be examined looking at the evolution of the monastic dress. This exemplifies the ways that trends developed, and the broader context of both the fashion industry and the improvement in sales by the end of the decade.

Sportswear was a key element in advertising campaigns, usually linked to seasonal lifestyle needs, such as holiday periods in summer and winter or the start of college in the autumn. As the 1930s wore on, sportswear shifted further from imagery of elite leisure to incorporate a wider range of social groups at different income levels. Not only were sports styles wearable in both formal and informal environments, but also they were usually made of simple, cheap fabrics, such as cotton, which meant they could be reproduced at various price points. This meant that there was less compromise in quality in sportswear copies than there were in many couture-led copies. Sportswear was therefore an attractive way for stores to lure customers in. It combined the consumer ideals of quality and ease of care, with elements of style and fashion, about which customers were unwilling to compromise. Winifred Wandersee has noted that, even during the Depression, many people tried to continue consuming at the same rate that they had in the previous decade, since:

> In order to maintain the standards achieved during the 1920s, families often went into debt or resorted to supplementary wage-earners. Although many families had to follow these measures simply to survive, for a wide range of middle-income families the choice was based upon relative values rather than absolute need.[2]

Department stores were keen to encourage customers to maintain their lifestyle standards and interest in fashion. This is apparent in sportswear advertising for New York's main department stores, which appeared in *Vogue* and *Harper's Bazaar* during the decade. These advertisements were usually placed in the prestigious early pages of publications that led readers into the magazine and established the fashion status of the advertiser. Store advertising had become increasingly sophisticated over the preceding decade, according to Margaret Case Harriman, pushed by 'Estelle Hamburger and Mary Lewis [who] gave department store advertising much of the spark it had long needed and even some of the proper organization it had lacked'.[3] Between them, the two women worked for several of the most important stores in New York, including Macy's and Franklin Simon. Lewis, like Hamburger, wished to address women directly through everyday language. She was a proponent both of New York as a source for fashion ideas and mass-produced ready-to-wear, having counselled Elizabeth Hawes that she 'should learn about clothes in the raw white light of city streets'.[4]

These ideals were connected to store identity through sportswear advertising. This ran in parallel to the growing congruence between sportswear and ideals of Americanness, which, in turn, was connected to images of New York and emergent New York designers. Such connections were intended to appeal to the consumer as an individual, in terms of building a relationship with a designer as personality. In the case of sportswear, this was often achieved through the notion of an American woman designer creating clothes for her countrywomen. It was also implied by advertisers and fashion journalists that American designers had greater understanding of their countrywomen's needs than a Parisian couturier would have. More generalised appeals to patriotism and long-held American ideals in fabric and dress were also included to entice women into the stores. This shift towards using American identity and ideals of Americanness may have been part of a wider move towards isolationism. Despite Roosevelt having 'once professed to be an internationalist', this was exemplified in February 1932 by his repudiation of 'the idea that the United States should join the League of Nations'.[5] It was further reinforced at the London Conference in July 1933, where he indicated that America would not be 'party to efforts at exchange-rate stabilization, nor would it return in the foreseeable future to [the] gold [standard]'.[6]

By the mid-thirties, department stores such as B. Altman confidently asserted America's fashion status, by naming their designers, as is the case in figure 4.1, and by using 'Early American design chintz' for play clothes that 'might have come from your great-grandmother'.[7] In 1935 Bergdorf Goodman was equally assured in its use of Americanness as a sales tool. This was made clear in the way that a model was placed against the New York skyline and the fabric is described as 'Manhattan chiffon'. These advertisements not only showed how ideals of Americanness were attached to department store sportswear, they also show the kind of clothes that increasingly were cast as distinctively American. The crisp, simple lines of the silhouettes, their careful co-ordination in terms of colour, pattern and design motifs and the quality of the designs, despite the fact that these were not from expensive ranges, were all particular to New York sportswear. In Paris and London clothing at this price point lacked the attention to detail and restrained design principles that were intrinsic to the best examples of American sportswear. Designers such as Tom Brigance and Clare Potter understood the restrictions of mass-production, which required basic pattern pieces and easy construction methods and made simplicity a virtue.

In 1932, Paul Nystrom had written of the recent reduction in 'institutional advertising', where stores relied solely upon their own name and reputation to sell goods, and the increase in 'direct sales advertising', which focussed advertisements on a specific product or clothing range.[8] He emphasised the need for retailers to be aware of their client base. Specialty stores were able to be more experimental in their advertising, since their customers were usually richer and more fashion conscious, and therefore more responsive to references to individuality and exclusiveness. As he noted, though, department stores had a wider consumer base, which was often more conservative. It is clear from the examples discussed above, that stores would also strive to balance between the more general statements about the clothes they sold, and specific

4.1. B. Altman advertisement, *Vogue*, 15 May 1935

4.2. Worsinger, Lord & Taylor Clare Potter windows for 'American Designers' campaign, 1933 © Museum of the City of New York Print Archives

4.3. Edward Steichen, Katharine Hepburn in Clare Potter, *Vogue*, 15 May 1933. Originally published in *Vogue* © Condé Nast Archive /CORBIS

references to particular ideals or qualities which might be less conservative. They could be given greater fashion edge by association with specific designers, or through fabric and detailing, which was elaborated upon in the advertisement's text. Thus, sportswear could once again represent a compromise, unthreatening to the less confident shopper, but capable, in the right designer's hands, of expressing innovative and high fashion capital.

It was important for stores to maintain their identity, and thus keep existing audiences, while simultaneously developing new ideas that might encourage new customers. Store loyalty could not be guaranteed:

> Some young women followed their mother's shopping patterns. For others, a store switch was a statement of independence. Still others were lured by newly developed Campus shops, college departments, or 'College Board' advisors – sales personnel and peers who were up on the latest fads and fashion within the stores or as store 'reps on campus'.[9]

College girls were a major target group for manufacturers and retailers. In the inter-war period, sportswear was sold in a wider range of sections of stores, such as the 'campus shops' mentioned above.[10] They represented what Gary Cross identifies as elements that were frequently employed during the Depression to encourage consumption: 'beyond trying to find new markets in previously neglected age groups, innovators redoubled their efforts to associate their products with pleasure and progress'.[11]

Such boutiques consequently sought to streamline the shopping experience, while simultaneously connecting buying clothes to positive lifestyle attributes, such as leisure and modernity. They created areas of the shop floor designed to cater to a specific market area, which could, therefore, lure a particular kind of customer. In-store shops would also affect the way customers moved through the store. Although department stores were nominally non-elite spaces, open to anyone, interior space was defined by type of goods, the way these were displayed, and by the audience they appealed to. In the late nineteenth century, stores had sold sportswear as active wear with associated equipment in an 'outing goods department'. However, by the thirties, sportswear was available in the resort shops and campus shops discussed above, which might be converted from one type of sportswear to another according to the season. Such spaces targeted middle-class women, who were able to afford not just the items on display, but also the activities connected to them, whether that meant going to college or taking a winter vacation. Saks Fifth Avenue listed a 'Tally Ho Sports Shop' in its advertisements from the period, but it was Lord & Taylor, under the guidance of Dorothy Shaver, which, with its 'special departments for small women, collegians, and teenagers … [became] the citadel for sporty femininity'.[12]

Shaver achieved this by a concerted campaign to promote American design. She began this with her 1929 commissions for Americana print fabrics from a range of artists, including Neysa McMein, Ralph Barton and Katherine Sturges, and then with her widely-publicised window and instore promotion of a selection of American fashion designers, which began in 1932.[13] As Elizabeth Hawes cynically noted, this was prompted by the Depression, since 'in the spring of 1932 … Buying French models was expensive. Moreover, they were sold by Klein for $4.75. Besides that, the French weren't paying their debts and the British were "Buying British". The public was holding onto its nickels. It needed something startling to pry them loose'.[14]

These promotions helped to encourage the use of designers' names in advertising and magazine and newspaper copy in *Vogue* and to a lesser extent, until the 1940s, *Harper's Bazaar*. Stores had previously opposed such a move, since they felt it would herald a loss of their own power and status..However, as a gradual shift towards personality-driven promotional techniques took hold in American fashion and national identity became a selling tool, the media began to name designers who had until then worked anonymously for stores and manufacturers. *The New York Times*, for example, in 1939 finally gave the name of designers whose work was featured.[15] Lord & Taylor had sufficient authority as a fashion store, through its choice and selection of Parisian labels, to be able to persuade the press and the public that the American designers it endorsed were credible. This unshakeable fashion status, combined with its already-noted use of instore specialist shops, was crucial to the success of the American designers campaign. Bernice Fitz-Gibbon, who worked in Macy's advertising department at the time claimed to have tried two years earlier to persuade Eddie Marks, Macy's President, to produce a salute to American designers under the banner 'Rue de la Seventh'. However, he resisted since the store – unlike Lord & Taylor – lacked the fashion prestige necessary to make such a venture viable.[16]

Shaver had seen the importance of this image from early in her career. In 1926, after three years at Lord & Taylor, she founded a special bureau to study fashion and style. By 1931 this had evolved into the store's Bureau of Fashion and Decoration that trained specialists to advise buyers on coming trends.[17] She had also cemented her own credibility, in the same year, by arranging the store's 'Exposition of Modern Art', which brought Art Deco style to New York. As early as 1927, in a training speech to store executives, she had identified the need for store buyers to be aware of wider social and cultural trends, or 'conditions' as she called them, which affected what women wear:

> Conditions affect style first of all … in the costumes and accessories of women's apparel … the main condition which has been affecting style is the activity of a woman's life – the age of the sportswoman – the business woman. Her clothes are built around that condition … She must have simpler clothes, she leads a very active life.[18]

New York designers were increasingly able to create this kind of fashion. Women such as Valentina and Elizabeth Hawes began to build their own made-to-order businesses that drew away from Paris as the main source for ideas, and mass-market designers were also sought by Shaver to present their ranges at Lord & Taylor. By the time the store issued a press release entitled, 'The American Designer's Movement', on 12 April 1933, Elizabeth Hawes, Muriel King and Annette Simpson were amongst the designers who had already been endorsed. The hyperbolic press release stressed the store's determination to promote American fashion, with its commissions for work from garment and textile designers such as those named above. Lord & Taylor claimed to have 'crystallized' the movement, which was now advanced by its promotion of three sportswear designers: Clare Potter, Alice M. Smith and Ruth Payne. Dorothy Shaver hoped that the store's sponsorship would encourage further recognition of American designers and the distinctive style that they were developing. On 12 April 1933, she reinforced this in a press release called 'The American Designer's Movement':

> Beyond even these women there is plenty of dormant creative talent in America. There are young people with alert minds who understand their contemporaries, who have a complete understanding of the activities, the sports and the social life of American women. It follows naturally that they should be able to design clothes for them with a verve, a dash and a spontaneity that are truly American.[19]

Shaver's own reputation for acute promotions and fashion awareness was successfully combined with Lord & Taylor's reputation to construct a merchandising display that would lure women into the store. The most significant part of this was the use of window displays to promote individual designers. The displays were part of a coherent structure of promotions that was designed to produce a schematic idea of Americanness, which consumers could easily comprehend and relate to their own identity aspirations. Store window displays represented a liminal space, at once inside the store, yet also part of the street scene. With their increasingly lifelike mannequins and carefully choreographed arrangements of goods, they were an uncanny switching station between, on the one hand, the two-dimensional representation of fashion in magazine photography and advertising and, on the other, the three-dimensions of the garments themselves as they presented a simulation of how they would look on the body of the wearer. Window displays offered a further setting for the dreams held out in fashion magazines, since they allowed women to inspect the clothes at close quarters, and turned the private contemplation of the fashion page into the public inspection of garments (seemingly) on the street. As such they were a transitory space that allowed people to pause and reflect on a store's goods despite remaining in the chaos of the city street. Window displays were designed to entice potential customers into the store to fulfil the fantasy of visual consumption through making an actual purchase.

In the case of Shaver's American Designer windows showing sportswear, as can be seen in figure 4.2, the displays included: a photograph of each designer turned to the camera, smiling and informal; a series of mannequins dressed in their outfits; and a card with a brief, lively introduction to the designer herself. The clothes were presented straightforwardly, with none of the ornate adornments sometimes used for high fashion. The only surreal note was an oversized reference to the designer's craft in each window: images of either a giant needle and reel of thread or paint brushes. Thus, the designer was presented as approachable, her work referred to in a witty, non-threatening way. The clothes themselves struck a note of authenticity, since they related more directly to the kind of clothes that the woman looking in at them from the Fifth Avenue pavement might herself be wearing, than more expensive and elaborate couture fashions did. The display's inclusion of a photograph of the designer aimed at an empathetic response from the consumer: the designer is simultaneously held up as a personality to be admired and a working woman to identify with. There is none of the couturier's hauteur in the poses adopted, the close-up focus on the designer's face would present a mirror double to the spectator's own reflection as she stared in through the glass window. In conjunction with the press releases, such as the one discussed above, and advertising material put out by the store, American designers are represented as in tune with their customer and aware of her needs. Both fashion designer and consumer are addressed as individuals, and, through the emphasis placed on their national identity, as a collective: they are separate personalities, yet bonded through their Americanness.

This idealised vision of American woman presents a supportive, unifying view that suggests all American women have the same lifestyles, needs, and desires, which are catered to by fellow-countrywomen who know how to incorporate these needs into their sportswear designs. Differences in class, ethnicity, and status are glossed over in favour of a coherent vision that uses discrete good taste and simple silhouettes to construct an American ideal. During the thirties this ideal was gradually being attached to particular fabrics, usually those which expressed simplicity and practicality, such as cotton and linen; to certain silhouettes, especially uncluttered lines; and to particular 'classic' garments, separates that could be worn from season to season. These elements were then enhanced through representational style. In the example of Lord & Taylor's window for Clare Potter, the 'authenticity' of the natural fabrics and appropriateness of the garments to middle-class American women's real lives was expanded upon and given an additional veneer of glamour in *Vogue's* photograph of Katharine Hepburn wearing Potter's white linen duster coat, as featured in the window display (fig. 4.3). Edward Steichen's image, although shot in a studio, uses a garden chair and the hint of foliage behind Hepburn, coupled with the sitter's pose, to create a relaxed atmosphere. This is enhanced by the accompanying caption that stresses the way the coat hangs from the shoulders as 'loose and insouciant'. Hepburn's star endorsement of Potter is invoked in the text as well as the picture, which states that the coat has 'a gay youthfulness', a quality 'that caused Miss Hepburn to choose [it]'.[20]

Since Hepburn was seen to epitomise a no-nonsense American approach to style, her sponsorship of the garment gave it further credibility and added to the complex interchange of signifiers denoting 'real' and 'fantasy' in the promotional material. She wears the coat as 'herself', not as a character from a film, yet her star persona is inescapable. The coat is shown in the window display and in the photograph as a comfortable, easy-to-wear garment to be thrown on over a simple dress. However, the coat is not as practical as it might at first seem, as it is white it would have been hard to keep clean. Potter's image is equally ambiguous, since she is an authentic American woman, conscious of other working women's needs, but she is also held up as a creator and the member of an elite group of designers known by her own name at a time of general anonymity for American ready-to-wear designers. Such inconsistencies are, however, disguised by the mask of fashion. The casual style of the sportswear aesthetic appears uncomplicated and direct, and thus elides problematic contradictions. Sportswear's image was itself contradictory and fluid, it was capable of representing different identities, which connected to the aspirations of middle-class American women during the Depression. The incorporation of individual and collective identity on the one hand and 'real' and fantasy on the other was designed to unify sportswear's image through its repeated tropes of Americanness combined with designer personality. This was carried from magazine page to

4.4. Clark-Rogers, James McCutcheon & Co Window Display, 1935.
      Photograph by Clark-Rogers, Museum of the City of New York, Gift
      of the photographers

4.5. Clark-Rogers, Saks Thirty-Forth Street Gstaad window display,
      1935. Photograph by Clark-Rogers Museum of the City of New
      York, Gift of the photographers

4.6. B. Altman, College window display, 1930s. Courtesy of Special
      Collections, Gladys Marcus Library, Fashion Institute of
      Technology

4.7. B. Altman, S. S. Manhattan window display, 1930s. Courtesy of
      Special Collections, Gladys Marcus Library, Fashion Institute of
      Technology

window display and through the store by further upbeat merchandising and signage.

Other stores' windows were equally efficient in their presentation of sportswear as a form of dress that linked to various desirable lifestyles and activities. Figure 4.4 shows specialty store James McCutcheon in 1935, where English tweed suits were accompanied by a worn velvet chair to infer old money and heritage, while Saks Fifth Avenue, in figure 4.5, showed a mannequin in winter sports outfit on skis against a poster advertising Gstaad. In each case, sportswear's elite European heritage was clearly demonstrated. However, a series of windows at B. Altman, a store more targeted at the middle market, placed sportswear firmly within an American milieu (figs. 4.6 and 4.7). One addressed college girls and showed campus styles against a 'Ten Minute Quiz' that encouraged spectators to appreciate the importance of fashion in college life, while another stressed sportswear's role in travel wardrobes combined with a model of the S. S. Manhattan and other promotions for the cruise liner. The outfits in store windows would be familiar, yet heightened versions of everyday wear, and would seem like a 'snapshot' of the women in the city crowd. The window was a mirror held up for women's contemplation, for them to identify with and aspire to mimic.

FASHION MEDIA

Vogue first used the idea of 'Smart Economies' in 1 September 1932 and stated that it was not 'merely a feature [in the magazine but has] … become an institution in the American home'.[21] The magazine had made a virtue of careful budgeting since the late 1920s and this was represented as part of the reader's greater knowledge of style. Extravagance may still have been part of many of the fashion spreads and editorials on dinner parties and travel, but there was continued interest in well thought-out and efficient spending. These were often termed 'smart' economies. The use of this adjective was an affirmation and a pun, since it referred to the magazine's, and by extension the reader's, cleverness as well as their chic approach to shopping and dressing. The 11 May 1929 edition was titled 'Smart Fashions For Limited Incomes' and the editor's letter declared that 'intelligent planning and a certain ladylike, yet firm efficiency have become the means for the smart woman to gain her ends'.[22]

The relationship between ideas of being 'modern' and economising was to be played out in subsequent issues, and extended in a 1933 article, 'Whispers to the Girl with Nothing a Year', which coached its readers to relate work practices to their personal finances:

> System saves just as much money in the wardrobe as it does in an office. Plan ahead – look over your closet and throw out useless things, setting aside any good carryovers. Then decide what you're going to need, eliminate the non-essentials, and set forth wearing imaginary blinders to keep you from seeing bargains which you can't resist because they're so cheap and later can't wear for the same reason.[23]

Once the Depression hit, and during its worst years in the early 1930s, *Vogue* was able to build upon its 'smart economies', since it had already successfully incorporated many seemingly problematic issues, such as lack of funds, into its archetype of a modern woman who was clever with her money as well as with her clothing. The magazine even produced a detailed chart of itemised wardrobes, with prices included for women on five budgets, which ranged from $1200 a year to spend on clothes to $12,000. Although these were clearly still aimed at wealthier women, during the 1930s the magazine did include wardrobes for $100 or $300 a year.

The magazine's shift between cheery camaraderie and a stern, dictatorial tone was already established in the fashion and beauty pages, which could equally sympathise over 'imperfect' figures or scold over lack of care and exercise. It was to be amplified during the Second World War as patriotism flipped between economising self-sacrifice and defiant statements of carrying on as before. In the Depression years, it was represented in a balance between simple styles, 'realist' imagery and practical advice paralleled by a continued reliance upon spectacle and glamour. The overall style and tone of the magazine carried sufficient authority to gloss over these apparent disparities and produce a coherent whole.

As the decade wore on, the economising ideal was frequently applied to stereotyped groups of women who were emerging within the magazine's fashion pages. Such groups, including the college girl and the working woman, led active lives and needed to put together adaptable wardrobes that would be fashion-conscious yet appropriate to their environment and would last for more than one season. The rise in sportswear and simplified styles from French, English, and American designers and manufacturers, made increasingly fashionable (to some degree by magazines such as *Vogue* itself), was part of this trend towards *Vogue's* idea of a 'rational' consumer. Such a consumer would buy thoughtfully and wisely, and with good knowledge of quality, design, and style. This apparent rationality would then be projected by the clothes themselves, which rejected 'frivolous' decoration, rich fabrics, and complicated pattern pieces. Indeed, in 1937, readers were told to 'be glad you're an American, when it comes to buying clothes on funds limited. Nowhere else in the world can you find such good-looking inexpensive … clothes'.[24]

The Depression's impact on the American people spread anxieties that punctured public confidence in financial institutions and businessmen. High fashion magazines had previously relied upon a seamless presentation of glamour and wealth, fractured only at times of extremity, such as the First World War. During the Depression, *Vogue* managed a balance between fantasy and authenticity through articles such as one from its 15 May 1931 edition entitled 'Rejuvenating the Wardrobe'.[25] This spoke about the need to refresh an existing wardrobe in the same terms as using new beauty products to enliven complexions, in order to connect wardrobe 'rejuvenation' to a practice already well-established within its canon of acceptable activities. 'Rejuvenation' presents a positive and dynamic vision of the activities it recommended, such as adding new collars or braid to last seasons' dresses, and dying faded bathing suits. The article's emphasis is upon practical steps towards reinvigorating clothing through careful cleaning and accessorising, never on mending or making do with old clothes because the reader might not be able to afford new ones. Articles encouraging women to update their wardrobes with separates, and interchangeable wardrobes were presented throughout the 1930s.[26] These would enable garments to be worn in various combinations to create the illusion of a larger wardrobe.

Separates, as well as colour co-ordinated and 'harmonising' outfits, had been discussed as an important way of economising as early as 1929, and were a staple part of sportswear ranges during the 1930s. As was so often the case, the interchangeable outfits which would come to be marketed as an American staple during the following decade were also attributed to French style in the 1930s, and thus to unquestionable fashion consciousness. In November 1930, an article entitled 'Practising Thrift the French Way' stated that: 'Thrift is in her Gallic veins. Whenever and wherever she can, [she] makes a costume do double duty. She is the arch-champion of the convertible ensemble … from the very beginning, there should be a continuity of plan. The fabrics must be related fabrics. Formal elements cannot be incongruously mingled with informal'.[27]

While *Vogue* attempted to integrate economy and luxury and introduced an increasing number of New York fashions into its pages during the 1930s, *Harper's Bazaar* was more oblique in its references to the Depression and did not really support the American ready-to-wear industry until the following decade. Throughout the 1930s, it sought to maintain its façade of elegant, fashionable living, with scant mention of the economic crisis. The magazines had similar audiences and, despite different approaches to the crisis, did not waver from their re-presentation of acceptable, 'good' taste. Very occasionally, a more direct comment would be made. In the worst year of the Depression thus far, for example, *Harper's Bazaar's* 'The Editor' section of June 1932 mentioned 'Speakeasy Shops' that would be set up quickly in New York to sell very cheap clothes. However, the main way in which a sense of 'authenticity' that related to wider realities of 1930s life was represented in the magazine was through the work of photographers such as Martin Munkacsi and Jean Moral. A modern sportswear aesthetic began to emerge during the 1930s. Jean Moral shot editorial pieces in Paris and Munkasci in New York, and, by the 1930s their style permeated the magazine, as they photographed sportswear, and, increasingly, high fashion stories, which integrated with Art Director Brodovitch's modern graphic style. Although their images were upbeat, their relationship to documentary imagery of the period created a very different atmosphere in high fashion magazines. While they did not make direct reference to the Depression, they interrupted the constant flow of high fashion pages and brought a dissonant note of realism to the fantasy landscape created by magazines such as *Vogue* and *Harper's Bazaar*.

Despite wider industry problems, the magazine market thrived during the Depression. Trade newspaper *Women's Wear Daily* published a telegram from *Harper's Bazaar's* Business Manager in its 5 January 1932 edition that praised the effectiveness of advertising in the magazine:

> Harpers Bazaars figures for nineteen thirty one show a gain of thirteen thousand nine hundred and forty four lines in ready to wear advertising stop proof positive in a year when advertisers demanded the best of their advertising dollar that harpers bazaar [sic] offers the most intensive market for fashion product.[29]

Advertising was crucial to a magazine's success and the quality and quantity of companies that advertised contributed to a title's fashion status. Both *Vogue* and *Harper's Bazaar* included a vast selection of advertisements in each issue and, as the decade wore on, more and more ready-to-wear was featured from manufacturers and department stores and chain stores, such as Carolyn or Peck & Peck. Despite the cost of buying advertising space, most of the big names bought pages in every edition of *Vogue* and *Harper's Bazaar*.

Two important new titles were established during the decade. *Mademoiselle* first appeared in 1935 and *Glamour*, subtitled, 'For the Girl With A Job', was a revamped creation of 1939 from an old magazine called *Glamour of Hollywood*. These magazines focussed on the youth market, and were joined in the following decade by *Seventeen*, which started in 1944, and *Charm*, which completed its first full year under this name in 1942. As demonstrated by *Vogue* and *Harper's Bazaar's* increased coverage of college girls, young career women, and debutantes, the teenage audience had become increasingly important and was catered to by numerous 'junior' and 'misses' clothes lines. Sportswear was also a feature of the younger market, as has already been noted. These titles, and the fact that such an audience did continue to gain significant ground, demonstrated the fashion industry's continued exploration and exploitation of new markets, at least in part as a response to the pressures of the financial crisis.

New magazines such as *Mademoiselle* were themselves, at least in part, a product of the Depression, as they represented publishing companies' search for new audiences to be exploited. However, none of them catalogued the wider industry's hardships, since, in common with other high fashion and women's magazines, fashion was presented as a seamless end product, with only occasional articles about American designers or craft skills breaking through this façade.

Fashion columns in newspapers, most notably Virginia Pope's articles for *The New York Times*, were equally focussed on fashion as news and trends forecasting, rather than discussions of the Depression's impact on the industry. The fashion media's focus upon trend dissemination was reflected by the fact that many fashion columns which originated in New York were syndicated across America. This practice, combined with free fashion news services, notably from Eleanor Lambert, ensured that fashion information was quickly transmitted across America.[31] It was only trade titles, the most important of which was *Women's Wear Daily*, that did include regular news relating to the economic crisis.

After Shaver's first window displays in 1932, more designers were named in advertising, mainly placed by Lord & Taylor at first, but then by a range of other stores and advertisers. This in turn meant that magazines used more American designers' names in their editorial fashion coverage. Individual named designers could be used to appeal to women consumers directly. In the 1935 advertisement for chain store Carolyn, the use of David Crystal's name adds an established name's endorsement to the styles (see figure 4.8). Described as a 'leading personality in the American sports couture', the accompanying text thus links his name to elite fashions, despite the fact that these were inexpensive, mass-produced garments. The text goes on to describe him as a 'personality', which implies his status as a noted individual.[32] Personality was also used to individualise less expensive clothing ranges, such as Betty Levay and Doris Dodson, and to give consumers a point of identification.

Although Lois Long had named American designers in her *New Yorker* columns since 1925, the practice remained rare in fashion publications and newspapers, as retailers and manufacturers were reluctant to give designers the potential bargaining power that becoming a known individual implied. During the Depression, this balance of power gradually began to shift, and since sportswear was most distinctive to New York, and by extension to America as a whole, it became a major market in which designers made their names.[33] In time, promotional tactics as much as design talent eroded the absence of names. This was helped by the professionalisation of women within the industry. It was also attributable to women's abilities in merchandising, forecasting, promotion, advertising, and even in some cases, fashion photography, to attract other women through language and imagery that was accessible to them and related more closely to their everyday lives. This representational shift and development in the range of fashion media during a period of general economic decline saw the rise of sportswear, its designers, and the modern sportswear aesthetic, which was used to idealise its values as a uniquely American form of dress.

Clare Potter and Tom Brigance were two of the most prominent designers of mid-range sportswear by the late 1930s, with their work frequently mentioned in elite fashion magazines' advertising and editorial content. Since her inclusion in Lord & Taylor's American Designer

4.8. David Crystal for Carolyn advertisement, *Vogue*, 15 May 1935

4.9. Toni Frissell, Clarepotter advertisement, *Vogue*, 15 December 1938. Toni Frissell Collection, The Library of Congress

promotions, discussed above, Potter had begun to establish a name for her smart spectator sportswear and beachwear ranges. Her designs were attuned to the modern sportswear aesthetic and ranged from madras cotton playsuits for holiday wear through crisp rick-rack trimmed day dresses, seen in figure 4.9 to streamlined pyjama suits worn with hair swept up into a turban. Known for her strong use of colour as well as her adaptable designs, Potter was sufficiently famous by mid-1939 to take part in a cross-promotion with Old Gold cigarettes that appeared in both *Vogue* and *Harper's Bazaar*.

Brigance, one of the few men to emerge within New York sportswear, was featured in Lord & Taylor's Sports Shop as an already formed creative force, who was now being introduced 'to his native America' as 'Brigance, young Texas-born genius who's left a brilliant career in Paris and London to create his imaginative, appealingly feminine sports clothes exclusively for our clientele'. His garments were concurrently on display in Lord & Taylor's windows and he had been appointed to the store's Bureau of Design.[35] In June 1938, *Harper's Bazaar* featured pieces from his collection photographed by Louise Dahl-Wolfe, in a shoot that emphasised youthful, summer pursuits and crisp white sportswear.

Brigance had designed for couture houses in France, before spending a year at Jaeger, and Simpson's of Piccadilly in London, as well as a period studying in Italy.[36] This combination of reference points fed into his work, which brought an air of elite femininity to mid-market sportswear. French and English sportswear was occasionally photographed for American fashion magazines in the same style as the New York designers. However, New York's fashion media had established an aesthetic that was used almost exclusively to represent New York designs and which had created effective ways to distinguish it, in relation to ideals of femininity, Americanness, and modern lifestyles. At the end of the 1930s, Seventh Avenue manufacturers were primed to respond quickly to new trends, trade papers gave daily reports on patterns in both production and consumption, and elite magazines provided an idealised vision of the development of new fashions.

THE MONASTIC DRESS AND SPORTSWEAR PROMOTION IN THE LATE 1930S

The contrasts in the ways different fashion media portrayed particular trends is illuminating, since high fashion magazines' longer lead times and their ethos of escape excluded coverage of rapid developments in ready-to-wear lines and underlying friction between manufacturers struggling to assert copyright of a design. This contradiction between the fast-moving pace of fashion trends on Seventh Avenue and high fashion magazines' less frantic approach to fashion promotion became apparent in 1938 when a new monastic silhouette trend swept the New York dress trade. Trade papers covered a constant struggle for new supplies and variations of the style, while *Vogue* and *Harper's Bazaar* showed only a few of the end products, masking the industry's machinations to present fashion as something that just effortlessly appeared for the consumer to enjoy. The rapid spread of the monastic, and the eagerness with which manufacturers at all levels of the market produced versions of the style was symptomatic of a more positive mood in America at the end of the 1930s. Despite a period of stagnation in 1937, increased government spending saw an improvement in the economy.[37] In 1938, *Women's Wear Daily,* in contrast to its gloomy coverage of the fashion industry's fortunes earlier in the Depression, carried glowing reports of predicted revitalization:

> Conviction grows that the outlook for prolonged recovery in the United States now is decidedly favorable. At the same time, clearly, the American people is making up its mind regarding aspects of our national and international relations and prospects. We are moving into that 'new era' about which we have in these last years so often talked.[38]

The simple style was first mentioned in *Women's Wear Daily* on 18 May 1938 as the 'Monk', and described as a beach coat design, by theatrical costumier Helene Pons.[39] This fluid shape hung from the shoulders and, in this case, was caught in at the waist by a drawstring belt. Its evolution during the autumn of 1938 and its genesis in the months before that clearly illustrate the complex interrelationship between Paris and New York, couture and ready-to-wear, formal and sportswear, and the attempts to curb copyists in all these areas of fashion. It also demonstrates the role of the fashion media in reporting fashion news and promoting particular styles.

The trend can be traced back to August 1937 when chain store Carolyn had advertised, in *Vogue*, plain campus dresses, seen in figure 4.10, that foreshadowed the style. However, it is

Clare Potter's Cuban-inspired blouse and skirt drawn in *Vogue* on 15 December that heralded the softer, simpler silhouette that was to become so popular and which the magazine reprised in its following issue as it had received such a favourable response. While the style had yet fully to evolve, *Women's Wear Daily* reported a series of modifications over the following issues, for example on 18 January, a 'balloon silhouette' is noted, with variations such as a 'little boy drawstring bloused blouse in a one-piece dress'.[40] Two days later, the paper showed another version by Helen Cookman, a New York sportswear designer.

This softer, more draped style can be connected to Grecian-inspired dresses that were similar to those by Madeleine Vionnet, for example, and shown at all levels of the industry. The monastic that was to evolve drew from the gathering range of trends that pointed towards a style that eliminated excess detail and focussed upon an adaptable, modern silhouette. Parisian couturiers had shown such styles for autumn/winter 1938/9. These shows took place in January 1938 and included kimono-sleeved coats, and unstructured dresses by Alix, such as the one in figure 4.11, photographed by Jean Moral for *Harper's Bazaar* in September 1938, and a 'monk's' coat by Bruyere shown in figure 4.12 from *The New York Times* in October 1938, which would later be erroneously credited as having begun the trend. London designers also presented the style in their January couture shows, and designers from all three cities produced variations of full styles, dirndl one-pieces and draped and pleated dresses such as Hattie Carnegie's, a soft blue jersey version featured in *Vogue's* 15 February 1938 issue. These elements would eventually evolve into the full-blown monastic fashion of autumn 1938.

Thus, even in the first months of 1938, the new silhouette was shown at couture and ready-to-wear levels and was part of high fashion, as well as cheaper sportswear styles. Rather than a fashion that was shown first by couturiers and then copied by mass-market manufacturers, it was a silhouette that was evolving simultaneously at all levels in Paris, London, and New York. Importantly, it is an example of a style that was both presaged by a New York sportswear designer, Clare Potter, and most famously espoused by Claire McCardell, who crystallised the style in autumn 1938 when she produced the 'Nada' dress [nada is Spanish for nothing, and implied a garment that was simple and unostentatious]. As is seen from the advertisement in figure 4.13, this was designed in August 1938 for Townley, the manufacturers that employed her, to be sold in the Best & Co. department store.

The 'Nada' was a range of dresses produced by Best & Co. since at least 1924, when it was advertised as 'typifying the American girl, youthful, chic and charming' and, rather contradictorily,

4.10. Carolyn advertisement, *Vogue*, 15 August 1937

4.11. Jean Moral, Alix, *Harper's Bazaar*, September 1938. Jean Moral, Paris, 1938.
       © Brigitte Moral

4.12. Bruyère, Town Wear, *The New York Times*, 16 October 1938. *The New York Times*, Archive.
       © Redux Pictures

as expressive of 'individuality', despite being mass-produced ready-to-wear.[41] Allied to the monastic in autumn 1938, the design that the store chose to be promoted under the 'Nada' brand was McCardell's bias-cut, circle skirted dress:

> An entirely new silhouette … An ageless, dateless silhouette simple as a monk's cassock, regal as a king's robe! … a design that might have come from the master hand of a Vionnet – flaring straight from the shoulders in soft folds gathered in a wide belt to make your waist look tiny. It fits everyone … it's comfortable; it's versatile – appropriate for business or tea! Exclusive with Best's.[42]

Potential consumers are assured that this dress is at once 'new', yet 'ageless', monk-like yet 'regal'. It is sold as a new design, but is validated by looking like something Vionnet might have made, and, indeed, she had shown a circular cut coat in her autumn/winter collection of 1938/9 that contains some elements of McCardell's design. Its claim to be suitable for all figures was due to its lack of fit, which would make it wearable for women of different sizes. However, one retailer warned that other stores would 'have to find customer types that flatter the monk's frock … the shorter woman should not wear it at all, and … it is becoming only to the small, slim, youthful figure'.[43] Another found that the monastic was selling well, although it had been difficult at first to introduce a 'quality styling', at 'popular price' points.[44]

Such simplicity was familiar within couture design, where it was interpreted as a mark of discernment and distinguished the wearer as able to appreciate a design for its intrinsic quality, rather than merely being attracted to obviously expensive decoration, elaborate design, or rich fabrics. It was also a feature of much New York sportswear, and was to become a signature of McCardell's style. In this case it was equally a marker of 'good' taste but, as the retailer quoted above observed, such simplicity was usually harder for mass-market customers to accept, as it lacked obvious selling points and looked better when worn than it did on the hanger. The monastic's enormous success was therefore an early example of a New York designer, albeit under a store's name, producing a fashion that was popular at all price levels.

Conservatism was a feature of American fashion, and also a factor in sportswear design, and can be seen in the gradual development of the monastic silhouette before it became a major trend in October 1938. While designers such as Claire McCardell would integrate more innovative elements into their work, in this case in the austerity of her version of the trend, these would usually be balanced by more familiar counterpoints that would prove less challenging to consumers. New York sportswear drew upon masculine tenets of restraint in dress and this conservative strain in sportswear's design provided women with clothing that was suitable for a variety of informal and formal situations, at home and in the workplace. McCardell's pleated version of the monastic from 1938 demonstrates these principles in figure 4.14.[45] Its plainness provides anonymity for the wearer that enables her to shift from one setting to another without drawing attention to herself, and its refined design ensures that she remains stylish and respectable. Made of open-weave wool and cut to hang from the shoulders, the box pleats on either side of the neckline act as a form of decoration and allows ease of movement while keeping the overall slim silhouette. It has zips either side of the neckline to allow the wearer to slip the dress over the head. There are concealed slit pockets below the waistline and a wide belt to add definition to the figure and emphasise the fullness of the skirt that is provided by the box pleats that mirror those on the bodice. The design, construction and fabric produce a dress that is sober and unostentatious. Its design was thus in keeping with current fashion trends, as well as being easy to mass-produce, since it contained so few pattern pieces. It therefore embodied several of New York sportswear's key principles, which were amplified by the promotional techniques used to sell them through newspaper and magazine copy and imagery and also through window display and store merchandising.

However, as has been discussed, it is difficult to attribute the design solely to McCardell. Although this dress went on to become one of her most famous designs, written about as original and innovative in all accounts of her work, it would in fact appear to be part of a far more complex fashion trend.[46] The style was promoted at all price points in department and chain stores, and advertised and editorialised in high fashion magazines, newspapers, and trade journals. Even during 1938, it was not seen as belonging only to Best & Co., who had commissioned the design, despite the store's registration of the design with the Fashion Originator's Guild on 20 September 1938. This is demonstrated by an announcement Best & Co. placed in *Women's Wear Daily* to attempt to underscore its ownership of the design. The style was widely copied, and was perhaps already too much a part of the existing fashion landscape to be easily attributable to one manufacturer. As the 'monastic', 'bishop', balloon', and 'angel's robe', versions of the trend had been current for several months and would continue into the first months of 1939. McCardell undoubtedly brought a fresh impetus to the silhouette by eliminating all extraneous details. Later accounts state that the design was inspired by a dress she made for herself after an Algerian tunic that hung straight from the shoulders, and although this may well be the case, her sketchbooks for the period reveal that she had been drawing designs that relate to the shifts in the trend, from straighter skirt with bloused bodice, to pleated versions and then to the daringly sparse design of the Nada dress.[47]

In 1938 it was still rare for an American sportswear designer to be named, and McCardell remained anonymous behind both Best's and Townley's names. *Women's Wear Daily's* round up of the year's fashion successes did not attribute the monastic to Best & Co.:

> This is the dress that appeared early in the autumn and made merchandising history. It created more comment and discussion than any dress in years, was claimed as an original by many designers and offered definitely new promotional ideas on the basis of a simple silhouette. It swept the country, featured under different names – 'Monk's robe', 'pinch bottle', 'angel robes'.[48]

The monastic's success spoke of the rise of sportswear as a potential fashion source, of the creative potential of designers such as McCardell and Potter, and of the interconnection between retailers and the fashion media to promote and exploit trends. It also demonstrated wider industry issues that were yet to be resolved, such as the role designers were actually to play within New York fashion. It exposed the ease with which simple designs like this could be mass-produced thanks to new technology, and the problems that not just Parisian couturiers, but also New York manufacturers had in trying to control copyists to protect their creations and ensure that profits from new trends stayed with their originators. Fashion trends could evolve out of several existing trends, at ready-to-wear and couture level. As styles were adapted for different national and economic tastes, they could be shown, as in this case, almost simultaneously in different cities, and be disseminated through cross-promotions between stores, manufacturers and the fashion media. Townley closed by the end of 1938, and this was ironically partly due to the success of the monastic's design. The manufacturer's owner, Henry Geiss was unable to keep up with the legal fees needed to fight the company's claim to the design.[49] This, combined with his own ill health, and a dispute with McCardell about putting her name on the Townley label, also precipitated the designer's move to Hattie Carnegie, whose name was attributed to two pleated versions of the monastic shown in *Vogue's* 1 November 1938 edition.

During the next decade Townley and McCardell were reunited and went on to create a highly successful sportswear range that drew upon the success of garments such as the monastic. One reason why McCardell's name has continued to be associated with the style is that it came to be a staple part of her collections. Her clothing ranges were themselves based upon the idea of simple adaptable clothes that were as easy to wear as they were to manufacture, and could be worn for more than one season. Once the monastic was no longer a trend, it could be promoted in the same terms that Best & Co. had used to advertise the Nada dress: as a 'timeless' classic. The style expressed the modern sportswear aesthetic of the 1930s in its spare, austere silhouette, but the simplicity that had made it so easy to reproduce by other manufacturers in 1938 also meant that it could easily be updated to adapt to fashions of the 1940s and 1950s. It therefore became part of McCardell's repertoire of signature designs, masking its fraught evolution and complex heritage to be promoted as part of her repertoire of sportswear 'classics'.

Vogue had been quick to feature New York ready-to-wear and integrate economising into its existing fashion profile during the Depression. It had first promoted the significance of New York fashion in its 15 April 1933 edition, which looked at designers such as Mrs. Franklin and Elizabeth Hawes, as well as including an article discussing Dorothy Shaver as a leading figure in retail and advocate of American fashion.[50] The magazine consolidated its patriotic message with its first Americana edition in February 1938. While high fashion magazines had always had 'American' or 'New York Fashions' editions, these had previously featured American imports of Parisian goods that had just arrived in New York stores, plus Seventh Avenue copies of Parisian couture. The 'Americana' edition, however, had quite different connotations. From its hyperbolic opening editorial piece, 'God's Country', through a succession of features and photographs shot on location across the United States, it established a tone that was to permeate fashion coverage during the Second World War:

> God may not prefer America to other places … but His hand is surely visible in its making. The great gesture is here, in this country. It is in the vastness of its plains and its mountains and its shores. There is no meanness in the contour of America, natural or man-made … And this grandeur has left its seal on the people. Americans may be fumbling and immature, but potentially they are a big people – as yet un-ridden by the suspicious, reservations, and rancours of older and wiser races. Blessed by the wealth and breadth of their land, and by the waters that guard it, they still breathe free air. Fundamentally they are pure in heart, perhaps as children are, from inexperience.[51]

This hagiography rehearsed binary oppositions of Old versus New World that had been played out on a smaller scale in the way fashion magazines spoke of the contrasts between Paris couture and New York mass-production and between the elite, leisured elegance of French women and the dynamic modernity of American women. It was a call to arms to consumers to buy American and to producers and retailers to look to the whole of America, including Latin America as a potential market, as well as a supplier of fabrics, accessories, and ideas. The article was followed by iconic images of America that showed high and low art, nature and culture, countryside and metropolis in a montage of chorus girls and cornfields, drive-by cafés and the Capitol. America was constructed as an ideal that could incorporate these contradictions.

New York sportswear had already been promoted using these ideas and images as a literal and metaphorical backdrop. At the end of the 1930s, the war and its build-up in Europe imbued discussions of American fashion with extra frisson, as they stood in contrast to reports of what Parisian women were wearing in wartime.[52] Some fashion imagery expressed a brooding darkness, seen in the gloomy skies above a sportswear-clad model overwhelmed by the monumentality of the structures being built for the World's Fair, as in this Toni Frissell photograph, of September 1939 in figure 4.15. Other images conveyed patriotic bravado as seen on the cover of *Harper's Bazaar's* 'American Fashions' edition in the same month, which showed the Statue of Liberty strewn with red, white, and blue feathers and glistening pearls. As the fashion industry began to explore the potential implications of war, *Vogue's* editor-in-chief, Edna Woolman Chase, spoke to the Fashion Group about her recent experience of leaving Europe as German troops marched into Poland. She compared this to her time in Paris at the start of the First World War, when American buyers had bought every Paris model they could find before leaving on the boats back to New York, with not enough to supply all the stores. At that time, Seventh Avenue, then essentially just a 'cloak and suit trade', could not adequately rise to the challenge of producing its own designs. In autumn 1914, Chase herself had therefore initiated a Fashion Fete, the first of its kind in America, backed by wealthy patronesses such as Mrs. Stuyvesant Fish and Mrs. Vincent Astor to promote New York stores' collections.[53]

In 1939, however, the New York fashion industry was more developed, in terms of production, retail, and promotion as demonstrated by the range of publicity in stores and magazines detailed above. The success of the monastic dress, seen in the rapid spread of its style, with manufacturers at different levels of the market emulating its design, implied that sportswear designers and manufacturers had the potential to capitalise on the growth in American-led design. While there were several successful American made-to-measure designers, such as Jo Copeland and Elizabeth Hawes, their work, in both design and manufacture, owed most to the French couture tradition. In contrast, New York sportswear embodied a machine aesthetic, was mass-produced and, as has been shown, was allied to cultural ideals of femininity, the body,

4.13. 'Nada Frock', Best & Co. advertisement, *The Washington Post*, 9 October 1938. Courtesy of Best & Co

4.14. Claire McCardell, novelty-weave wool 'Monastic' dress, (1938). The Metropolitan Museum of Art, Gift of Claire McCardell, 1949. Photograph © The Metropolitan Museum of Art 1998

4.15. Toni Frissell, Saks Fifth Avenue, *Vogue*, 1 September 1938. © Toni Frissell Collection, The Library of Congress

lifestyle, and cleanliness that had been combined with iconic American imagery to create the modern sportswear aesthetic. Although some commentators were sceptical about America's ability to survive on its own fashion talents, Edna Woolman Chase remained upbeat: 'And of course here in America we are prepared to give a much better account of ourselves as designers today than we were a quarter of a century ago, so I do not think we need fear for fashion's future'.[54]

Thus, even in the earliest days of the war, the leading career women of New York's fashion industry were devising ways to sell its merchandise whatever the conflict might bring. The Depression had already shaped their responses to crisis, and women, as designers, promoters, retailers, and consumers were to play a crucial part in New York sportswear's continued success in the coming years of the war. The key features of 1930s sportswear were to be crucial to this success – interchangeable wardrobes of separates; colour co-ordinated ranges of garments; simple, adaptable designs enlivened by a few bold accessories such as the monastic, and hardwearing, easy-to-clean fabrics – along with its status as America's archetypal style of dress, expressive of an ideal of national character and a unified feminine identity.

1   David E. Kyvig, *Daily Life in the United States, 1920–1940: How Americans Lived Through the 'Roaring Twenties' and the Great Depression* (Chicago: Ivan R. Dee, 2004), 209.

2   Wandersee, *Women's Work*, 3.

3   Margaret Case Harriman, *And the Price Is Right* (Cleveland and New York: The World Publishing Company, 1958), 129.

4   Elizabeth Hawes, *Fashion is Spinach,* 189.

5   David M. Kennedy, *The American People in the Great Depression: Freedom from Fear: Part I* (Oxford and New York: Oxford University Press, 1999), 101.

6   Kennedy, *The American People in the Great Depression,* 155.

7   Advertisement caption for B. Altman, *Vogue*, 15 May 1935, 3.

8   Paul H. Nystrom, *Fashion Merchandising,* 172.

9   Nan Tillson Birmingham, *Store* (New York: Putnam's Sons, 1978), 268.

10 Dorothy Shaver recognised that 'teen age' girls were a significant potential market. In 1937, she initiated a contest for them at Lord & Taylor. The twenty-four winners (there were ten thousand entrants) were invited to have lunch with the store's staff to discuss their needs and ideas about fashion. See Tiffany Webber Hatchett, 'Dorothy Shaver: Promoter of the "American Look",' in *Dress*, vol. 30 (2003): 82.

11 Gary Cross, *An All-consuming Century: Why Commercialism Won In America* (New York: Columbia University Press, 2000), 81.

12 Cross, *An All-consuming Century*, 219.

13 *Department Store Buyer*, August 1939, 16.

14 Hawes, *Fashion is Spinach*, 195.

15 Daves, *Ready-made Miracle*, 53.

16 Bernice Fitz-Gibbon, *Macys, Gimbels and Me: How to Earn $90,000 a Year in Retail Advertising* (New York: Simon & Schuster, 1967), 205.

17 'The Progress of An Executive', *The Christian Science Monitor*, July 28 1931.

18 Dorothy Shaver, 'Appreciation for Style: Presented by Dorothy Shaver to the Assistant Buyers' Class on Color, Design, and Style In Merchandise, on May 25, 1927', Dorothy Shaver Papers no. 631, Folder 3, Box 16, The Archives Center, National Museum of American History, Smithsonian Institution, Washington D. C.

19 Dorothy Shaver, 'The American Designer's Movement', 12 April 1933, Dorothy Shaver Papers, no. 631, Folder 4, Box 15, The Archives Center, National Museum of American History, Smithsonian Institution, Washington D. C.

20 Picture caption, *Vogue*, 15 May 1933, 60.

21 '*Vogue's* Smart Economies', *Vogue*, 15 April 1933, 69.

22 '*Vogue's* Eye View of the Mode', 75.

23 'Whispers to the Girl on Nothing a Year', *Vogue*, 15 May 1933, 70.

24 'More Taste than Money', *Vogue*, 1 May 1937, 105.

25 'Rejuvenating the Wardrobe', *Vogue*, 15 May 1931, 90–91 and 116.

26 See for example, 'A Wardrobe for a Limited Income', *Vogue*, 31 August 1929, 56–58, and 'Interchangeable Economies', *Vogue*, 15 May 1932, 80–81.

27 'Practising Thrift the French Way', *Vogue*, 1 November 1930, 69.

28 'The Editor … Speakeasy Shops', *Harper's Bazaar*, June 1932, 31.

29 Telegram reproduced in *Women's Wear Daily*, Section 2, 5 January 1932, 7.

30 See for example, 'What Makes a Thing Expensive', *Vogue*, 1 February 1937, 84 – 85 and 128. This article uses a discussion of various craft skills to justify the high cost of made-to-order garments.

31 Jessica Daves, *Ready-Made Miracle*, 176.

32 Carolyn advertisement caption *Vogue,* 15 May 1935, 24b.

33 Los Angeles' reputation for sportswear was growing during this period. However, its designs were not regularly featured in high fashion magazines, and were not as well known as those from New York.

34 Lord & Taylor advertisement caption *Vogue*, 15 May 1938, 1.

35 'Lord & Taylor Designer of Sportswear Speaks Up for More Feminine Styles', *Women's Wear Daily*, 12 May 1938, 20.

36 'Lord & Taylor Designer of Sportswear Speaks Up for More Feminine Styles', 20.

37 See Susan Ware, *Holding Their Own*, xiv–xv.

38 'Latest Retail Selling Slants – In Trends of the Times', *Women's Wear Daily*, 19 October 1938, 6.

39 'Monk and Peasant Styles for the Beach By a Designer of Stage Costumes', *Women's Wear Daily*, 18 May 1938, 12.

40 'Stop and Look at …,' *Women's Wear Daily*, Sportswear Section, 18 January 1938, 36.

41 Best & Co advertisement caption, *The New York Times*, 27 January 1924, 7.

42 Best & Co advertisement caption, *The Washington Post*, 9 October 1938, S2.

43 'Sunday Night Frocks and Monastic Adaptations', *Women's Wear Daily*, 1 November 1938, 15.

44 'Sunday Night Frocks and Monastic Adaptations', 15.

45 CI.49.37.15a and b, The Costume Institute, Metropolitan Museum of Art, New York. The Costume Institute also has a plain 'Monastic' from 1938, which resembles Best & Co'.s 'Nada' dress: CI.49.37.14a and b. The basic style and fabric is the same as the one described, except that it is bias-cut and falls from the shoulder with no waistline.

46 See, for example, Osborn Elliott, 'The American Look', *Time*, 2 May 1955, 89–90.

47 Kohle Yohannan and Nancy Nolf discuss McCardell making a dress for herself based on an Algerian tunic she owned, and suggest that this design formed the basis of the later monastic dress. See Yohannan and Nolf, *Claire McCardell* 41. Claire McCardell's sketches for Townley Frocks are collected together in a series of chronological sketchbooks that show her designs for each season. Sketchbook 43, for Summer 1938, shows the early form of the style. Sketch no. 113 is of a dress that pleats over the yoke and has zips to fasten at the shoulders. Sketchbooks 44 and 45, also for Summer 1938, show further evidence of the influence of the trend for fuller skirts and simple bodices. In sketchbooks 46 to 48 for Fall 1938, the style has crystallised, for example, sketch no. 778 in sketchbook 48, shows a dress that follows the 'Nada' silhouette and seems to be cut on the bias. See Sketchbooks 43 to 48, Claire McCardell Sketches, Townley Frocks, The Anna-Maria and Stephen Kellen Archives Center of Parsons School of Design, New York.

48 'Fashion Significances and Successes of 1938', *Women's Wear Daily* Section I (30 December 1938), 3.

49 See Yohannan and Nolf, *Claire McCardell*, 42.

50 See *Vogue*, 15 April 1933.

51 'God's Country', *Vogue*, 1 February 1938, 61.

52 'Passed on by French Censor', *Vogue*, 15 November 1939, 58–9.

53 Edna Woolman Chase, speaking to The Fashion Group, 27 September 1939, The Fashion Group Archives File 6, Box 73, New York Public Library.

54 Chase, speaking to The Fashion Group, 27 September 1939, The Fashion Group Archives.

CHAPTER FIVE

SPORTSWEAR AND THE NEW YORK FASHION INDUSTRY DURING THE SECOND WORLD WAR

EFFECTS OF THE SECOND WORLD WAR

Sherna Berger Gluck has described America in the immediate pre-war period as 'a country just beginning to recover … from the depression. Its social institutions were largely intact, and its people were still sustained by the essentially traditional values that had served them so well in a simpler society. But the inescapable complexity of the world was gradually changing the fabric of society'.[1] The contrast between America's apparent domestic stability and the growing international crisis was brought to the otherwise secure environment of the Fashion Group by talks from women such as Elizabeth Penrose, editor of British *Vogue*, who told members of London's suffering during the Blitz. Her speech interwove personal concerns at the volatility of the situation, with fears for future trade and industry: 'what chance then have you and I in New York at this moment to conjecture about the shape of things to come in England, and more particularly about the future of trade between England and the United States when we cannot even keep pace with the present?'[2] The fashion industry's success was predicated, at least in part, on its ability to predict the future in its trends forecasts, and the uncertainty that Penrose spoke about threw it into turmoil. When Paris fell to the Nazis on 14 June 1940, the American fashion industry began to feel the full impact of the Second World War. This event signalled the temporary end of the French capital's influence on fashion in New York.

The Depression had provided America with templates of potential strategies to ride out the war. Magazines, retailers and manufacturers had experience of creating and promoting clothing that embodied ideals of thrift, 'good' taste and patriotism. During the Second World War, in the absence of French influence, these ideas would be consolidated and amplified to construct a coherent ideal of American fashion. New York sportswear, with its simple designs and focus on cheap, washable fabrics, was a key category within this assertion of American fashion's status. When America entered the war in response to the Japanese attack on Pearl Harbour on 7 December 1941, these attributes made sportswear a practical response to ensuing shortages and women's role on the home front. Sportswear's representation in fashion magazines drew upon ideas of America that could be exploited as patriotic. This chapter will examine the ways that the war impacted upon the New York fashion industry and the crucial role sportswear played in the continuing development of a distinct ideal of American fashion and femininity. The ways in which this ideal was expressed through design and representation will be analysed in con-nection with the rise of named designers, in particular Claire McCardell. The chapter will also discuss the work of specific photographers, such as Toni Frissell and Louise Dahl-Wolfe. Together they contributed to the construction of New York sportswear as the ultimate expression of the American Look.

During the summer of 1940, the Fashion Group had held a series of important meetings to continue the industry's debate about potential responses to the fall of Paris. On 7 July, Mary Lewis asked, 'Are we mice or designers?' and called for individual designers to be promoted by name.[3] The importance of coherent promotional techniques echoed through the Group's meetings. Although New York was still pre-eminent within the American fashion system, insiders were anxious about its ability to continue without Paris. Despite advances in the promotion of a distinct American style and New York fashions during the 1930s, Paris' absence fundamentally shook the New York industry's confidence. This fear reflected American fashion's contradictory relationship to Paris. The French capital had functioned as both a positive and negative myth. It had been employed by the New York industry to indicate both sameness, in relation to high fashion ideals and the authenticity of copies, and difference, in its role as foil to America's emergent fashion identity.

By October 1940, the first New York fashion shows since the fall of Paris had been held, and Carmel Snow and Dorothy Shaver spoke to the Fashion Group about the current and future potential of American designers. Snow praised the collections, but was clear that the industry needed to reform to take on the challenge of 'leading' fashion.[4] Her praise for American design was measured, tempered as always by her reverence for Parisian couture above all other fashion forms. However, Dorothy Shaver was optimistic. Her mood echoed that of New York's mayor, Fiorello La Guardia, who had announced at a Fashion Group meeting in March 1940 that 'New York is the center of fashion of the entire world'.[5] In his speech he went on to support the industry's recent progress and potential, and linked this to America's democracy, which provided fashion for all women, not just, as in Europe, the aristocracy. He saw this as 'another reason why our style should be typical New Yorkese … because we have a greater field in this country for women's clothes than in any country in the world'.[6] La Guardia continued in his role as spokesperson for the New York fashion industry during the war.

Both La Guardia and Shaver used overstated language to rally Group members to the cause of New York fashion, eager to establish the city's pre-eminence as an international fashion centre with the potential to continue in this position after the war. Such hyperbole reached back to Shaver's American designer promotions of the 1930s, which were given extra significance now that New York was forced to be more self-reliant. Advertisements amplified this patriotism: L'Aiglon claimed to have 'caught the spirit of the American woman' in its print dresses of autumn 1940, shown in figure 5.1. The accompanying image of a smiling model raising the American flag emphasised the relationship between simple sportswear pieces, in this case in Enka rayon, a fashionable synthetic of the period, and ideals of patriotic Americanness. Editorial shoots used similar tactics. Figure 5.2 shows a John Rawlings spread of sportswear trouser suits from *Vogue's* 1 December 1940 edition, in which more subliminal references to the Stars and Stripes are employed. Both garments and backdrop are red, white and blue, the models inspect astrological charts, and the clothes are bold sportswear fashions, designed for the magazine's privileged middle-class readers' winter holidays in Palm Springs. The first outfit is emblazoned with a gold eagle and military style buttons; the last is described as being 'as blazing white as a Navy officer's uniform'.[7]

Images such as these evoked the war effort through signifiers that stimulated positive feelings of nationhood and pride. Military motifs were transposed onto women's bodies through design elements and decoration, which linked their visual identity to the war. It is, however, reductive to view only military-inspired garments as representative of national pride. For fashion magazines, the overriding message was that it was fashionable and patriotic to wear simple clothes, especially easily adaptable suits and separates. Military-related garments may have been most obviously linked to the war, but they made up only a small part of the fashion industry's output. Once America had entered the war in 1941, fashion magazines repeatedly used a range of signifiers to construct a more complex visual landscape, which showed everything from red, white and blue colour combinations to explicit references to the war effort. These contributed to the cultural formation of feminine ideals in terms of appearance, dress and behaviour during wartime.

Newspaper articles were equally concerned with the future of the American fashion industry. They used jingoistic language to connect the fashion industry's own efforts to those of the Allies, and continually to link back to fundamental ideals of Americanness to justify such claims and give them validity. Barbara E. Scott Fisher of *The Christian Science Monitor* drew together current political and world events to introduce her article on the American fashion industry in October 1940: 'America always seems to have her brawny hands full, what with war, elections, and refugees. But not content with these small items, she rolls up her sleeves and takes on fashions'.[8] America is thus personified as both feminine and strong, able to cope with global and local

5.1. L'Aiglon advertisement, *Vogue*, 15 November 1940

5.2. John Rawlings, Saks Fifth Avenue, Jaeger and
      Abercrombie and Fitch, Bonwit Teller, *Vogue*, 1 December
      1940. Originally published in Vogue © Condé Nast
      Archive/CORBIS

issues. Fisher's strident tone is employed to promote New York fashion collections as embodying 'with striking authority the courage and integrity of our designers, and their striking ability to create and carry through this magnificent adventure'.[9] This use of propagandistic language elevates all endeavours to those of a noble cause, and provides a linguistic foil to the imagery used in fashion magazines. It turns America's struggle to assert its fashion status into a positive action, rather than a panicked reaction to an extreme situation. Fisher cites the fact that 'our sports clothes stand alone and unchallenged anywhere in the world', as further proof of the industry's potential to succeed.[10]

There were a series of practical responses to the war, which aimed to consolidate New York fashion's position and to continue the industry's streamlining and professionalisation, which had grown during the 1930s. To this end the New York Dress Institute was founded in 1941, after discussion by unions and manufacturers, who anticipated America's entry into the war and feared a drop in trade. It was funded by 0.5 per cent volume of sales from each dress manufacturer (it only represented dress, not, for example, coat or suit manufacturers), and aimed to comprise a coherent means of promoting the trade nationally. It placed regular advertisements in fashion magazines during the war, and its label was attached to garments that were part of the campaign. Eleanor Lambert felt its early campaigns reflected weaknesses that related to wider problems about designers' ambiguous role within the design and promotion process at this time:

> It was almost impossible without identifiable clothes [that stated designers' or at least manufacturers' names] ... I finally got some of the executives together and said, 'Just forget the whole thing unless we can use designer names, and you yourselves must pick your leaders, the people who are the most creative'. That was the beginning of the couture group of the New York Dress Institute.[11]

The original Institute, plus the specialist couture group, helped to promote New York fashion design and linked its qualities to those of the city itself. This organisation gave focus to dress manufacturers' promotional strategies. Wider scale events, such as the coordinated press shows for made-to-measure garments, and the Coty awards, again initiated under Lambert's auspices in 1942, provided focussed media coverage for the industry.[12] The Coty awards were presented to the full range of New York's design community, and sportswear designers were included amongst the winners. Middle-market designers benefited from these promotions too, as they raised New York's fashion status in general.

Fashion's psychological importance was multi-layered. It could enable women literally to construct a sense of self, which was allied to contemporary ideals of femininity, status and beauty at a time of uncertainty. This could provide a feeling of continuity for both men and women, despite unfamiliar situations and behaviour patterns precipitated by the war, such as more women entering the workplace. The female labour force grew by 55 per cent between 1941 and 1945. Support for married women workers increased enormously. Whereas four out of five Americans had disagreed with married women working in 1938, a 1942 public opinion poll showed that 71 per cent of Americans felt that more should take jobs.[13] Although this demonstrates greater acceptance of women in the workplace, or at least recognition that they were needed as part of the war effort, women's wages tended to be less than men's. Susan M. Hartmann cites the average wage of a skilled female industrial worker at the wartime peak level in 1944, as $31.21, while a male worker would have received $54.65.[14] In view of these changes, fashion imagery and advertising helped to normalise new attitudes, and were part of the contemporary

> visual representation [which] helped to define a wartime culture even as it revealed the contradictions within any effort to present a unified image of home-front America. In times of crisis, such as war, representation revealed ruptures and fissure normally concealed by the process of ideology. The demands of the home front and the disruption of war unsettled gender roles and class structures.[15]

These contradictions are apparent in the way that fashion could simultaneously be used to encourage women to take an active part in the war effort, while reinforcing their 'natural' alliance to dress and appearance. Melissa Dabakis identified 'glamour … [as] yet another strategy that lured women into the workforce'.[16] However, imagery reinforced gender segregation and, as Ruth Milkman has written, while 'women could do "men's work," this was only for the duration'.[17]

Sportswear was able to bridge the seemingly contradictory ideals of women as wives and mothers, as well as those of women as workers. Sportswear's flexible designs signalled the possibility that women could embody either or both of these ideals, as garments could easily be adapted to home or office. Fashion could also play an important part in boosting women's morale, through identity construction, and through pleasure. It provided a selection of identities to women, as it had done during the Depression. The stereotypes of working woman, college girl, and 'Woman of Fashion' remained intact. Sportswear was central to the creation of the first two ideals, as it was for the leisured woman, who was shown in holiday wear throughout the period.

Successful appropriation of the current ideals of style and beauty could provide pleasure for the individual, as could the act of consumption. This was the case whether consumption itself was literal or merely through the fantasy provided by looking at fashion magazines or window-shopping. Gary Cross has noted that, despite the undoubted hardships of the Depression and war, consumerism became increasingly central to Americans' sense of identity, and that they remained unwilling to give up luxuries and:

> The federal government lifted the United States out of the Depression by preparing for and waging World War II. The federal budget rose from about $9 billion in 1939 to $100 billion by 1945, elevating the GNP from $91 to $166 billion. Naturally much of this money made its way back into the private sector. Home-front workers found their wallets and purses full, many for the first time in a decade.[18]

During the war, consumption of clothing and grooming products not only provided a means to formulate ideals of femininity. They took on other connotations, as they were also now seen as a duty, and this was, as noted above, partly to maintain individual and collective ideals of femininity. It was also to present a sexually alluring image for men, and to act as a reassurance to soldiers on furlough that nothing had changed. For the first time, men began to appear regularly alongside the female models in magazines and advertisements as seen in figure 5.3, which promotes Clare Potter. Although high fashion magazines had always included photographs of men, these were normally in personality-driven articles on actors, writers or statesmen, and it was a significant shift that they now entered the previously feminine realm of the fashion plate. Magazines aimed at younger women such as *Charm* had sporadic picture stories, often depicting models 'on holiday' in an exotic resort, but incorporating a male figure, usually in uniform, to the side or in the background of the image.

Sportswear shoots lent themselves especially well both to escapist resort spreads that signified a fantasy holiday environment, and to more realist town clothes stories that showed soldiers leaving from train stations. Indeed, while male models were not seen in every edition of fashion magazines, a more sexually-charged aura was discernible in many images of the period. One fashion spread from *Harper's Bazaar* presented a heady dreamscape to spectators, with models reclining in hot-coloured play clothes in a 'Hawaiian' backdrop, suggested by bamboo and palms. In one shot a model lies back on a makeshift bed of mats, framed in a tight shot by bamboo poles and a patterned backdrop. She wears a fuchsia and powder pink Tom Brigance wrap dress that slips down from her slightly parted knees, her tanned legs stretched out beyond the frame. She is barefoot, and seemingly caught in private reverie, her eyes shut in apparent ecstasy, as she inhales the perfume of the exotic blooms that she holds up to her face. The distancing 'otherness' of the tropical setting perhaps allows these images greater sexual license, which would not be possible in a more straightforward 'American' setting. The final shot of the story, reinforces the sexual message as it shows the model, still clad in simple Brigance sportswear pieces, once again laid back on mats and throws, smiling up at a male figure. The lighting is dark and intimate, at its brightest across her body and on her flowing blonde hair. Her companion is contrastingly dark-haired and leans into the picture. He is dressed in a dark blue and white patterned Hawaiian shirt, of the type sold to tourists and off-duty soldiers and sailors stationed on the island's military bases.[19]

Such imagery provided escape and fantasy, but fashion magazines had to strike a difficult balance during the war. While they strove to maintain a semblance of normality with regular fashion, beauty and cultural coverage, this material had to be combined with practical advice on how to cope with shortages. Images from the front, for example Lee Miller's war reportage in *Vogue*, fractured the normal fashion environment further. This balance between reality and fantasy had been rehearsed, albeit in a less violent way, during the 1930s when documentary-style photography entered fashion magazines' pages.

When the government began to introduce a series of laws to ration fabrics and limit amounts used within clothing design, magazines had to search for a means to present this to readers in as positive a way as possible. The Limitations Order L–85 regulations that were instigated by the War Production Board in April 1942, 'introduced what was called the "silhouette." It attempted to control fabric yardage and set certain restrictions but permitted all to make apparel under a general plan or silhouette. It did not attempt to set the details of style'.[20] L–85 comprised a detailed breakdown of fabric allowances according to clothing size and type of garment.[21] On 30 March 1942, Stanley Marcus, then Chief of the Apparel Section at the War Production Board, notified the Clearance Committee in a memorandum that L–85 was issued because:

> In view of present and prospective shortages, it seems essential to attempt to produce the maximum number of garments out of existing and future yardages … [Furthermore] In view of the fact that women's and children's apparel is subject to extreme variation in fashion, it also appears desirable to establish such restrictions that may prevent radical changes which would render obsolete existing clothes in women's wardrobes.[22]

Various elements of the regulations applied to sportswear, for example those that concerned dresses and coats, but the most direct reference was made in a section devoted to 'Slacks, Play Clothes, Separates', which was presented in illustrated form in *Women's Wear Daily* on 8 April 1942. This showed the maximum lengths of garments and also restrictions placed on items such as the number of garments that could be sold as one 'unit', and the disallowance of bibs, suspenders or accessories being sold as a single unit with a sports garment.[23]

L–85 called for simplification of design and a slim silhouette. In the 1930s, these design ideals had been established within sportswear, as it was usually designed to comprise a minimum number of pattern pieces, and to avoid elaborate, extraneous decoration. They gained added resonance in the 1940s because of their association with the war effort and therefore with patriotic, rather than purely technological and commercial, imperatives. Fashion magazines conveyed the contents of L–85 to their readers through articles that reassured readers that the regulations would make little difference to fashions, other than through design devices introduced to restrict, for example, the use of metal fastenings. *Vogue's* article on the first collections since L–85, in its 1 September 1942 edition, stated that the restrictions would have limited effect on the fashionable silhouette. The article is couched in patriotic tones to reinforce the need for these regulations, while simultaneously asserting that they merely make into law what American women have always wanted from their clothes: 'You'll admire them for public and patriotic reasons … Clothes must be simple. That's the Government rule – but hasn't it always been your own personal Golden Rule?'[24] Despite the over-enthusiastic tone of the article many of these design elements, as well as the slim silhouette, were an established part of New York sportswear's style, and had been connected to patriotism and Americanness in the 1930s. The fashion media therefore continued and consolidated a process that had begun during the Depression, of presenting restrictions as a means to reinforce existing 'good' taste, which already favoured simplicity and restraint.

Magazines also made suggestions about how readers might continue to add personal touches to their clothing while they saved resources. This might take the form of articles on dressmaking, or, as in *Vogue's* 1 July 1942 edition, a series of illustrations that encouraged women to take an active part in the styling of their outfits and, with 'An Ounce of Invention', dye, revamp or decorate garments they already owned. This innovativeness, albeit guided by *Vogue*, was accompanied by ideas that had evolved during the Depression, including interchangeable wardrobes, such as that in figure 5.4. Along with the suit, these became a cornerstone to aid women to build small wardrobes of garments, which could be worn in different combinations to create the illusion of a larger range of clothing.

It was important for the fashion industry to find other means to source inspiration and extend their markets. Various schemes were run to encourage designers to work with museum collections to find inspiration, and, in some cases, to emphasise America's rich cultural legacy. The Brooklyn Museum opened its storerooms to designers, and developed its links to Morris de Camp Crawford, the avid proponent of American fashion. The Museum of Modern Art hosted an exhibition in 1945, 'Are Clothes Modern?' curated by Bernard Rudofsky, and the Metropolitan Museum held 'American Fabrics and Fashions' in spring 1945. The advertisement shown in figure 5.5 names each participant in the collaboration: Claire McCardell designed the sun dress, which is made up from Wesley Simpson's 'Dynasty Print', based on patterns in the Museum's collection, and the fabric itself was designed by Bemelmans textile mill. This is an example of the raised profile of designers, as well as textile mills themselves, both of which were, by this stage, frequently named in advertisements. The use of museums' names could also help to promote the status of all involved since, along with the promotion of American identity, such tactics implied the museums' relevance and currency, and provided the designers' with incontestable 'cultural capital'.[25]

In the 1930s and 1940s, Americanness was connected to patriotic spirit and to the United States' democratic political system. In *Vogue's* 1940 Americana issue, Americanness was extended to include Latin America. While this inclusiveness meant that a wider range of nationalities, and therefore national clothing styles, were included within fashion's realm, it was not a purely altruistic exercise. South America was discussed in magazines, and visited by designers such as Carolyn Schnurer, who sought inspiration for their own work. It was described in the Fashion Group's meetings as a vast resource of ideas, fabrics and accessories, to be used by the New York industry and, importantly, also as a major market to be conquered.[26] Sportswear designers used these influences widely, its simple lines smoothing out the 'otherness' of such reference points to temper them for North American ideals of femininity and 'good' taste.

Immigrants had long been encouraged to assimilate American style self-presentation. In a similar way fashion incorporated and played with 'exotic' styles, but always converted them into designs and images that would be acceptable to high fashion magazines' audience. Colours and design devices might be taken from South America, but the overall impression did not deviate from a white, middle-class ideal. The growth of South American inspiration was linked to the reduction

5.3.   Clare Potter advertisement, *Vogue*, 15 May 1942

5.4.   ColoRelated Fashions advertisement, *Vogue*, 15 February 1942

5.5.   Wesley Simpson advertisement, *Vogue*, 1 April 1945

in the domestic, and, more significantly, the international market during the war. Chain store Burdines even produced a 'Good Neighbor' print dress in 1944 that harked back to Roosevelt's 1934 policy of the same name, which had signalled a less interventionist approach to relations with the western hemisphere.[27] This policy had been intensified after the start of the war in Europe in 1939, and it prompted greater exploration of South America in particular as a potential friendly market, as well as inspiration, for the fashion industry.[28]

Other allies courted by the United States included China, and the fashion industry was equally interested in assimilating its culture. This took the form of articles on Madame Chiang Kai-shek and other Chinese women who visited or lived in America, particularly those deemed to be especially stylish.[29] American policy towards China immediately before and during the war reflected the hope that a 'liberal and pro-American China' would help to prevent both imperialist interventions in Asia, especially by the Japanese, and 'counter the appeal of revolutionary doctrines among the masses in the East'.[30] Popular representations reflected official policy, Michael Schaller writes, since 'for a variety of reasons, both pragmatic and romantic, Roosevelt sought to include China among the ranks of the Grand Alliance'.[31] In fashion terms this connection drew upon the perceived exotic potential of non-white influences and was expressed through a range of fashion designs and promotions. Cosmetics brand Chen Yu embodied a heady femme fatale aesthetic that extended the Asian influence not just to its name, but also to its seductive advertising campaigns. Sportswear designers used Chinese references in various ways. Joset Walker, who was known for her use of South American and Asian textiles and detailing, produced for Spring/Summer 1945 a Chinese collection, which was staged in Lord & Taylor's windows with Chinese screens and "coolie" hats. As with the South American designs, exoticism was used, in this case in the form of Orientalism, but was presented through the trope of recognisably American forms in its overriding design principles. These internationally-inspired designs thus functioned in a number of ways. They mined potential new business markets and provided an escapist exoticism at a time of limited travel. They also enabled American women to masquerade as 'other' while maintaining a unified American identity, linked to the war effort by promoting allies.[32]

SPORTSWEAR DESIGN AND REPRESENTATION

Crisp, neat and ready for the day ahead, the model stands against floral wallpaper, which adds a dainty, feminine air to a Louise Dahl-Wolfe image from *Harper's Bazaar* in November 1942. Dressed in a denim pop-over dress designed by Claire McCardell for Townley Sports, the model represents the seemingly contradictory ideals of femininity that flourished under war conditions. The dress referenced women's traditional domestic role, in the quilted 'pot holder' attached to the pocket with tapes, as well as employing the masculine authenticity of the American West in its sturdy workwear denim fabric. The text that accompanied the photograph reinforced the pop-over's purpose. Written in the first person, it sought to establish an empathetic connection between magazine, designer and reader. The copywriter adopted the persona of a busy wartime housewife: 'I'm doing my own work – the ideal garment for it, for cooking, dusting, scrubbing, painting, or any odd job about the house'.[33] As women were forced to take on a wider range of tasks in the home, Townley and *Harper's Bazaar* had collaborated to create a dress that would be appropriate to developing needs. Carmel Snow and *Harper's Bazaar's* fashion editor Diana Vreeland had approached McCardell to design a garment that could address the lifestyles of housewives and mothers, while remaining stylish and fashion-conscious.[34] During the Depression, there had been occasional mentions in high fashion magazines of women having to dismiss their servants and take on increased housework, and even more occasional advertisements for cheap 'house dresses' at the back of magazines. However, it was not until the Second World War that a high fashion publication such as *Harper's Bazaar* made explicit reference to the subject, and acted to create a sartorial solution that would provide middle-class women with an appropriate garment. Vreeland and Snow aimed to boost New York fashion and encourage innovative design. The pop-over was mass-produced and cost $6.95, well below the normal cost for a McCardell design, thus addressing financial as well as lifestyle concerns.

The pop-over was to become a bestseller for Townley, and raised both manufacturer's and designer's profile. Indeed, McCardell went on to win the Coty award in 1943 when, amongst other key trends, she helped to launch the leotard, discussed below. The pop-over style was repeated in various forms in later collections. This was because Townley patented it immediately to protect the company from the type of losses incurred by the monastic dress. McCardell was rarely credited in *Harper's Bazaar* before the pop-over, although designers such as Clare Potter and Vera Maxwell had been named since the late 1930s. One of the first instances of McCardell

5.6.   Claire McCardell, cotton 'Pop-over' dress, 1942. The Metropolitan Museum of Art, Gift of
       Claire McCardell, 1945. Photograph © 1998 The Metropolitan Museum of Art

5.7.   Vera Maxwell, cotton twill jumpsuit, 1942. The Metropolitan Museum of Art, Gift of Miss
       Vera Maxwell, 1945. Photograph ©2000 The Metropolitan Museum of Art

5.8.   Davidow design, early 1940s. Courtesy of Special Collections, Gladys Marcus Library,
       Fashion Institute of Technology

being named as a garment's designer was in June 1942. Even after this, advertisements were also more often for Townley than for McCardell, an early example that bore the designer's name appearing in September 1942.[35] After the pop-over's success she was named more frequently, as were an increasing number of sportswear designers during the later years of the war.

The original 1942 pop-over, shown in figure 5.6, demonstrated McCardell's ability to design clothes for mass production that lost none of their attention to detail and cut.[36] The bodice was cut in two pieces, with one section crossing diagonally over the other to produce a wrap-over effect, which fastened with five white buttons on the left of the body. The buttons are distinctive, a feature that would become one of McCardell's signatures. Each has a triple set of holes to enable them to be sewn onto the fabric. This provides a simple decorative addition, without distracting from the garment's clean lines. The collar is small and neat and fastens at the neck with a single white button. The waistband is concealed by a slim buttonhole placket attached to the bodice, which fastens with the same white buttons that are used throughout. This is cut to look like a belt, although it is integral to the dress. It represents another example of an intrinsic decorative element, since it adds detail while also functioning to join bodice to skirt. The skirt wraps around the body from right to left and has a large quilted patch pocket on the right side, with a matching red cotton-backed oven mitt. This is attached to the dress with a tape that buttons onto the waistband.

This pop-over's patriotic red, white and blue colour scheme is reinforced by its designed purpose: to ease women's dutiful contribution to the home front. McCardell's tongue-in-cheek use of the oven mitt comments on women's new role. This was echoed in other pieces, such as her evening dresses with matching aprons, to enable women to move elegantly from kitchen to dining room, and thus from being cook to hostess. Such outfits embodied what *Vogue* wrote of in 1942 as 'the two roles you'll be seen in most often this summer … the war-worker-by-day (look cool, look neat, look efficient) and the lovely-lady-by-night (look feminine, look pretty, look serene)'.[37] Women were constantly reminded of their need seamlessly to maintain existing ideals of femininity and beauty, while simultaneously assimilating those of the career woman.

American and French designers had made designs based on working dress before, for example Balenciaga's 'vegetable-seller' dress of 1940. However, it was American sportswear designers who most effectively exploited work wear's potential as a source of inspiration during the war. The pop-over related to other equally innovative examples of fashion designs that addressed women's more active lives, such as Vera Maxwell's jumpsuit that, like the pop-over, was created in 1942 (fig. 5.7).[38] It included similar design details, such as the concealed waistband, which enabled women to unbutton the jumpsuit at the waist to detach bodice from 'trouser' section, and enable them to dress and undress more easily. The narrow line of these outfits would have fitted within L–85's prescriptions. McCardell, like other successful sportswear designers such as Maxwell, was able to understand and apply the restrictions placed upon their designs, not just by the mass-production method, but also by the wartime regulations. These designers were able to produce innovative designs during the Depression and even more so during the war, focussing on the inherent properties of the fabric, the natural form of the body and the machine process employed in their manufacture. Such sportswear designs foregrounded women's practical needs, as well as their desire to remain stylish. These design imperatives were carried through into the development of civilian uniforms for women, such as those created by New York designer Muriel King in 1943 for aircraft workers, and military nurse's uniforms, such as those designed by Hattie Carnegie. In each case these designs used masculine elements, such as denim fabrics or trousers, to produce an image of women ready for action. In the 1930s, sportswear had done this for actual sporting activities such as golf and tennis, as well as for career women. In the 1940s, this search for feminised versions of men's work and office wear continued to gain importance, with greater emphasis placed upon connotations of duty, patriotism and national identity.

High fashion magazines enthusiastically promoted, as the smartest and most appropriate attire for women working in the city, suits such as those produced by Davidow, seen in figure 5.8. As in the 1930s, suits and practical accessories for working women, such as big bags and comfortable shoes, were frequently promoted in relation to images of Manhattan. Fashion features also recalled those of the Depression, the 'thirties term 'tubbables' may have been changed to 'washables', but the message remained the same: that in straitened times easy-to-clean fabrics were the most sensible choice.[39] McCardell supported this easy-to-wear, easy-to-care-for ethos in her use of fabrics, such as cottons that could be washed repeatedly. Women continued to be encouraged to maintain hygiene standards for themselves and their clothes, and to police their bodies to attain the American ideal. Slimness was promoted as youthful and desirable and women were expected to balance attention to 'care of the self' alongside a variety of work roles, inside and outside the home, as they had been during the Depression.

In the 1940s, though, such attentions were portrayed as a part of the war effort. An article entitled,

'What Price Physical Fitness', from *Vogue's* 15 May 1942 edition, admonished women that: 'it's up to you, in the interest of your own defence to be as physically prepared as possible for the job to come, whether it's ambulance driving, desk work, motor mechanics – or just sittin' knittin'.'[40] This sense of preparedness for whatever might happen reinforced the potential precariousness of everyday life during the war, and therefore encouraged women to maintain constant vigilance. *Vogue*, for example, ran an article in August 1942 that gave women specific exercises to do according to the type of war work they were engaged in. The text that accompanied the images of women carrying out each exercise echoed the tenets of Taylorism in its statement that 'tiredness and tenseness and muscle-weariness are the great enemies, not only of your looks, but of your efficiency and ability, as well'.[41]

Pat Kirkham has written of the association of 'beauty and duty' in Britain during the Second World War, as part of the government's 'concern to boost morale and create a common outlook and *national* identity amongst all women'.[42] This was to be achieved through the 'emphasis [that] was placed on features of women's culture which closely related to the shaping of their *individual* identities. The personal paralleled the collective … [and] what had previously been matters of personal pleasure and pride now became patriotic issues central to the war effort'.[43] Clearly, official and media attitudes were similar in America. Kirkham discussed fashion magazines as a key site in which women's individual and collective identity was shaped. This is borne out in American *Vogue* and *Harper's Bazaar's* contents' continual balance between war duty, personal appearance and fashion.

On the one hand, war added to pressure on women to create an external self that conformed to current ideals. On the other, it provided women with justification for the pleasure they took in such practices. During the early 1940s, these issues became the concern of psychiatrists, who pathologised women's constant search for beauty and linked it to their sense of lack. This trend was to grow apace after the war, but had already entered fashion magazine pages by 1942. In an article, 'The Psychology of Beauty', psychiatrist Dr. Louis Bisch discussed the relationship between women's search for beauty and the 'love urge'. It also gave practical advice, based upon clinical techniques, of how to avoid anxiety and depression. *Vogue* saw this as necessary because: 'Today, since the advent of the war, personal and practical problems have multiplied a hundred-fold … [and] the preservation of some form of personal beauty is a genuine psychological need for women'.[44] Bisch saw good posture and exercise as two important means to achieve greater confidence and sense of self. Body image, clothing and well-being were all connected to the war's impact.

This focus on exercise culture was evident within sportswear design during the war. Mildred Orrick was a peer of Claire McCardell's from Parsons School of Design in the 1920s and went on to become an illustrator and stage and fashion designer. During her career she explored forms of bifurcated garment that moved with the body. Her sketchbooks and cuttings reveal early work on figures as they perform yoga positions for Natacha Rambova's 'Techniques for Living' in the 1920s. Other folders include extensive research into American pioneer dress, Shaker clothing, Native American and other folk costume from, for example, China, Turkey and Inuit culture, which incorporated trousers and leggings. Together they demonstrate the range of Orrick's work, and also the relationship between her theatrical and fashion designs, since in each case she considered how clothing could be designed to follow the anatomy closely and allow the body to move. Her 'Bifurcation Sketches' show how she drew upon these studies, developing ideas for trousers and finally leggings that used her studies of other cultures, as well as examples of nineteenth-century bloomers from the Brooklyn Museum's collection, to formulate garments that could be worn in the 1940s.

Orrick took an ideas board to Diana Vreeland, fashion editor at *Harper's Bazaar,* that showed the evolution of her ideas and a selection of possible outfits based upon her research. The Anna-Maria and Stephen Kellen Archives Center of Parsons School of Design contains what appear to be the original components of this presentation, shown in figure 5.9. The text that accompanied Orrick's drawings set out her ideas: 'the foundation of all these clothes is the acrobat's leotard, or tights. We selected it in closely-knit cotton jersey, and we think it a fine idea for cold weather indoors and out, as pants, stockings, and undershirt combined … This is one of our signposts-to-the-future garments. We see no reason why it shouldn't be worn some day soon for general wear'.[46]

It is significant that Orrick positions her work as 'signposts-to-the-future'. Several accounts of sportswear from the 1930s and 1940s note that some of Claire McCardell's work, in particular, was deemed too avant-garde for the mass consumer.[47] Sportswear's simplicity of form and modern aesthetic was undoubtedly in contrast to more obviously 'feminine' fashions that relied upon decoration and (before 1940) links to Parisian style for its appeal. The designs that women such as Orrick and McCardell produced were perceived as of the present, since they addressed the lifestyles of contemporary women, while also incorporating both avant-garde and orthodox elements. This was particular to New York sportswear. While Paris had embraced a similarly modern aesthetic in twenties and thirties couture sportswear ranges such as Schiap Sport, which was also sold in America, this had not been translated into ready-to-wear, mass-produced clothing. London's sportswear lacked this deceptively simple design style too, and continued to reference traditional styles rather than to produce innovative designs for cheaper ranges. In the absence of Parisian influence and with the limited amount of fashions London was able to produce during the war, New York designers such as McCardell, Schnurer, Maxwell and Leser were prolific in their creation of high quality designs for mid-price sportswear ranges.

Fashion media and design both sought to elide potentially challenging notions of femininity as productive and independent necessitated by the home front, in favour of traditional ideals that could present a façade of normality and stability. Sportswear presented design and representation that incorporated old and new and its strong association with a coherent ideal of national identity could enable it to transcend this potentially threatening ambiguity. It could also therefore be reassuring, although in its most forward-looking incarnations could disrupt consumer expectations. Any such potentially unsettling elements could harm sales, and so it was crucial, from the fashion industry's perspective, that the overall image that sportswear presented would assuage concerns about its ambiguities.

There is a tacit acknowledgement of this issue in the way that *Harper's Bazaar* attempted to introduce Orrick's ideas gradually, to accustom its readers to the non-western style of combining leggings and dress. In the January 1943 *Harper's Bazaar*, 'The Leotard Idea' was presented in the form of text and illustrations based upon Orrick's work. Her sketches showed variations on the leotard theme, and described this as 'a new idea leading toward the twenty-first century and the cosmic costumes of Flash Gordon … it's an old idea, based on every ballet dancer's traditional rehearsal costume'. This was developed seven months later in *Harper's Bazaar's* July edition, under the title 'It's Something'. By this point Diana Vreeland had involved Claire MCardell in the project, since she felt that McCardell's name and Townley's manufacturing capabilities were needed to launch Orrick's design. Landshoff's photograph showed two young models, windswept and casual, clad in tabard-style dresses worn over stripy sweater and leggings combinations. The caption recalled the magazine's earlier trial of Orrick's idea, and linked this potential new fashion to college girls, who were frequently associated with new sportswear trends. It reminded readers that 'in January we tossed out an idea, a new silhouette based on the leotard or ballet school tights', and went on to assert its fashion authority and suggest how the clothes might be worn: '*The New Yorker* ribbed us but fashion followed us. This month we present leotards for the college girl. Under them, wear nothing but brassiere and pantie girdle'.[48] The garments were cited as Claire McCardell's designs, available at Lord & Taylor. However, despite

5.9.   Mildred Orrick, Leotard Fashions, c. 1942. © The Anna-Maria and Stephen Kellen
       Archives Center for Parsons The New School for Design

5.10. Claire McCardell, Ensemble, wool, leather (Leotard, overdress, belt, ballet slippers).
       1944. The Metropolitan Museum of Art, Gift of Claire McCardell, 1945.
       Photograph © 2007 The Metropolitan Museum of Art

5.11. Claire McCardell, wool and rayon jersey diaper bathing suit, 1944. The Metropolitan
       Museum of Art, Gift of Mrs. A Moore Montgomery, 1970.
       Photograph © The Metropolitan Museum of Art 2007

publicity in other magazines and a cover shoot for *Life* magazine on 13 September 1943, the design was unsuccessful in the long run. The knitting process required to produce the wool jersey was to prove too expensive for McCardell's mid-range price point.[50] As seen in figure 5.10, The Costume Institute in New York's collection contains a surviving outfit of 1944 that shows a variation on the leotard theme, in this case a wraparound striped tweed dress with matching bottle green bodysuit and belt and tweed ballet pumps.[51] It demonstrates the care McCardell took to co-ordinate complete outfits, and the forward-looking silhouette that the streamlined bodysuit would have produced. The dress echoes the wrap-over design of the pop-over, while extending the wrap to the whole garment, rather than just the bodice.

The 'leotard idea' suggests the various factors that could contribute to the success or failure of a particular design. While the monastic dress was a success on the macro level, in that it crystallised a trend, it was a failure on the micro level, since the lack of adequate legal protection for the designer's ideas meant that it contributed to Townley's bankruptcy at the end of the 1930s. The pop-over was successful since it was patented early, its design fitted with women's lifestyle trends, and it was given strong support from its inception by a major fashion magazine. Importantly, it was also a design that could be manufactured cheaply. The leotard idea fitted all but the last of these criteria, and thus remained unavailable to its target consumer market of college girls and other young women on limited incomes. Indeed, Henry Rosenfeld, a designer, who frequently created garments based on mid-range sportswear manufacturers' work, produced a more basic, easy to produce version of this outfit in August 1944. It did away with the leotard that had proved so difficult for Townley to manufacture and, instead, showed a simple sweater, worn beneath a dress that drew upon McCardell's design.

These designs were promoted on young, slim models and several revealed the body in such a way that favored those whose bodies conformed to the fashionable ideal. This was especially the case with resort wear, which often focussed on the natural body and was shown in magazines on lithe, tanned models. McCardell's diaper suit, shown in figure 5.11, was a prime example of this, since it brought together key elements of 1940s beach and swim clothes in its reference to children's clothes, and use of simple design and basic cotton fabric.[52] As this example shows, it was made in dark jersey knits that would cling to the figure to produce a more grown-up silhouette, as well as in cotton prints that related more closely to babies' diapers. Although the diaper suit comprised two pieces of fabric sewn together at the waist that were tied around the wearer's neck then passed between the legs and folded back round the waist to tie at the front,

Life magazine felt it needed further explanation. During the war, *Life* tended to focus on fashion stories that exposed women's bodies and could thus function as both news of clothing trends for women, and pin-ups for male readers. In its 17 January 1944 edition, a young 'beach beauty' was used to demonstrate how new swimsuits and beach clothes should be worn, and a four-picture strip presented a 'how to' guide for putting on the diaper suit.

McCardell's work demonstrates the innovation apparent in 1940s sportswear, despite wartime restrictions. Along with other designers who rose to the fore in the early 1940s, she built upon techniques that had evolved during the Depression to produce clothing that was appropriate to contemporary social and fashion concerns. New York fashion insiders, such as Vreeland and Snow, were keen to encourage this type of work, which could consolidate an ideal of American fashion that had the potential to carry the industry through the war and beyond. Stereotypes that had developed in the 1930s, in particular the career woman and the college girl, continued to act as ideals of active, modern femininity. Their relevance extended beyond the purely representational, to reach out to potential consumers who could relate to their 'real', though idealised, lifestyles.

THE MODERN SPORTSWEAR AESTHETIC II

Toni Frissell established her photographic style during the 1930s. Encouraged by Edward Steichen to focus on natural settings, she used the outdoors as a backdrop to her images of sportswear in action. Frissell's work epitomised the modern sportswear aesthetic, and her interest in realism was brought to bear on both her fashion and war photography during the 1940s. It married sportswear and documentary-style imagery to construct the atmosphere of casual, holiday snapshots.

This ethos extended to her choice of models. She favoured women who could bring 'naturalness' to the photograph. This had been revealed in a *Vogue* internal memo from Carmel Snow, which discussed the photographer's use of non-professional models:

> I am told that the reason we use the Pulitzer-Patterson type so little is that the photographers prefer to use the old-time models, who are too skinny for the modern idea of beauty … Do believe me when I say that the average reader, looking over both *Vogue* and *Harper's Bazaar* is sick to death of this type of model both magazines are using. There are many beautiful American girls, and I think that photographers should be flexible enough to get their eye in for the new type.[53]

Frissell continued to favour society women such as Patsy Pulitzer and Joan Patterson, who embodied Frissell's own privileged, sporty ideal of Americanness in their lean physiques, angular features and love of the outdoors.

On 20 July 1943 *The Christian Science Monitor* described her work as official photographer 'for the new WAC recruiting activities'.[54] This work showed the women recruits as an efficient, unified collective, dressed the same and acting together, while also capturing more individual moments. Frissell's technique grew out of her constant experimentation, which meant, 'she developed an eye for blending together naturally both model and landscape'.[55] This is demonstrated in one image which shows two uniformed recruits walking through a field with kit bags (fig. 5.12). Frissell used the soft grey tones of her black and white shots to unite body and nature. She favoured images that showed women working or moving with purpose, happy and forthright or focussed on the task in hand.

This extended to her portraiture and personal work, and dominated her fashion photography. As

5.12. Toni Frissell, WAACs, c.1943. Originally published in *Vogue*. Originally published in *Vogue* © Condé Nast Archive / CORBIS

5.13. Toni Frissell, Peck & Peck, *Vogue*, 1 July 1940. Originally published in *Vogue*. © Condé Nast Archive / CORBIS

5.14. Toni Frissell, Contact Sheet, 1940s. © Toni Frissell Collection, The Library of Congress

figure 5.13 shows, sportswear worked best with her visual style. She frequently set her subjects against big skies that rose up behind their bodies, as in this photograph which was used on *Vogue's* cover for 1 July 1940. The vivid blue of a summer sky emphasises the warm red of the model's sweater, as she stands on a ship's jib boom. Although, as with all fashion imagery, the photograph has been carefully orchestrated by fashion editor and photographer, the aesthetic conventions are designed to lend realism to the artificial.

Frissell's contact sheets, an example of which is shown in figure 5.14, demonstrate how she achieved this, since rather than placing them in a series of preconceived poses, she would put the models into an environment, and then photograph them as they looked around, talked and smiled. She therefore engaged with the models: rather than imposing specific gestures upon them; in some shots the model is clearly speaking to her while she photographs. For Frissell, as Snow's above memo demonstrated, this approach was more modern and in tune with fashion magazine readers, since it was easier for them to relate to than more posed, studio-bound shots. Along with 1940s sportswear, it portrayed an idealised form of the everyday and made the mundane appear special. Sportswear and the modern sportswear aesthetic were given extra validity by association with serious photojournalistic representation and linked to glamour once printed in high fashion magazines.

Louise Dahl-Wolfe and Frissell's work was instrumental in the formulation of the modern sportswear aesthetic during the 1930s and 1940s. However, they had different preoccupations and technical approaches. While both women photographed all kinds of fashions, they were perhaps most innovative when depicting sportswear. Frissell's images presented an idyllic vision of body and nature united. They showed sportswear as a further 'natural' element in the busy, outdoors life of the bourgeoisie of which she was herself a part. The nonchalant way that the clothes were integrated into the image suggested how easily women might integrate them into their own wardrobes, and by extension, their lives.

While Dahl-Wolfe also favoured outdoor settings and natural light, she was more interested in colour and form.[56] She drew upon her art school training in colour theory, and the influence of Edward Weston, to focus on the contours of the posed body as a modernist object. This is clear in her black and white work, as well as the richly coloured imagery that was frequently featured in *Harper's Bazaar*. In this photograph of a model in a rubber swimsuit from 1940, seen in figure 5.15, both similarities to and differences from Frissell are apparent. Martin Munkacsi's influence on each woman was noticeable. In this case it is apparent in Dahl-Wolfe's use of a jarring angle:

a view down onto the beach where the model is lying. Both women related body to landscape, but for Dahl-Wolfe this was often done through texture and form, rather than through a unifying use of soft grey tones. Thus, the model becomes as smooth as the stones that stand to her side, and both rock and body cast sharp black shadows on the soft sand. Her hair and body are contained in white rubber swim cap and suit, the only inorganic elements in the picture, but their potentially harsh shine is dulled by the shadow that her raised leg throws across her body. The texture of the rocks, sand, water and body are harmonious, each form is distinct, yet visually connected through the print's clarity and thematic concerns. Dahl-Wolfe's Kodachrome photography used colour as a formal element that helped to organise the composition and heighten its impact and meaning.[57] This could take the form of a subtle exploration of tone and texture, or vibrant, contrasting colours to draw attention to the clothes and to enhance the effects of sunlight on cloth and flesh. Dahl-Wolfe worked closely with Diana Vreeland and was always conscious that fashion photography's primary purpose was to promote current trends, whether couture or 'pearls of little price', cheap designs that had less obvious visual appeal.[58]

In the case of sportswear, this frequently entailed a visual articulation of themes of American identity in Dahl-Wolfe's imagery. As has been seen, Americanness as a useful trope through which to promote New York fashion became dominant during the war years. In Dahl-Wolfe's work, contemporary cultural imperatives that related to, for example, morale, were balanced with commercial imperatives to display and sell clothing effectively. The pull between the mythic open plains of the West (nature) and the dynamism of the metropolis (culture) were central to constructions of American identity. These seemingly contradictory impulses were amalgamated on the fashion pages, which helped to communicate a coherent ideal of American identity. Dahl-Wolfe's use of colour and light to create form and texture in a photograph could produce a unifying aesthetic that provided a visual and stylistic link between city and nature. This is explicit in figure 5.16, her photograph of a model in Jay Thorpe slacks and fringed shawl posed against the Arizona skyline, leaning against Frank Lloyd-Wright's house at Taliesen West. Lloyd-Wright's architecture is quintessentially modernist. It foregrounded geometric forms, the authenticity of materials and the relationship between architecture and environment, as exemplified by Taliesen West's jutting balconies of warm wooden panelling, set against rough stone walls that merged with the colours and textures of the surrounding rocky landscape. The skyline's deep blues throw the house into stark relief, and the photograph is cropped to emphasise the monumentality of both building and mountainous terrain beyond. The model is also presented monumentally. Her tanned skin is emphasised, and is related to, the colours of her environment.

5.15. Louise Dahl-Wolfe, Model in Rubber Bathing Suit, California, 1940. Gift of Helen Cumming Ziegler. Courtesy of National Museum of Women in the Arts

5.16. Louise Dahl-Wolfe, Jay Thorpe, *Harper's Bazaar*, January 1942. © Courtesy of the Museum at the Fashion Institute of Technology, New York. Photograph by Louise Dahl Wolfe

5.17. Louise Dahl-Wolfe, Russeks, *Harper's Bazaar*, August 1944. © Courtesy of the Museum at the Fashion Institute of Technology, New York. Photograph by Louise Dahl Wolfe

5.18. Martin Munkacsi, Henri Bendel, *Harper's Bazaar*, October 1944. © Joan Munkacsi. Courtesy Howard Greenberg Gallery, NYC

This photograph depicts the allure of America's natural heritage, while simultaneously recognising man's agency within this vast landscape. The city acted as the binary opposite of nature within the construction of American identity. New York was the ultimate expression of America's technological and economic evolution. In this image, from August 1944, the city's modernist horizon becomes a hazy backdrop for the model's confident figure, as she looks out on the city from an expansive window in figure 5.17. She wears rich, autumnal shades: a deep bronze three-quarter length coat by Roxspan from Russeks and red scarf-style hat by Hattie Carnegie, with matching gloves. Manhattan had become an established venue for fashion shoots during the 1930s, and was increasingly popular in the war years. It offered metaphorical significance to an image, as it could stand for the chaos and excitement of modernity, reinforce the modern design of the clothing, or the modern lifestyle of the woman who would wear sportswear in the city. It also offered the practical advantage of being cheap and easy to access from the fashion magazine's Manhattan offices, during a time of limited travel and fuel restrictions.

Martin Munkasci's work continued to inspire his fellow photographers and remained influential throughout the war period. He frequently used scale to affect a photograph's impact. In figure 5.18, a picture from October 1944, the shining metallic form of the plane dwarfs the model. The photograph is shot from beneath the plane, which becomes an abstract modernist symbol of speed and technology. The model is smart and efficient, in a Henri Bendel jersey dress and pale wool bolero. The plane provides a reflective surface to mirror her form and that of the runway on which she stands. Thus, Munkacsi was able to incorporate the disruptions of war into the modern sportswear aesthetic. Both the photographic style and the clothing depicted fitted together to comprise assertive images of dynamism, which accorded with the ideals of a strong and confident home front.

When Paris was occupied, there was a rise in sportswear imagery in New York fashion magazines, although high fashion and made-to-order clothing by American designers such as Valentina and Traina-Norell were still shown in a more traditional way, as was London couture. The modern sportswear aesthetic was developed by younger practitioners, who were clearly influenced by Frissell, Dahl-Wolfe and Munkasci. Frances McLaughlin and Genevieve Naylor's work made direct references to that of Frissell and Dahl-Wolfe and continued to view sportswear through the prism of Americanness.

However, it was Richard Avedon and Irving Penn whose photography brought a dynamic, graphic abstraction to the modern sportswear aesthetic during the war years. Penn used sharp cropping to slice the model's figure, parodied the model's studied poses and played with the ambiguity of the 'live' model. In a graphic photo-spread from 15 October 1944, Penn showed models in sportswear by Claire McCardell and Tina Leser amongst others. The images were stacked in boxes on the page; each model shot against white to foreground the bold colours of her sportswear separates worn with dark tights and primary coloured ballet pumps. Several held emblems of sporting activities: a bowling ball, tennis rackets or archery target. These objects acted as shorthand for the dynamic potential of each outfit. Such imagery referenced the realist imagery of other sportswear photographers, while demonstrating how both sportswear, and the modern sportswear aesthetic, were sufficiently embedded within fashion's visual culture by the mid-1940s both to be referred to in shorthand and even to be parodied by younger photographers.

Penn and Avedon were able to transpose the sensibility and atmosphere of Frissell, Dahl-Wolfe and Munkacsi's aesthetic to studio-bound shots. Penn and Avedon mainly worked on teenage fashions and, just as college girls remained the ideal audience for more avant-garde sportswear designs, so they provided an audience for more daring photographic styles. Penn did this by cropping the photographs to focus on details, while Avedon lightened the formality of studio shots by showing the model seemingly caught off guard, laughing and awkward, as seen in his work for *Junior Bazaar*. Their work not only fitted with that of the other photographers discussed above, but worked in unison with the modernist style of page layout that had been brought to America by Alexey Brodovitch in the 1930s.

In the absence of Paris, and through the impact of the Second World War, sportswear had come to represent a real alternative to high fashion. New York sportswear was inextricably linked to ideals of Americanness that made it appear patriotic, while its 'everyday' simplicity linked it to ideas of normality, which could boost morale at a time of instability and insecurity. However, American fashion was still a relatively new concept, even in 1944. In January 1944, *The New York Times* backed the fashion industry's push to promote American designers, with a series of fifteen biographical profiles.[59] *Vogue* was still cajoling its readers to take national styles seriously. In the magazine's annual Americana edition of 1 February 1944, an article, 'Fashion ... Our brand U.S.A.,' echoed comparisons made between Paris and New York since the early years of the twentieth century. It showed that, despite the advances made in New York sportswear (and made-to-order), readers still had to be reminded that they and their countrymen were not 'individualists', and that this was why ready-to-wear was so important in America. American fashion was still an emergent, rather than an established force, and, in *Vogue's* words, bore 'the earmarks of Democracy – "The greatest good for the greatest number," without quenching the right of individual expression'.[60] While the article praised made-to-order, it recognised that America's 'very well-made "ready" clothes fill a place in our fashion scheme which was not duplicated by the clothes of France'.[61] *Life* was also supportive of the drive to assert America's fashion industry, and had a cover story 'American Designers', for its 8 May 1944 edition. The accompanying article discussed the public's growing awareness of designer names, and contained images of ten designers, including Claire McCardell and Clare Potter, plus an example of their work.[62]

Europe's influence on American fashion was greatly diminished by this time. English fashions were seen in the regular features on London couture, from designers such as Molyneux and Victor Stiebel, but Paris fashions were not seen in Allied countries until the city's liberation on 25 August 1944. This event had special significance for the American fashion industry, since it called into question the permanence of its position within international fashion. *Vogue* was quick to print a report on Paris couture on 15 October 1944, eager to show what French women were wearing in a series of images from its war correspondent Lee Miller. Paris' return forced the New York fashion industry to take stock for the second time in four years. At a highly charged Fashion Group meeting on 25 October 1944, designers, store buyers, fashion forecasters and journalists spoke to a large audience about what might happen. Attempts were made to sound positive and confident, Claire McCardell said simply that she would continue 'to make clothes to solve ease and comfort problems'.[63] However, other speakers expressed a series of anxieties, primarily about America's ability to continue to hold its own. Others feared that New York fashion might be unfairly judged against Paris, which made clothes directly for individual clients rather than through mass production or that American designers would not get proper recognition. Alternatively, there were concerns that Paris would not be able to produce work of the pre-war standard, given what the city and its people had experienced.[64] For the final year of the war, these concerns were played out within the fashion industry. As Paris sought to convince the rest of world that it had lost none of its fashion status, the New York fashion industry returned to its pre-1940 interplay between reverence for Paris and its commercial potential as a source of ideas. However, this now had to be balanced with the New York fashion industry's patriotic (and business) investment in its promotion of American design and designers.

1   Sherna Berger Gluck, *Rosie the Riveter Revisited: Women, the War, and Social Change* (Boston: Twayne Publishers, 1987), 9.

2   Elizabeth Penrose speaking to The Fashion Group, 26 June 1940, The Fashion Group Archives, File 8, Box 73, New York Public Library.

3   Mary Lewis speaking to The Fashion Group, 11 July 1940, The Fashion Group Archives, File 8, Box 73, New York Public Library.

4   In fact the previous season's New York fashion collections had already been interpreted by *The New York Times* as having 'a predominantly American emphasis', despite inspiration derived from Paris. This was attributed to New York designers' 'alertness to the opportunity offered by war conditions abroad'. Kathleen McLaughlin, 'The Fashions of Spring Review at Four New York Shows Yesterday', *The New York Times,* 6 March 1940, 5.

5   Fiorello La Guardia speaking to The Fashion Group, 20 March 1940, The Fashion Group Archives, file 8, Box 73, New York Public Library.

6   La Guardia, The Fashion Group Archives.

7   Photograph caption, *Vogue,* 1 December 1940, 99.

8   Barbara E. Scott Fisher, 'Over the Top! On Your Shoulders Now Fall Mantle of French Couture', *The Christian Science Monitor,* 5 October 1940, FA1.

9   Fisher, 'Over the Top!' FA1.

10 Fisher, 'Over the Top!' FA1.

11 Eleanor Lambert interviewed by Phyllis Feldkamp for the Oral History Project of the Fashion Industries, no. 29. TT139.073v.13 (8 December 1977), Gladys Marcus Library, Special Collections, Fashion Institute of Technology, New York.

12 The Coty Awards were founded in 1942 by Eleanor Lambert in collaboration with Grover Whalen, Coty's chairman of the board. The Award's purpose was to 'draw attention to the originality, scope and power of American fashion and bring it to equal prominence with European fashion'. Committees comprised members of the fashion media selected designers, who were felt to have made 'an outstanding contribution to contemporary style in the previous year', or who were deemed to be a significant new talent. There was then a ballot of fashion industry people to choose winners in each category, plus an overall winner, in women's and in men's fashion. The latter would be awarded a 'Winnie'. Eleanor Lambert, *The World of Fashion, People, Places, Resources* (New York and London: R. R. Bowker Company, 1976), 284.

13 See William H. Chafe, 'World War II as a Pivotal Experience for American Women', in Maria Diedrich and Dorothea Fischer-Hornung, eds., *Women and War: The Changing Status of Women from the 1930s to the 1950s* (New York and London: Berg: 1990), 22–23.

14 Susan M. Hartmann, *The Home Front and Beyond: American Women in the 1940s* (Boston: Twayne, 1982), 87.

15 Melissa Dabakis, 'Gendered Labor, Norman Rockwell's Rosie the Riveter and the Discourses of Wartime Womanhood', in Barbara Melosh, ed., *Gender and American History since 1890* (London: Routledge, 1993), 184–5.

16 Dabakis, 'Gendered Labour' in Melosh, *Gender and American History,* 190.

17 Ruth Milkman, *Gender at Work: The Dynamics of Segregation by Sex during World War II* (Urbana and Chicago: University of Illinois Press, 1987), 61.

18 Cross, *An All-Consuming Century,* 83–84.

19 H. Thomas Steele notes the rise in the tourist and military market for such shirts from the mid–1930s. See Steele, *The Hawaiian Shirt* (London: Thames and Hudson: 1984), 11–12.

20 Frank L. Walton, *Thread of Victory* (New York: Fairchild Publishing Co., 1945), 76.

21 An amended version of the Order was issued in May 1943, the content of which was summarised in *Control Without Regulation, The New L–85* (Washington, D.C: War Production Board June 1943). This extended the regulations to all fabrics and asserted that manufacturers must control the silhouette to limit yardage.

22 H. Stanley Marcus, 'Reasons for Issuance of this Order', Memorandum to Clearance Committee Record Group no. 179, WPB 2–55, (30 March 1942), 1. The National Archives, Washington D.C.

23 'Diagram Specifications and Limitations: Authorized Measurements for Slacks, Play Clothes, Separates', *Women's Wear Daily*, Section 2, 8 April 1942, 18.

24 'Autumn Openings: American Designers Make their First Complete Collections Under Government Regulations', *Vogue*, 1 September 1942, 43.

25 Pierre Bourdieu, *Distinction: A Social Critique of the Judgement of Taste* (London: Routledge, 1996), 52–53.

26 These discussions had begun in the Fashion Group even before the outbreak of war, as industry insiders anticipated the need to widen their markets. See notes on speeches at the Fashion Group meeting held on 25 November 1940, The Fashion Group Archives, Box 73, File 9, 8–27.

27 Martin Folly, *The United States and World War II: The Awakening Giant* (Edinburgh: Edinburgh University Press, 2002), 7.

28 Folly, *The United States and World War II*, 10.

29 See, for example, 'Chinese Women: Eight Aristocratic Women who are Living, Working, Creating in this Country', *Vogue*, 1 June 1942, 30–33.

30 Michael Schaller, 'The U.S. Failure in China', in Mark A. Stoler and Melanie S. Gustafson, eds., *Major Problems in the History of World War II* (Boston and New York: Houghton Mifflin Company, 2003), 203.

31 Schaller, 'The U. S. Failure in China', in Stoler and Gustafson, *Major Problems in the History of World War II*, 203.

32 For further discussion of relationship between foreign influences and American identity in fashion, see Rebecca Arnold, 'Looking American: Louise Dahl-Wolfe's Fashion Photographs of the 1930s and 1940s', in *Fashion Theory, the Journal of Dress, Culture and the Body*, Fashion Photography issue, vol. 6, issue 1 (March 2002): 45–60.

33 Picture caption, *Harper's Bazaar*, November 1942, 54.

34 See Yohannan and Nolf, *Claire McCardell*, 67–8.

35 See *Harper's Bazaar* (June 1942), 58, and *Harper's Bazaar* (September 1942), 17.

36 C.I.45.71.2a and b, Costume Institute, Metropolitan Museum of Art, New York.

37 'Two Performances a Day … 3 Pages of desk-to-dinner clothes', *Vogue*, 1 June 1942, 52.

38 47.60.1, Costume Institute, Metropolitan Museum of Art, New York.

39 See for example, 'Washables', *Vogue*, 1 May 1942, 43.

40 'What Price Physical Fitness?' *Vogue*, 15 May 1942, 88.

41 'To Ease the Strain', *Vogue*, 15 August 1942, 42.

42 Pat Kirkham, 'Beauty and Duty: Keeping Up the (Home) Front', in Pat Kirkham and David Thoms, eds., *War Culture: Social Change and Changing Experience in Work War Two Britain* (London: Lawrence and Wishart, 1995), 13.

43 Kirkham, 'Beauty and Duty', in Kirkham and Thoms, *War Culture*, 13–14.

44 'The Psychology of Beauty', *Vogue*, 1 March 1942, 116.

45 Sketches based upon this research were included in *Harper's Bazaar*, July 1943, 26–7. Orrick was also included in the 'Editor's Guest Book' at the front of this edition. A photograph and short biography were given, which helped to establish the designer's presence and to reinforce the magazine's support for her ideas. *Harper's Bazaar*, July 1943, 9.

46 Mildred Orrick, 'Bifurcation Sketches', The Anna-Maria and Stephen Kellen Archives Center for Parsons The New School for Design, New York.

47 Valerie Steele, for example, notes that many of Claire McCardell's designs lacked 'hanger appeal', and needed to be seen on the body to be appreciated. See Valerie Steele, *Women of Fashion*, 108.

48 'The Leotard Idea', *Harper's Bazaar*, January 1943, 35.

49 'It's Something', *Harper's Bazaar*, August 1943, 65.

50   See Yohannan and Nolf, *Claire McCardell*, 68.

51   45.71.1a–c, Costume Institute, Metropolitan Museum of Art, New York.

52   C.I.1970.153.3, Costume Institute, Metropolitan Museum of Art, New York.

53   No date is given for this memo, but since it is from Snow when she was still at *Vogue*, it must be from between 1931, when Frissell began to produce fashion photography for the magazine, and 1932, when Snow left to take up a job at Harper's Bazaar. Quoted in George Plimpton, 'Introduction', *Toni Frissell: Photographs 1933–1967* (London: Andre Deutsch, 1994), xxv.

54   Inez Whiteley Foster, 'Pictures Keep Toni Frissell on the Move', *The Christian Science Monitor*, 20 July 1943, 8.

55   Whiteley Foster, 'Pictures Keep Toni Frissell on the Move', 8.

56   See Arnold, 'Looking American': 45–60, for further discussion of Louise Dahl-Wolfe's techniques and significance.

57   Kodachrome photographs began to appear in fashion magazines during the second half of the 1930s and altered the dynamic of magazine design, by breaking up the previous dominance of black and white imagery, with colour only used in fashion illustrations. Kodak's Kodachrome colour transparency film had been launched in America in 1935–1936 in conjunction with the promotion of 'miniature' still cameras that used 35mm film. The processing of kodachrome was improved in 1938 to gain greater colour permanence. See Jack H. Coote, *Illustrated History of Colour Photography* (Surbiton, Surrey: Fountain Press, 1993).

58   Louise Dahl-Wolfe, *A Photographer's Scrapbook* (New York: St Martin's/Marek, 1984), 37.

59   See Sandra Stansbery Buckland and Gwendolyn S. O' Neal, '"We Publish Fashions Because They are News": *The New York Times* 1940 through 1945', in *Dress*, vol. 25 (1998): 39. This article also contains a detailed discussion of the importance of the newspaper in covering American fashion during the war years, and the increased number of articles it carried on American designers, despite paper shortages that cut the paper's overall length.

60   'Fashion ... Our Own Brand U.S.A.,' *Vogue*, 1 February 1944, 54.

61   'Fashion ... Our Own Brand U.S.A.,' 54.

62   See 'American Designers', *Life*, 8 May 1944, 63–69.

63   Claire McCardell speaking to The Fashion Group, 25 October 1944, The Fashion Group Archives, File 3 Box 74, New York Public Library.

64   Claire McCardell speaking to The Fashion Group, 25 October 1944.

CHAPTER SIX
THE AMERICAN LOOK AND THE RISE OF THE DESIGNER

THE AMERICAN LOOK

The phrase American Look was already in circulation during the war years, as domestic designers and promoters strove to find a collective term that would distinguish the country's national style.[1] On 20 November 1943, *The New York Times* carried an article on the Fashion Group's annual luncheon, at which *Vogue's* editor Jessica Daves gave a slide show of New York fashions 'to demonstrate how "the new American look" has developed since 1941'.[2] Daves' description of what the look comprised is illuminating: '[it represented] a freshness, a genuineness and a suitability to American women'.[3] This perception echoed the ideal of restraint constructed during the 1930s, which was combined with the pared-down silhouette that the L–85 regulations necessitated: 'a narrow silhouette, with nearly normal shoulder; arm-sized sleeves, or none, and almost-knee-length skirts. But it would be a mistake to call this new look of clothes simplicity. It is really a triumph of premeditated elimination'.[4] Thus, Daves drew upon an established narrative of American style, which related it to authenticity and appropriateness, and to a rejection of any unnecessary detail or decoration. Daves' deployment of the phrase 'premeditated elimination' was an attempt to guide the way that American Look clothing was interpreted, since this reinforced the role of the designer, who used her skills carefully to refine a design to its essential form. *Vogue* had already identified the main elements of the American Look in its 'Personal Planning' edition of 1 January 1945. The magazine encouraged its readers to 'unclutter' their lives, their houses and their clothing. This 'uncluttered' style in dress was identified by a wearer's knowledge of how to wear simple clothes with only a few, well-chosen accessories. The article went on to state that 'the difference between clutter and unclutter is the difference between order and disorder … Unclutter is not merely emptiness; it is arrangement … It means, in the best sense, the achievement of simplicity out of complexity'.[5] *Vogue* explicitly associated this style with contemporary modern art and design in a photo-shoot that placed American fashions next to iconic examples of modernist design, for example, a Claire McCardell design was placed with a Robsjohn-Gibbings interior design. It was just such a clean, modern style that was epitomised by the sportswear of the American Look.

In 1945, Dorothy Shaver took up the American Look as a rallying cry. This was primarily to give renewed focus to her ongoing promotion of New York designers at Lord & Taylor. However, as with her 1932 publicity for the same cause, she aimed to link this to the wider fashion industry, and, by implication, also to America's needs. The *New York Times* reported a press conference at which Shaver, while welcoming the 'one world of fashion' she envisioned after the war, was keen to stress that, 'the traditional American look will be copied widely'.[6] Shaver also asserted that the American figure, '"always considered the finest in the world," [due to] ... its "lack of artifice,"' was, as usual, linked to youth, and American clothes were, she therefore stated, 'designed for the active, vigorous life lived by American women'.[7]

The American Look had evolved in the 1930s and was then honed during the war years. What is notable during this time is the continuity both of this image, and the system of promotional tropes employed to market it. Sportswear had altered over the same period, developing from active-wear to include spectator wear and a wide range of smart, casual clothing. It had been designed in line with fashion trends for particular colours, accessories and silhouettes. However, the ideals it represented had remained remarkably stable. This chapter will consider the promotion of sportswear under the banner of the American Look, and how the New York fashion industry responded to the return of Paris after the Occupation. The rise of sportswear designers, whose names began either to replace, or be used alongside, those of manufacturers and retailers will be analysed in relation to the American Look as manifested by particular designers' signature styles. The rise of consumerism in the post-war period will form a backdrop for this examination, as will the problematic formulation of a coherent ideal of femininity in the mid to late 1940s. Finally, these issues will be related to the Costume Institute's 'Woman of Fashion 1947' exhibition, and its formulation of both American femininity and fashion before Dior's New Look was shown, and Paris fully reasserted its dominance.

There were practical reasons for the stability of sportswear's style. As has been shown, this related in part to the focus on designs that were easiest and cheapest to manufacture and, ultimately, such designs were able to fit the maximum number of women. Sportswear designers' focus on washable fabrics increased their longevity and meant they cost less to care for, in terms of time. Sportswear had developed into a type of clothing that ran parallel to high fashion styles. It connected with main trends, while also representing a more constant, and therefore 'reliable', component of women's wardrobes, since it was designed to be mixed into existing outfits and to transcend seasonal fashions. While these elements made sportswear desirable, they did not ensure that consumers would regularly purchase new items. It was necessary, therefore, for promoters such as Shaver to ensure that publicity was regularly generated to reinforce its status and to turn sportswear into 'news'.

The American Look campaign was a key example of this, as it built on earlier Lord & Taylor promotions, and was made newsworthy by being connected to what might happen to American fashion after the war. On 9 February, *Women's Wear Daily* reported that a second bank of American Look window displays had been unveiled at the store. Shaver exploited the publicity that the first round of advertising had gained to generate more interest, since each window contained a card that read: 'in newspapers, magazines and over the radio – countrywide – it is being discussed, praised and acclaimed – "The American Look"'.[9]

Print advertisements widened the exposure of Lord & Taylor's promotion. High fashion magazines carried a series of these, which developed the themes that Shaver had ex-pounded at the initial press conference. On 15 May 1945, *Vogue* carried a morale-boosting advertisement, which simultaneously promoted New York designers and praised American women. This showed a fluid fashion drawing of a hazy figure in a simple striped dress. The focus was on the strident mood of the text, rather than the specific design. Adele Simpson's credit is in much smaller typeface and is placed at the bottom of the page. The copy began with the statement that 'you can thank your ancestors for the American Look', and ended with praise for 'that natural, unaffected air – it marks you as a citizen in the world's greatest democracy'.[9] This eulogy to America represents each woman as an embodiment of the country's ideals and, by extension, each New York designer's work as an encapsulation of these ideals. Thus, to wear a simple cotton dress is to demonstrate citizenship and patriotic fervour. This promotional style was extended to various groups of women, there was, for example, a college girl version in August 1945.

Just as the campaigns that began in 1932 asserted Lord & Taylor's (and Shaver's) pre-eminence in American fashions at the worst point of the Depression, so the American Look campaign positioned the store at the forefront of American fashion as Paris was liberated and the Allies moved towards victory. In this way, Shaver was able to project a strong profile for the store, and its focus on American fashion, at a time when Paris itself had launched an attempt to regain its fashion stature. Shaver received a widespread response for the campaign, not only in the press, but also from a variety of people who wrote to her privately. Esther Lyman, *Harper's Bazaar's* Merchandise Editor, congratulated Shaver on the publicity that the advertisements had generated, and confirmed the magazine's support: 'we feel that they are exceedingly timely and also that Lord and Taylor is maintaining an envious leadership in fashion presentation and merchandising'.[10] Stores such as Best & Co. had been seen as especially important for sportswear in the early 1930s, but Lord & Taylor had become the pre-eminent store for American fashion and sportswear by the mid-1940s.[11]

Lord & Taylor's American Look campaign therefore contributed to elevating various designers' status across America. This was helped by Marjorie Griswold, one of the store's buyers, who, since the early 1940s, had worked closely with manufacturers such as Adolf Klein of Townley.[12] She ensured that Lord & Taylor stocked a representative range of New York labels, and also that she obtained each designer's strongest work. The American Look was, therefore, the result of a number of influences: the designers and manufacturers, advertisers and public relations experts, together with the encouragement of magazine editors and of important store buyers, who had the ultimate choice of whose work, and which pieces, would be sold. Manufacturers, who were aware of their power, courted buyers such as Griswold, and it was Klein's approaches to her in 1940 that had been instrumental in bringing Claire McCardell's work to a wider public.[13] Shaver's association of such designers' work with a recognisable phrase, the 'American Look', reinforced their collective identity. This made their work easier to market as a 'genre' of clothing. It also made it more comprehensible to potential consumers, who could link individual designs to an existing idea already seen in various advertising media. It was a phrase that persisted beyond the war period.

Once the war ended in Europe on 8 May 1945, and in Japan on 15 August 1945, the American fashion industry was keen to consolidate its own gains made during the war. It was also still imperative to see whether Paris couture could recover from the war's deprivations and from accusations of collaboration with the Germans.[14] On 25 October 1945, Beatrice Auerbach, who had surveyed the European market for her own fashion stores, encouraged Fashion Group members not to abandon American designers as soon as French fashion became available:

> I feel that we talked so much about American designers that we now have a chance to be on the same footing with designers from overseas … until the L–85s … are taken off that we shouldn't hurry and scurry and see what somebody else is going to do as much but let us take and back our own.[15]

New York designers had already started to seek ways to test the L–85 regulations and find a different silhouette. The small-waisted look that began to evolve during 1945 suggested the direction that fashion was to take for the last half of the decade and beyond, and demonstrated American designers' role in shaping trends.

However, *Vogue's* editorials during autumn and winter 1945 demonstrated conflicting impulses of caution and optimism. On 1 September, a report on the recent New York collections celebrated the end of the war in the Pacific and used dramatic language to connect this to native designers' new direction:

New York fashion houses designing for Americans who had rather shop for their clothes and take them home than order-them-and-wait have simultaneously staged a sort of bloodless silhouette revolution. And no L–85 rules broken. It is part pendulum swinging. Part Paris. Part reaction to the narrow tube silhouette, which is still a fashion form in high favor. Waists are as small as inner or outer lacing can make them. They look as small as panniers, peplums, hip-padding or leg o' mutton or puffed sleeves can make them.[16]

This romantic, historicised style constructed a more defined silhouette, which was visible in the ready-made garments that the article praised. Sportswear designers experimented with the silhouette and *Vogue* noted this shift in January 1946 describing designs by Tina Leser, Joset Walker, B. H. Wragge and Claire McCardell as 'Play Clothes Going Seductive. Less Nice-Little-Boy, More Round-Pretty-Woman. Less Midriff. More Shoulders'.[17] These clothes, like those from the preceding year, managed to maintain the fluidity, lack of extraneous decoration, and reverence for the natural body that was distinctive to the American Look. This contrasted with the various embellishments that were part of Paris' version of this silhouette, which had been shown in *Vogue's* 1 May 1945, including a Balenciaga ensemble with swatches of contrasting fabric wrapped around the hips to produce a neat upper body, small waist and fuller hips.[18] Basques and other restrictive corsetry were placed alongside these designs to demonstrate the way such an artificial figure could be achieved.

This silhouette had been hinted at in the last collections before the war, and American designers had shown similar forms in the early 1940s, including department store designs for 1941. Fashion trends were clearly evolving in much the same way as they had done before the war: a radical new style would be apparent in a few examples, but would not necessarily become popular immediately. In this case, the restrictions of L–85 and concurrent rejection of extravagant fashions as unpatriotic interrupted its development. During 1945, both Parisian couturiers and New York ready-to-wear designers began to promote a nostalgically feminine shape that turned away from the slimmer figure that had dominated wartime fashion. This was gradually to take hold in New York, London and Paris in 1946, before Dior crystallised the look in his 'Corolle line' of 1947, seen in figure 6.1. His example was completely coherent in its authentically historical use of padding and multiple petticoats to achieve the most extravagant version of the style, and, importantly, it came at a point when both press and consumers were ready to accept a 'new' look from Paris. They had been prepared for the style by American and French precursors, as well as those from London couturiers such as Hardy Amies, and were

6.1. Christian Dior, silk "Chérie" dinner dress s/s 1947. The
      Metropolitan Museum of Art, Gift of Christian Dior, 1948.
      Photograph © 1996 The Metropolitan Museum of Art

6.2. B. H. Wragge advertisement, *Vogue*, 15 September 1946

eager for fashions that revived couture skills and, indeed, paid homage to earlier feminine ideals. As with the monastic dress, this shows the complex interchange that led to a new trend's evolution within all three fashion cities, before it became the dominant theme. It is also significant that it was American, British and Parisian designers who had heralded this style, even if it was Dior, a French couturier, who was seen as its creator.

Paris couture gradually became more visible in fashion magazines during 1946, as more fashion stories were devoted to its creations. However, it was yet to be fully re-established, and during 1946 the only advertisements for French names in *Vogue* and *Harper's Bazaar* were those for perfumes by Chanel and Lucien Lelong. High fashion magazines continued to report news from Paris when they could, and there was, for example, a lot of coverage of *Le Théâtre de la Mode*.[19]

American sportswear had continued to establish its niche within fashionable dress since the 1930s. In 1946, it began to be promoted in relation to the full range of fashion sub-categories seen before the war, as active sportswear re-entered the fashion pages on a more regular basis. The L–85 regulations were lifted in October 1946, but there were still fabric shortages. However, as *The Christian Science Monitor* noted, some shifts in style had already been seen within resort wear collections: 'in many cases designers, looking forward to the lifting of L–85 restrictions, have included styles which violated restrictions, though they did not sell them. Sometimes they were shown to buyers as indicating what they might look forward to when the ban on fabrics was lifted. These will now undoubtedly go into production and soon be released'.[20] Sportswear, particularly resort wear, was frequently worn in more relaxed contexts where women could be more daring. It was therefore possible to experiment with new ideas and styles within these collections. Thus, while Paris gradually re-colonised fashion pages during 1946 and 1947, American sportswear continued to be shown, although not in the same quantity. Sportswear was still able to cater to different audiences and different occasions, when the American Look of smart casual clothing was more appropriate.

Resort wear had a stronger potential audience after the war, as it became easier to travel internationally, and also popular American domestic destinations, such as Palm Springs began to regain their status as holiday centres. Carolyn Schnurer recalled that Tobé discouraged buyers from purchasing play and beachwear immediately after the war, because holiday resorts on the Atlantic coast would, she claimed, still be covered in barbed wire.[21] However, when Schnurer went to Florida, she found the beaches full of people: 'so quietly I [built] … the best and biggest line that I ever had … And we had the most successful line in the market'.[22] Many designers managed to bridge the transition from war to peace-time, and to develop their market by allying their designs to women's contemporary lifestyles, in the same way that they had done in the 1930s and early 1940s. William H. Chafe has discussed the complex picture of women's roles and attitudes to work after the war. He described the immediate post-war period as one of 'joy and anticipation', with seventy-five per cent of female war workers initially wanting to retain their war jobs, even if ultimately 'the total number of women in manufacturing jobs declined by nearly one million between spring 1945 and winter 1946'.[23] However, by the end of the 'forties the overall percentage of women in work was thirty-two per cent, a rise of five per cent since the previous decade, with middle-class (and often married) women, in their mid-'forties and 'fifties, most committed to retaining their jobs.[24]

Younger women were still addressed as career girls by magazines such as *Glamour* ('for the girl with a job') and *Charm* ('the magazine for the Business Girl'). Both these popular titles used smart sportswear ensembles and city backdrops to construct a modern, dynamic image. In November 1945, after over a year as a special 'magazine' insertion within *Harper's Bazaar, Junior Bazaar* was launched as a separate entity, focussing on young women's fashions. It drew upon the sportswear aesthetic described in this book. This was apparent in its integration of modernist graphics, 'realist' photography by Landshoff and Richard Avedon amongst others, and foregrounding of New York designers.[25]

Other magazines were more interested in the trend towards domestic life. For many of their readers, jobs were seen as an interlude between college and marriage, and, 'after the war, both marriage and birth rates soared. From the mid-depression low of 18.7 births per 1,000 population, the rate increased to 24.5 by 1949, or about the same as it had been in 1925'.[26] Depression and war had slowed birth and marriage rates but, even by 1946, young women's fashion magazines had begun to integrate this shift into their fashion pages. Advertisements for engagement rings and maternity clothes became increasingly frequent in *Mademoiselle*, which had always been more aligned to a domestic lifestyle.

In the years after the war ended, it was necessary for sportswear manufacturers and designers to find a balance in both the clothing itself and, by extension, in the way it went on to be promoted. They needed to appeal both to women who wished to remain in work, and those who wanted to stay at home, as well as continuing to promote garments for active pursuits and leisure time. As already demonstrated within this book, sportswear mimicked the fluidity of modern life in its anonymous designs that managed to incorporate potentially problematic changes in gender roles and attitudes towards, for example, women and work. The emergence of individual, named sportswear designers since the 1930s meant that the differences between designer and consumer image and identity could profitably be collapsed. Designers were discussed in promotional material as both creators and wearers of the clothing they made, and this blurred the distinction between producers and consumers.

NEW YORK SPORTSWEAR DESIGNERS
AND CONSUMERISM

In her book, *Fashion is Our Business*, Beryl Williams notes that, unlike fashion consumers earlier in the twentieth century, who 'accepted slavishly' designers' pronouncements on style, American women of the late 'forties were more active in their choice of clothing:

> Nowadays the status of designers has changed again, because their customers have changed. Those customers have learned to think for themselves about clothes, and have come to the conclusion that things should be wearable as well as a badge of one's ability to 'keep in style'.[27]

Williams connected this to developments in ready-to-wear, which reinforced the idea of its availability and accessibility. This was contrasted with couture which sought to construct women as passive receivers of designers' whims. American designers were positioned as benign collaborators, eager to assimilate the needs of the consumer into each garment: 'So American designers today … are sensitive, intelligent reflectors of what American women want them to be, creating what American women want to wear'.[28] Thus, designers are cast in contradictory ways, both as creative individuals, an assertion that was crucial to try to compete with the European notion of the 'artistic genius', and, simultaneously, as mere interpreters of the customers' needs.

American designer names began to be promoted in the early 1930s, but it was often the designer's character that was foregrounded rather than her/his creative genius. Eleanor Lambert drew on her earlier experience in the promotion of artists and, later, film stars, to emphasise aspects of her client's lifestyle and character that consumers could empathise with and admire. Interviews with McCardell and other New York designers reinforced these ideals. Designers were quick to reassure potential customers that they understood the problems of finding the right clothes to wear. This is apparent in a 1946 interview with Clare Potter, in which she is quoted saying that 'the best-dressed women are generally the most uncluttered and simply dressed … I think my first rule for dressing well is to dress to fit the occasion, and then to dress in the most becoming fashion to fit your own particular style'.[29]

While the need to dress appropriately was always present, women were flattered into the illusion that they made their own choices and that they could take control and be above fashion. They were encouraged to feel that sportswear would allow them to develop their own individual style, however far removed this possibility may have been in the context of mass-produced garments and restrictive notions of 'good' taste. Since the 1930s, sportswear had been a part of a cultural shift that saw the gap between 'respectable' and mass culture closing. In the hands of both mid-range designers such as Potter, and in cheaper lines that drew upon the same styles such as those of Henry Rosenfeld, it comprised a form of dress that was at once inexpensive yet modern and stylish. While sportswear's wide availability at different price levels was continually presented as part of its 'democracy', this idea is in fact more complex and problematic. Firstly, the most fashionable lines did cost more. Secondly, despite its 'simple' design tenets, sportswear had evolved from European elite style, and although it was increasingly associated with ideals of Americanness, it was a white, middle-class vision of national identity. As has been seen, other ethnic and cultural identities were seamlessly integrated into its overall style to create a homogenous image of femininity, which was given unity through its allegiance to modern design tenets.

In the 1940s, Robert Warshow wrote of the encroachment of mass culture on American life since the Depression in these terms:

> The chief function of mass culture is to relieve one of the necessity of experiencing one's life directly … Mass culture … seeks only to make things easier. It can do this either by moving so close to reality as to destroy detachment of art and make it possible for one to see one's own life as a form of art … by providing a fixed system of moral and political attitudes, it protects us from the shock of experience and conceals our helplessness. The movies, the theater, the books and magazines and newspapers – the whole system of mass culture as creator and purveyor of ideas, sentiments, attitudes, and styles of behavior – all this is what gives our life its form and meaning. Mass culture is the screen through which we see reality and the mirror in which we see ourselves. Its ultimate tendency is even to supersede reality.[30]

This tendency is discernible within sportswear design and representation. Fashion magazines, newspapers and retail promotions constructed sportswear within a system of behaviours and attitudes. This system presented sportswear as an idealised 'escape' into authentic Americana, while at the same time also suggesting a less conservative connection to contemporary modern design. This was epitomised by the tenets of the American Look promotions, which were also frequently characterised as 'American Modern' in high fashion magazines and advertising, as seen in figure 6.2, a B. H. Wragge advertisement of 1946.

The designers' lives and personalities were presented as 'authentically' American, in their ability to balance sport, career and family life. Through interviews and promotional material, the designer became an empathetic figure of identification for consumers. There was a constant shift within editorial and advertising material, between the general (mass-produced clothing) and the specific (the individual consumer), and designers could act to connect the two sides. The visual 'world' of sportswear had already been established during the 1930s by photographers such as Martin Munkasci, but passed through several stages. It was at first only inhabited by 'unreal' women, models, who were purely aspirational figures, and society women, whose lives were far removed from most women's experience. Sportswear was then linked to specific groups, such as college girls. They represented a more accessible ideal than models and society women, and this was emphasised by magazines' and retailers' use of real college girls in promotions. From the early 1930s onwards, this process of 'normalising' sportswear also involved providing consumers with individual identification figures in the shape of designers, who were portrayed as both the authoritative creators of the garments, and as stand-ins for the consumers themselves. The designer was projected as a woman who, like them, needed practical clothing to suit a busy, modern life.

These promotional techniques were designed to sell idealised visions of 'real' everyday life. Sportswear itself was shown as the most 'real' form of dress, allied to fashion, yet less transitory and ephemeral, and more connected to 'real' women (whether designer or consumer), and their 'real' lives. Meanwhile the sportswear aesthetic amplified these meanings in its appropriation of 'snapshot' photography to display the clothing as representations of potential consumers' own experiences. Thus, sportswear design and representation, like ready-to-wear fashion in general, was part of mass culture's ideological discourses of gender, morality and race. As has been seen though, sportswear, through both its design and representation, was more closely allied to ideas of authenticity and realism than other fashion forms. Promotional material represented sportswear as accessible and easily comprehensible, and linked to pleasurable and desirable lifestyles, while simultaneously replacing diverse ethnic and class identities with a unified ideal of restrained good taste. This restraint was mediated by the sensuality of the natural body upon which the designs were displayed, the visually rich landscapes, both urban and rural, in which it was placed, and by the seemingly infinite varieties of activities it catered to, from city career to beach holiday. Sportswear appeared to open up opportunities, while reinforcing respectability and conformity.

New York sportswear designers' style was united in its focus on clean silhouettes and minimal decoration. They tended to prefer either hardwearing natural fabrics, such as cotton, which also related to ideas of Americanness, or new synthetics, including the rayon processes developed since 1942 such as Enka, that added fluidity and movement to garments. However, it was important for each designer to project a particular image through their designs, in order to distinguish him– or herself within a growing market. Potter was known for her painterly use of colour and for sophisticated, fluid dresses, as well as more practical daywear. This was apparent in a Louise Dahl-Wolfe photograph from *Harper's Bazaar* in November 1945, which showed a softly draped mint-green wrap dress. Pictured against bright white walls and fireplace, the setting simultaneously evoked modern American design and more traditional styles, as did the Native American-influenced turquoise jewellery.

Although there are similarities between designers' styles, each was either known for a specific type of garment, or for continued reference to particular influences. Carolyn Schnurer designed clean-cut beach and playwear, which drew upon childrenswear and, sometimes, South American craft decoration. This was demonstrated in one of her designs for 1945, a white linen-type rayon smock with red, blue and green floral embroidery on the yoke. The design, with its flounced sleeves, rounded yoke and rick-rack trim, was based on blouses worn by women in Otaralo, Ecuador, and demonstrated Schnurer's interest in travel as a major source for her ideas. She was not the only designer to use such influences: Joset Walker was equally well-traveled. However, her design style related more to the use of printed fabrics from, for example, South East Asia, to distinguish the simple lines of her clothes.

Tina Leser was associated with exoticism through both her designs and her background, as her first boutique was in Honolulu. While Schnurer and Walker's clothes had a youthful air to their cut and design, Leser, in common with Potter, focussed on more sophisticated lines. During the 1940s, she created collections that used soft, natural colours draped onto the figure to evoke Greek statuary and accessorised with simple, gold jewellery and sandals, as well as hand-painted designs that added the cachet of exclusivity to her ready-to-wear lines. The evening ensemble shown in figure 6.3 is from 1945 and comprises a white crêpe blouse painted with hands holding doves, embellished with translucent sequins and tiny red beads for the birds' eyes. The blouse was worn with aquamarine shorts, which fastened with a decorative gilt button.[31] This was typical of Leser's grown-up design style that integrated sportswear style into evening, as well as daywear. Figure 6.4 shows Leser's original drawing for a similar outfit with a variation on the imagery used

6.3.   Tina Leser, white crepe 'Doves' blouse and shorts, 1945. The Metropolitan Museum of Art, Gift of Tina Leser, 1945.
       Photograph © 2007 The Metropolitan Museum of Art

6.4.   Tina Leser design, c.1945. The Metropolitan Museum of Art, The Irene Lewisohn Costume Reference Library, Tina
       Leser Collection. Tina Leser Collection Image. © The Metropolitan Museum of Art

6.5.   Claire McCardell beach wardrobe, 1945. Courtesy The Museum at the Fashion Institute of Technology
       Photograph Rebecca Arnold

6.6.   Macy's exercise suit, c. 1920s. National Museum of American History Courtesy of Smithsonian Institution
       Collections, National Museum of American History, Behring Center

on the shirt and the uncomplicated way that she imagined it could be worn. The model is shown with upswept hair and black ballet pumps, the plain shorts a backdrop to draw focus to the delicate watercolour style of the painted blouse. Her vision was still clear in a 1946 advertisement for a version of the style with butterfly-decorated blouse and a sash added to the shorts.[32] In each case, Leser's signature is reasserted: from sketch to actual garments and advertisement. It was important for designers and manufacturers to try to establish and maintain an identity that customers would become aware of through both clothing collections and their representation in editorial and advertising. This would, they hoped, encourage women to identify themselves with a particular designer, whose work 'fitted' with their idea of themselves, either as they really were, or as they aspired to be.

Claire McCardell, like the others discussed above, produced a wide range of garments, and had a selection of signature outfits. Sportswear designers sought to create 'classics', garments that they would repeat with slight variations in each collection, to reinforce their design image, give customers a sense of continuity, and to maximise sales of successful styles. For McCardell, interchangeable wardrobes became one of her recurrent motifs, adaptable for beach, travel and daywear. They were an effective way of encouraging multiple garment purchases, to develop a coherent look and to fit with ideals of respectability and appropriateness that favoured well-co-ordinated outfits and matching colour schemes. Wardrobes, such as Claire McCardell's, four-piece blue cotton chambray ensemble from 1945, are typical.[33] The spaghetti-strapped bra top, shorts, skirt and jacket could be worn, in a variety of combinations, for beach and daywear. They are given unity through the fabric, and the repeated use of the same design details, specifically the distinctive white buttons and double stitching along seams. The practical fabric, minimal number of design pieces and signature McCardell detailing recalled work wear and, especially, school and college exercise wear. Figure 6.6 shows an exercise suit from the 1920s that clearly demonstrates these connections, in its use of blue cotton drill fabric and white double stitching to reinforce seams.[34] Active sportswear such as this was a continuing influence on casual sportswear worn for more leisurely pursuits. The bloomer-style pants of the exercise suit inspired various designers' playsuits. Thus, beachwear could combine reference to both sporting activities and childrenswear, which lent much sportswear its playful air. In much the same way that New York's Seventh Avenue manufacturers had always used Paris couture for trend and style direction, so Seventh Avenue manufacturers made clothes that mirrored American designers' work. Figure 6.7 shows a checked cotton ensemble by Loomtogs from the late 1940s that echoes McCardell's neat, round-necked jackets cut to fit into the waist, and in the simple style of the sundress, with its spaghetti straps to tie around the neck.[35]

A successful designer identity did not just inspire copyists; it could also lead to lucrative cross-promotions with other companies. It is notable that, whereas the Sportswear Guild had used outfits by named American designers to promote their work and link contemporary fashion to a soap brand in 1934, the National Cotton Council used photographs of the designers themselves to publicise American cotton in 1947, as seen in figure 6.8. Textile companies frequently used garments by popular designers to advertise new fabric designs or types, and designers promoted beauty products. Old Gold cigarettes, amongst other brands, had used sportswear designers to promote its cigarettes since the 1930s, but it was not until the late 1940s that this kind of advertisement began to gain in popularity. By this point the growth in consumerism meant that car sales were steadily rising, and could only be enhanced by their association with sophisticated sportswear designers such as Tina Leser, as seen in figure 6.9. It was important that there was a match between each brand. In this case both Leser and the Kaizer-Frazer Corporation represented leisure, modern design and streamlined silhouettes.

Sportswear's image, like that of its designers, fitted well with the American consumer dream of the postwar period. The 1944 GI Bill of Rights had provided war veterans with loans to buy houses, and these increased the growth of the suburbs, which had been developing since the late nineteenth century.[36] Over a million new housing units were built per year between 1940 and 1950, and the number of people living in homes that they owned rose from fifteen point two million to twenty three point five million over the same period.[37] Sportswear's relaxed, yet smart style spoke of leisure and respectability and its adaptable designs could be worn in the home, at social events or to go shopping. Sales of consumer durables rose commensurately, as Americans sought to furnish their homes with modern conveniences, and assert their freedom through purchase of a car: 'between 1946 and 1950', Hartmann notes, 'they purchased 21.4 million automobiles, more than 20 million refrigerators, 5.5 million electric stoves, and 11.6 million television sets'.[38]

Although this spoke of growth and prosperity, it was also a result of conflicting emotions that harked back to the uncertainties of the 1930s. Gary Cross argues that American post-war spending 'fulfilled the dreams that the years of hardship had nourished. The postwar period was an era of unprecedented prosperity, built on an extraordinary, fortuitous confluence of economic and social opportunities … This consumerism reflected often confused hopes and fears: desires for both innovation and tradition, participation and privacy'.[39] Sportswear could accommodate

6.7. Loomtog's dress and jacket. 1947—55. National Museum of American History. © Smithsonian Photographic Services

6.8. Cotton Council advertisement, *Mademoiselle*, January 1947. Courtesy of the National Cotton Council

6.9. Kaiser-Frazer advertisement, *Vogue*, 15 June 1947

these apparently contradictory emotions and impulses. The promotion of named designers meant that it could seem individual, its plain forms able to allow the designer's, and, by implication the wearer's personality to shine through, while its reliance on 'classics' and mass-produced aesthetic meant that it looked familiar and reassuring, immediately linking the wearer to established themes and ideals of group identity.

Fashion magazines occasionally acknowledged the problems of mass production. In August 1945, *Harper's Bazaar* had cautioned its readers: 'There has never been a generation of American girls whose individuality is so challenged, because what is available to one and to all ... There's a million of everything ...The mass uniformity is a challenge to your diversity'.[40] *Harper's Bazaar* saw this as a problem of style, rather than ethnic or class, homogeneity. The magazine advised women to choose clothes that suited them and to accessorise carefully, to ensure that they would be stylish, rather than slavishly following fashion. This article crystallised the problem for the American fashion industry. On the one hand, it did produce clothing that was to a great extent uniform, and which was sold in such quantities across the United States as to eliminate regional differences. On the other hand, manufacturers and promoters needed to assert difference in order to sell one company's goods, rather than those of another. Thus, American ready-to-wear was marketed as democratic for the very same reasons that it could be criticised as homogenous. Its pervasiveness meant that it was at once easily obtainable, yet ultimately could be seen as limiting consumer choice. This was true of all mass-produced goods, and it was therefore imperative that manufacturers were adaptable, able to forecast new trends and markets and to project latent problems within their designs as positive attributes. The flexible image that the fashion industry had constructed to promote sportswear had managed to sell its anonymous style as quintessentially American. It had already weathered the anxieties of both Depression and war, and its image as simultaneously modern and dynamic, yet relaxed and leisured, enabled it to fit into the lives of suburban housewives, as easily as it had those of career women and college girls. Designers such as Claire McCardell had anticipated this major market growth in her mid-1940s designs for hostess gowns with matching aprons, and, of course in the 'popover'.

Young women were encouraged to view design as a viable career option, as they had been during the 1930s. Career guides and magazines such as *Mademoiselle* had various features on fashion jobs, that encouraged girls to view fashion as one of the few industries where they would be able to expect 'good prospects, good pay', since women were actually favoured over men.[41] Fashion and women were viewed as inextricably connected and, in America at least, the identities of designers and customers were sometimes blurred, as promoters sought to assert their similarity of outlook as a marketing tool. In the immediate post-war years, the way in which both were represented became increasingly complex, under the influence of concerns about women's shifting role and the stability of New York fashion's status.

THE WOMAN OF FASHION 1947

In the second half of the 1940s, ideals of femininity became increasingly problematised. Once relief at the end of the war, and joy at the return of soldiers from overseas, had subsided, women were caught between the independent and resourceful gender model of woman as worker, and increasing pressure to return to a domestic ideal of wife and mother. Women had been negotiating this apparent dichotomy since the late nineteenth century, when middle-class women began to enter clerical jobs. However, the process had been accelerated by the economic needs of the Depression, and then the rapid increase in women war workers. It was difficult to assimilate such a succession of changes, and convincingly to create a revised version of femininity, which could somehow unite women's experiences during the preceding years with their return to the private, domestic sphere.

In the later 1940s, this problem was frequently discussed in terms of the contemporary fascination with psychoanalysis and psychology as a means to explain such issues. This confusion was encapsulated in an article, 'Anxious Women', published in *Harper's Bazaar* in October 1946. Its introduction aimed to summarise the concerns of its readers:

> She thinks she is alone. In reality she is one of hundreds of thousands of women haunted by anxieties, flummoxed by everyday problems, jostled in a traffic jam of insecurity and fear ... her husband has returned from the war, setting up new patterns of confusion … Because she loves him, she feels guilty that she cannot help him find his way back to satisfaction with his old job and his old life … she has trained her intellect to handle a responsible office job, but now finds herself servantless, holding the mop. The atom bomb comes to her breakfast table with the marmalade – with it, other headlines, challenging and difficult to understand, demanding her opinion as a woman of conscience and education, yet leaving her with a feeling of utter helplessness.[42]

Once again, the fantasy world constructed within fashion magazines was punctured by anxieties from the outside world. However, these concerns were not like those during the Depression and Second World War, when problems were more easily apparent, and widely discussed in newspapers and other media. These new concerns were hidden within the home, and tinged with a sense of shame at feeling confusion and distress at a time when, with victory in the war still so recent, there was social pressure to construct an image of happiness and perfect family life. These anxieties were psychological, as much as they related to 'real' issues, such as the atom bomb.

Such fears were often seen exclusively as a problem for women. Dorothy Sayers highlighted this cultural bias in *Vogue* in January 1947. She discussed the way in which women were continually judged in relation to gender ideals, and noted that: 'probably no man has ever troubled to imagine how strange his life would appear to himself if it were unrelentingly assessed in terms of his maleness; if everything he wore, said, or did had to be justified by reference to female approval'.[43] Ironically, but perhaps unsurprisingly, in the years immediately after the war fashion magazines engaged with questions of women's status, and the very nature of femininity, more explicitly than ever before. The last years of the 1940s contain a complex discussion embracing how women are represented, how this contrasted with masculinity, and feminist and psychological examinations of these issues. Simone de Beauvoir even published an early extract from *The Second Sex* in *Vogue* for 15 March 1947. In this she set out the main tenets of her forthcoming book, and expounded upon the ideal of the 'eternal feminine', which was used to control and oppress women by pressuring them to behave according to restrictive rules of etiquette and decorum.[44]

Women's dichotomy was stereotyped by contemporary fashions. The nostalgic ideal of round-hipped femininity that was embodied by Dior's New Look constructed an elite vision of the pull of domesticity, with its focus on a fecund figure of womanly, flower-like curves, which in turn epitomised the artificial 'eternal feminine' that de Beauvoir condemned. Despite, or perhaps because of, its view of femininity as rarefied and delicate, it appealed to women who wanted an escapist vision of fashion after the harshness of the war years. Although this is frequently presented as the only fashion in existence during 1947, there was a wider choice, as will be seen in this section, with sportswear a more functional alternative. It could incorporate the fashionable line, while rendering it easier to wear, by focussing on lighter fabrics and fewer layers, and represented an ideal that was more independent and active. Sportswear also offered the range of clothes described within this book, which catered to a broader spectrum of feminine roles than just that of 'Woman of Fashion' or housewife.

Attitudes towards femininity were constructed and 'learnt' through fashion and beauty photographs, as much as through articles and fashion advice books. Fashion occupied a fraught position within the culture: while an awareness of new styles was acceptable, and even desirable, women who associated themselves too closely with fashion and, in turn, avid consumerism, were often viewed askance. Ferdinand Lundberg and Marynia F. Farnham's 1947 book, *Modern Woman: The Lost Sex*, which was originally serialised in the *Ladies Home Journal*, represented the extreme manifestation of this view. They condemned: 'the vast palpitrant [sic] anxiety betrayed, as a group, by the "Woman of Fashion"… [and the] clearly morbid narcissistic preoccupation of contemporary women with appearance stems directly from sexual failure, from basic failure as women. In the advertising of perfumes particularly the desire [for] orgiastic attainment is most directly played upon'.[45] As was the case with other pop-psychology texts of the period, Lundberg and Farnham saw fashion as a prop to disguise inadequacy and lack.[46]

Lundberg and Farnham's book was also controversial in its condemnation of women who prioritised their careers. While *Glamour* magazine gave Farnham a column on the role of psychiatry within contemporary society, other areas of the fashion industry were far less supportive of her opinions.[47] Speaking to the Fashion Group on 16 July 1947 to defend the book she had co-authored, Farnham appealed to the members to use their influence over other women to convince them that they should consider whether they really could combine career and child-rearing. In Farnham's opinion, women were unhappy, despite having achieved 'probably the greatest collection of privileges and satisfactions that any group has ever gotten for itself in time'.[48]

Thus, in these authors' view, femininity was constrained by the biological imperative and any deviation from a domestic role was highly problematic. Sportswear was situated comfortably within the mainstream scale of acceptability. It was connected to a set of images of 'natural' beauty, photographed on beaches, boats and sunny countryside locations that reinforced its alternative proposition to the fashionable Parisienne or Hollywood 'glamour girl'. Sportswear's target market was largely conservative, while it managed simultaneously to incorporate many women's altered status over the eighteen-year period discussed in this book, and, as has been seen, it included innovative designs.

These competing impulses, and the interchange between Paris, London and New York fashion, are visible in the twenty-six outfits that Bloomingdale's donated to the Costume Institute in 1947. The exhibition of these outfits, under the title 'Woman of Fashion 1947', was the idea of Tobé, who brought together work by leading American designers It suggests comparisons to *Le Théâtre de la Mode exhibition*, which sought to promote the work of Parisian couturiers, in order to revive haute couture internationally after the war. The New York exhibition differed in important ways. It was, after all, a selection of full-size garments that were available to the public to buy, rather than miniature outfits shown on tiny mannequins. However, it functioned in a similar way, in that it consolidated the idea of a fashion city, in this case New York, and highlighted the designs of key individuals, who were felt best able to represent national ideals of fashion and femininity. By placing the clothes in the context of a museum, contemporary fashion was given gravitas. The inauguration of the Costume Institute ten years earlier in 1937 had placed fashion in the context of serious studies of decorative arts and design, and marked an important shift in the way fashion itself was regarded. By 1947, the Institute had found a permanent home at the Metropolitan Museum of Art, and both the Museum and the department store that gave the collection were aware of the historical significance of the gift.

In its 1 March 1947 edition, *Vogue* noted that the wardrobe was 'chosen from the first ready-to-wear collections made since the Government's war-time restrictions were removed'.[49] This in itself gave the clothes added meaning, especially since they had been designed in 1946, and therefore represented American designers ideas for 1947, before Dior's New Look was shown.

The collection was conceived of as a wardrobe for a 'Woman of Fashion', a term that had seemed anachronistic, not to say unpatriotic during the war, but which was now resurrected as part of the shift away from the ideal of an independent ideal of femininity. The catalogue that accompanied the exhibition demonstrated the ambivalence surrounding this term, and the realities of even wealthy women's lives in the immediate post-war period in the definition it gave: 'a woman essentially of the so-called "leisure class," although she may very well have a real business career instead of her many activities; with a cultural background that assures her taste; with an established social position that calls for participation in smart social functions; with money to buy the right clothes for these'.[50]

The 'Woman of Fashion' is thus portrayed as living between city and country residences, and leading a leisured, yet active lifestyle. This is shown in the choice of outfits: of the twenty-six shown, two were nightwear, and one was lingerie. Many of the remaining ensembles were either active sportswear, or town and country or resort wear. Six of these showed a strong resemblance to 1930s styles: Picard and Yeoman's simple golf dress and tennis outfit recalled the previous decade's active sportswear; Davidow's heavy tweed coat and skirt suit paid homage to English tailoring; Claire Potter's 'shirtwaist dress' harked back to both her own designs of the 1930s, and to the Gibson Girl as the original propagator of the style; while the crisp blue and white cotton suit presented by Dorothy Cox and the fluid evening pyjama one-piece by Joseph Whitehead were equally familiar in their styling.

This showed the continuity within sportswear design, but was also representative of fashion's growing nostalgia. There had been such references during the war, but as fabric restrictions were lifted, designers had more scope to experiment with Victorian and Edwardian silhouettes, which not only evoked a more sedate manner of dressing, but also implied a more demure feminine ideal. This was seen most clearly in the outfits that looked to Paris for inspiration. These showed more sculpted silhouettes, which employed peplums, flounces and drapery to enhance the natural figure. Ben Gershel's hourglass shaped coat was closest to the New Look figure that would become so important by the middle of 1947, although its waistline, like several of the ensembles, was longer and its shape less defined.

In contrast to these couture-led designs was a selection of garments by New York sportswear designers. Joset Walker's scoop-necked cotton print dress was typical of her work, and, while it had a fuller skirt that indicated the more voluminous silhouette that was developing, its light fabric and simple cut eschewed any overt nostalgia. The fabric was by Everlast and was printed with designs inspired by Polynesia. Such exotic references were a signature of Walker's, who was none the less known for her typically American style. Sportswear was able to incorporate a variety of historical and/or ethnic influences into its smooth lines. This integrated approach even extended to the identity of the designer herself, as is shown in the text that accompanied the picture of her design: 'Joset Walker is a French-born designer, who has accomplished the remarkable feat of becoming one of the leading American designers of sportswear clothes – a field in which America leads the world'.[51]

It is interesting to note the different impression given by the studio-bound images of the clothes included in the catalogue, and the more naturalistic, uncluttered way they were shown in fashion magazine editorial shots. The studio setting gave a unified air to the outfits, and focussed attention on the garments themselves, but the accessories and fixed poses of the models were less convincing for the sportswear pieces. In Walker's case, her dress was shown on a groomed model, who wears bold jewellery and a corsage at the waist (fig. 6.10). In contrast to this was *Harper's Bazaar's* photograph from its December 1946 edition of a similar dress from the same season, which showed the model in long grass, devoid of accessories, her long hair swept away from her face.

This is also the case with Carolyn Schnurer's swimsuit and beach coat. In the studio shot a beach is suggested by the addition of driftwood and netting in the foreground of the picture (fig. 6.11). However, in a photograph taken by Toni Frissell for *Harper's Bazaar* in December 1946 of a bronze version of the swimsuit, the model lay in crystal clear waters, which reinforced the environment in which it would be worn, and makes sense of its daringly revealing cut. The magazines aimed to contextualise the garments and display them through the, by this point, established trope of the modern sportswear aesthetic, while the museum catalogue's role was to present the clothes as objects of study, as well as of contemporary fashion.

Thus, Claire McCardell's multi-coloured check beach wardrobe of bra-top, shorts, culottes and jacket, is photographed in two different combinations against the same white background as the other outfits in figure 6.12.[52] Along with the other sportswear ensembles, the exhibition demonstrated the shift in attitude towards ready-to-wear clothes made by New York designers by the late 1940s. McCardell and her colleagues were presented as equals to designers who focussed on more elite, Parisian-inspired fashions, such as Jo Copeland, who had always been named in publicity. This was, at least in part, due to the publicity that they had received since the 1930s, which meant that their names were as recognisable across America, as was their design style. It is also clear from both the number of sportswear designs included in the collection, and the way in which these clothes, and their designers, are described in the catalogue's text, that sportswear was established as the definitive American style, the American Look promoted by Dorothy Shaver in 1945. Both the designers and the 'Look' they had helped to create gained further publicity through the exhibition.

However, while the 'American Look' was gaining international exposure, Parisian couture was also recovering its position. As already described, some of the outfits in the 1947 wardrobe showed this fuller silhouette, and even Schnurer's beach coat was more voluminous than those made during the war, with pleats at the back, and puffed sleeves. In the 15 March 1947 edition of *Vogue*, reports and sketches from the Paris couture shows heralded the impact of Christian Dior's opening, with its curving silhouette, 'a direct steal from the heavily padded, canvas-stiffened skirts [worn by] the women in Les Halles near Notre Dame. Cinched at the waist with a corselet; the bodice Victorian tucks or pleatings; the skirt full and circular'.[53] This elite expression of historicised, couture femininity was to continue to grow in notoriety as the season wore on. The style represented an escapist fantasy of feminine artifice, which was welcomed by many after the restrictions of the war, and Dior was written of as the 'agent provocateur and hero of the day'.[54]

Thus, 1947 saw conflicting ideals of femininity in fashions, a product of confused gender roles in the aftermath of the war. While New York sportswear was able to integrate the overall silhouette of the New Look into its style, couture fashions returned to their dominant position within high

6.10. Joset Walker "Noon-Day Sun."Photograph by Ben Studios, reproduced *A Woman of Fashion, 1947, spring/summer.* © The Metropolitan Museum of Art"

6.11. Carolyn Schnurer, "Sun-Swept". Photograph by Ben Studios, reproduced in *A Woman of Fashion, 1947, spring/summer.* © The Metropolitan Museum of Art

6.12. Claire McCardell, "Gay Weekend". Photograph by Ben Studios, reproduced in *A Woman of Fashion, 1947, spring/summer.* © The Metropolitan Museum of Art

fashion magazines. However, the modern, active ideal that sportswear had helped to construct during the Depression and war years did not completely recede. As the 'Woman of Fashion 1947' showed, even the leisure classes were expected to be active by the late 1940s, and many of them had careers. During the Depression and especially during the war years, sportswear had paralleled both shifts in women's lives and fashionable ideas of femininity. In the late 1940s, gender roles became increasingly problematised, as men and women struggled to readjust to peacetime lifestyles. However, sportswear had come to represent an intrinsic set of ideals that projected American feminine identity to the domestic market and, increasingly, abroad. It thus retained its place as an adaptable form of clothing for work, home and holidays. Despite its middle-class respectability and popularity with suburban housewives, New York sportswear, in its most avant-garde incarnations, was able to suggest that there was an alternative to the 'eternal feminine'.

1   There are various examples of the phrase being used before Shaver's campaign of 1945. However, these were isolated instances, rather than part of a sustained campaign. See for example the advertisement for Landsburgh's sportswear, which stated that English style has been adapted to have 'the striking long-legged, slim-waisted American look'. *The Washington Post*, 29 October 1935, 2. It was even noted as evident within Parisian couture fashions in Bonwit Teller's advertisement for 'the Skyscraper Look' foundation garment by Camlin: 'clean and soaring as modern architecture – the trim-lined "American Look" Paris Openings emphasized'. *The New York Times,* 11 February 1940, 5.

2   'Lauds Fashions of Today: Editor Says They Presage Our Style Independence After War', *The New York Times*, 20 November 1943, 10.

3   'Lauds Fashions of Today', 10.

4   'Lauds Fashions of Today', 10.

5   'Unclutter', *Vogue*, 1 January 1945, 86.

6   'Style Leadership For America Seen', *The New York Times*, 12 January 1945, 18.

7   'Style Leadership For America Seen', 18.

8   '"The American Look" – "New York Look" – In New Windows', *Women's Wear Daily*, 9 February 1945, n. p.

9   Advertisement caption for Lord & Taylor, *Vogue*, 15 May 1945, 1.

10 Esther Lyman to Dorothy Shaver (19 January 1945), Dorothy Shaver Papers, Box 8.5, 88, The Archives Center, National Museum of American History, Washington, D.C.

11 Carolyn Schnurer interviewed by Mildred Finger for the Oral History Library of the Fashion Institute of Technology, no. TT139.073v.110 (16 April 1989), 1, Gladys Marcus Library, Special Collections, Fashion Institute of Technology, New York.

12 Yohannan and Nolf, *Claire McCardell*, 76–81.

13 Yohannan and Nolf, *Claire McCardell*, 76–81.

14 For discussion of these issues, see Dominique Veillon, *Fashion under the Occupation* (New York and Oxford: Berg, 2002), 142–45.

15 Beatrice Auchbach speaking to the Fashion Group, 25 October 1945, The Fashion Group Archives, File 9, Box 74, New York Public Library.

16 'New York Collections', *Vogue*, 1 September 1945, 122.

17 'Play Clothes going seductive. Less nice-little-boy, more round-pretty-woman. Less midriff. More shoulders', *Vogue*, 1 January 1946, 76.

18 'What's the New Look in Paris? It's "Hanché" – Full-figured, Definitely Hippy', *Vogue*, 1 May 1945, 144–45.

19 See Valerie Steele, *Paris Fashion: A Cultural History* (Oxford and New York: Berg, 1998), 269–70, and Veillon, *Fashion under the Occupation,* 144. The mannequins and sets are now in the permanent collection of the Maryhill Museum of Art, Goldendale, Washington.

20 Barbara E. Scott Fisher, 'Few Fashion Changes With End of L–85', *The Christian Science Monitor*, 24 October 1946, 12.

21 Carolyn Schnurer interviewed by Mildred Finger, 11–12.

22 Carolyn Schnurer interviewed by Mildred Finger, 11–12.

23 William H. Chafe, 'World War II as a Pivotal Experience for American Women', in Diedrich and Fischer-Hornung, *Women and War*, 26–30.

24 William H. Chafe, 'World War II as a Pivotal Experience for American Women', in Diedrich and Fischer-Hornung, *Women and War*, 28.

25 Although the magazine's first 'birthday' edition of November 1946 stated that its circulation had increased from an initial twenty-five thousand to one hundred and twenty-five thousand, it ceased publication in May 1948, when it was reincorporated into *Harper's Bazaar*. 'Self-Portrait of a Young Magazine', 119. Martin Harrison cites a decline in sales of advertising space as a reason for this. See Martin Harrison, *Appearances, Fashion Photography Since 1945* (London: Jonathan Cape, 1991), 30.

26 Berger Gluck, *Rosie the Riveter Revisited*, 17.

27 Beryl Williams, *Fashion is Our Business* (Worcester and London: Ebenezer Baylis and Son, 1948), 4.

28 Williams, *Fashion is Our Business*, 4.

29 Clare Potter, quoted in Virginia Pope, 'Clare Potter Designs', *New York Times Magazine*, 28 April 1946, 90.

30 Robert Warshow, 'The Legacy of the '30s', (first published in 1947) *The Immediate Experience: Movies, Comics, Theatre and Other Aspects of Popular Culture* (Cambridge, Massachusetts and London: 2001), 8–9.

31 Acquisition number C.I.45.74A–B, Costume Institute, Metropolitan Museum of Art, New York.

32 See Tina Leser at Gidding's advertisement, *Harper's Bazaar*, January 1946, 43

33 85.174.2, The Museum at Fashion Institute of Technology, New York.

34 1984.0825.01, Division of Sports, Leisure and Entertainment: Sports, National Museum of American History, Smithsonian Institution, Washington D.C.

35 1990.388.15, Division of Home and Community Life: Clothing and Accessories, National Museum of American History, Smithsonian Institution, Washington D.C.

36 Cross, *An All-Consuming Century*, 87.

37 Hartmann, *The Home Front and Beyond*, 8.

38 Hartmann, *The Home Front and Beyond*, 8.

39 Cross, *All-Consuming Century*, 67.

40 'State It', *Harper's Bazaar*, August 1945, 55.

41 Carolin Compson, 'Clothes: Start Picking up Pins', *Mademoiselle*, October 1945, 147.

42 'Anxious Women', *Harper's Bazaar*, October 1946, 203.

43 Dorothy Sayers, 'The Woman Question', *Vogue*, 15 January 1947, 86.

44 Simone de Beauvoir, '"Femininity, the trap"… a French View', *Vogue*, 15 March 1947, 171. Her book *Le Deuxième Sexe* was first published in 1949, and translated into English in publisher Jonathan Cape's edition of 1953.

45 Ferdinand Lundberg and Marynia F. Farnham, Modern Woman: *The Lost Sex* (New York: Harper and Brothers, 1947), 219.

46 See, for example, Richard Curle, *0*(London: Watts and Co, 1949) and Albert Ellis, *The American Sexual Tragedy* (New York: Twayne, 1954).

47 The first of these, 'Let's Talk About the Modern Woman', was published in *Glamour*, September 1947, 144–45.

48 Marynia Farnham, 'Career – Privilege or Penalty?' *The Fashion Group Bulletin*, October 1947, 3.

49 1947 Wardrobe in the Museum', *Vogue*, 1 March 1947, 212.

50 *A Woman of Fashion Spring/Summer* 1947 (New York: Costume Institute, Metropolitan Museum of Art, 1947), n. p.

51 *A Woman of Fashion Spring/Summer* 1947, 46.

52 C.I.47.74.24A–D, Costume Institute, Metropolitan Museum of Art, New York.

53 '*Vogue's* Eye View: First Impressions of the Paris Openings', *Vogue*, 15 March 1947, 151.

54 'First Notes from the Paris Collections', *Harper's Bazaar*, April 1947, 186.

CONCLUSION

On 2 May 1955, *Time* magazine's cover bore a tribute to Claire McCardell. An illustration of the designer's face was surrounded by pictures of models in the kind of sportswear that had evolved over the past twenty-five years, and which was now a staple of many women's wardrobes. The illustrations included several of McCardell's signature designs that have been discussed throughout this book: a version of the diaper suit, a playsuit and a light cotton printed summer dress. The accompanying article looked back over McCardell's career to date, and connected the rise of her work, and American fashion in general, to changes in leisure. The article's author, Osborn Elliott, listed some of the informal activities such as car trips, 'backyard barbecues' and golf weekends that distinguished the American way of life and which, he argued, had shaped the American Look.[1] The impact of shifts in leisure activities on sportswear had been noted by *Women's Wear Daily* as early as 1938. 'Dress Trade More Attentive to Resort Wear', an article from its 11 November edition, spoke of retailers' acknowledgement that more people were going on trips all year round, which negated the idea of sportswear as a purely seasonal clothing form: 'In spite of the general setback to business incident to the depression year[s] a growing portion of the public has shown a real preference for short or extended vacations to break up the winter months … So the opportunity for specialized apparel has broadened out, and is likely to attain even more breadth in the nearby future'.[2] This trend was to continue, despite the war's travel limitations, as people travelled inside the United States or ventured to South America, as evidenced by the number of fashion editorial shoots on resort wear that were carried in magazines such as *Vogue, Harper's Bazaar* and *Charm* between 1941 and 1945.

Time magazine's article demonstrates how Americans aspired to this leisured lifestyle, and aimed to incorporate relaxation and travel into their everyday existence. The ideals attached to New York sportswear, which had been crystallised during the 1930s, were deployed throughout the article: American designers' inherent understanding of what kind of clothes their countrywomen need; Paris couture's focus on elite style; and New York sportswear's focus on comfort, practicality and affordability were all detailed. These ideas were then related to McCardell's design skills, to explain her success. Her ability to produce clothing that was creative in its design, as well as appropriate to a wide variety of lifestyles and activities, had come about, Osborn felt, because for McCardell, 'garments must have a reason'.[3]

The idea that rationality and an understanding of American women's needs informed New York sportswear's design had become intrinsic to its promotion since the Depression. As has been shown, sportswear was imbued with symbolic meanings. These had been constructed by repeated motifs in imagery and text, which were used to market and advertise sportswear as a type of clothing that could be worn beyond the confines of active sport. Promotional material asserted sportswear's link to national identity as a reassuring constant. Advertisers' morale-boosting tone was continued in editorial material, as discussed in this book. It connected sportswear with an ideal of 'normality', based on American heritage, as well as contemporary national identity. Sportswear was, thus, perceived to be appropriate both to these women's lives, and to their needs during this period of history. Jessie Stuart described the central place of this interrelationship to the (American ready-to-wear) fashion process:

> Fashion is not a superimposed thing that is forced on the public, but rather one that grows out of the lives and activities of the women it serves. Fashion is not just an intangible and nebulous idea in the mind of some artist, but rather an idea translated into an object, for fashion does not operate in a vacuum.[4]

Sportswear's growth was as much connected to developments in consumerism and mass-culture as it was to the fashion industry's increased targeting of the career woman, college girl and servantless middle-class housewife who needed to do her own household chores. There was a greater dissemination of ideas and information, through magazines, cinema and radio. During the Depression, such media increasingly associated goods with ideas of quality and usefulness, as well as of fashion. This built upon the growing sophistication in advertising in the first three decades of the twentieth-century, which had, as Gary Cross argues, already meant that 'Products increasingly embodied what people in a "mass" society wanted, a reassuring and inspiring friend. Ads were far more than manipulations, "forcing" people into performing their passive duty of spending to keep the mass-production economy humming. Ads linked material goods to immaterial longings, blending social, psychological, and physical needs indivisibly'.[5] This was significant to sportswear, since it was a clothing genre that was at once appropriate to modern lifestyles, to fashion and to psychological needs. Important promotions, such as the American Designers windows that Lord & Taylor began in 1932, and *Harper's Bazaar's* encouragement of designers such as Mildred Orrick and Claire McCardell during the war, had shaped the way sportswear was perceived by consumers, and within the fashion industry.

The fashion industry's increasing desire to build up sportswear's position was in turn linked to the promotion of New York as an international fashion centre, and America as a country with its own fashion identity. *Vogue's* annual Americana issues were part of this search for a coherent means to represent American fashion, firstly to the domestic market, but, increasingly during the

1940s, to an international market as well. The tenth Americana issue, published on 1 February 1947, showed the significance of these changes since the first edition in 1938:

> turned its usually international eye singly on the ideas, the women, the life, the fashions of its own country. In those days when France was the fashion heart of the world, it was dramatic, unique, and even newsworthy for a fashion magazine to produce an issue with no touch of Europe in it. It was a new direction not only for Vogue but for the fashion publishing world.[6]

The article went on to list the wide range of authors and intellectuals who had written for the first issue, including Ernest Hemingway. It mentioned the second issue's inclusion of South America. It also referred to the discussions in later editions about the impact of Paris' fall to the Germans, and the general effects of war on America. Thus, it connected *Vogue*, and its Americana editions, not only to the gradual maturation of New York as an international fashion city, and American fashion as a distinct entity, but to the wider issues that had concerned and affected the country over the past nine years.

The 1947 Americana edition went on to discuss the significance of American fashion, detailing the enormous amount of ready-made clothing that the country produced: 'More than a billion pieces of clothing for women in the past year'.[7] *Vogue* acknowledged both the advantages and disadvantages such quantities of mass-produced clothing created. It provided vast choice at a wide price range, but it could also lead to poor quality and uniformity. However, the article was keen to praise American fashion, partly by connecting it to America's other consumer goods:

> The wonder of American fashion, like the wonder of American cars and of the by-products of American peanuts, is the result of a certain happy mix of national idiosyncrasies. The miracle of millions of pleasantly well-dressed women is the direct result of mass production, sound basic design, and a strange unexplained talent, of American figures and designers, for ready-made fit. The three are as inter-involved as a monkey-puzzle tree, of course. Clean simple lines are the obvious choice for mass manufacture; they also adapt themselves to many sizes, and leave small room for wayward paths of careless taste. If this statement brings to mind a race of neat little women wearing adjustable uniforms in a sort of national sister act, it is because it is a generalization. Generalizations have a habit of being at once reasonable and misleading.[8]

This description of 'clean simple lines' immediately recalls descriptions of New York sportswear and the American Look, already cited throughout this book. The mention of 'careless taste' is a reminder that, while mass-produced fashion was widely available, high fashion still only placed value on those items that fitted within a narrow definition of 'good' taste. Finally, the idea of 'uniforms' being produced due to the sheer quantity and wide distribution of ready-made fashions raises another important point that has been suggested by this book's study of New York sportswear. As has been shown, it was frequently used to indicate American women's visual identity within high fashion magazines, and indeed, it still is today. This is embodied by the stereotypes of career women, college girls, sports women, and tanned holiday-makers, whom models represented in the visual culture of New York sportswear. As the 1947 *Vogue* article itself pointed out, while over a billion garments were made, not all manufacturers distributed to all American cities and, importantly, 'three quarters of the dress dollar volume is spent on dresses from nine dollars down', that is from the cheaper ranges.[9] This would still have made some, but not all, of the clothing by the designers discussed in this book out of the reach of most American women. However, this does not reduce its significance as a driving creative force within the ready-made market, as is evidenced by this article's accompanying photographic spread. The images showed how cheaper ranges frequently looked to designers such as Claire McCardell and Vera Maxwell for ideas and trends (just as they always had done with Paris couture). New York had therefore been able to generate its own replacement for Paris as sole provider of fashion influence and inspiration.

It is also important to note that, while mid-range New York sportswear was not necessarily bought by the masses, it was used as the symbol of wider American identity. In a nation as vast and disparate as America, and with such a huge clothing market, it was necessary for the fashion industry to create an identity that could encompass and make sense of difference in order to produce an effective selling tool. This was applicable to both the fashion industry's need to create an image that could be sold abroad, and to its need to communicate efficiently with the home market. New York sportswear and the American Look provided an ideal of American femininity that incorporated national stereotypes and characteristics, which derived from the most visible and, in relative terms, powerful women: the white middle classes. It was women from this social group who had helped to professionalise the fashion industry, who made up the membership of the Fashion Group, who designed the clothes, worked on fashion magazines, and in promotions, advertising and retail. They were able to construct an image of American fashion and taste that was modelled on their own. While this may have been conservative, in that it related to such a specific element of the general population, it did produce an ideal that had wider resonance, and which helped to build the American fashion industry's success after the Second World War.

In 1946, Helen Augur had written in *Mademoiselle* about the fragmentary nature of American identity and the problem of trying to conceive of it as a coherent whole:

> In a curious sense we Americans live in an invisible country. No mental image can contain the whole United States, from sea to sea, from the Great Lakes to the Gulf. Though we feel and react as Americans, we can visualize America only piecemeal, for geography and history have agreed in making us sectional people.

> … Actually we are united by virtue of being sectional. We are not so much a federation of states as a tissue of large and small geographic-cultural parts, whose contrasts in climate, occupation and way of life are often profound. A thousand things unite us, but two of them are fundamental. We all live on this continent together, and we share ideals of liberty and equality. It is a dual fact of being a continental people working out a democracy that makes us American.[10]

In this account, America is given coherence through belief in democracy, which provides a philosophical union between its people. It was just such a conviction that became a major element within the New York fashion industry's promotion of American fashion, especially its sportswear, as embodying these democratic ideals. Augur goes on to ask: 'Are we a mosaic of cultures, or are we all-American jello?'[11] Sportswear, along with the panoply of other consumer goods that were linked to ideals of democracy, from Ford cars to Coca-Cola, was shaped by designers, manufacturers and promoters to signify all-American unity. In the post-war period, the mass culture that had come to fruition during the 1930s enabled these goods to be seen in the same magazines across the country. They were often available in chain and department stores and specialty shops nationally, and, by the end of the 1940s, were beginning to be advertised not just on radio and in the cinema, but on television too. This provided another connection between the diverse peoples of America, and made products, such as sportswear clothes, that had the potential to appeal to a wide range of women, all the more saleable.

Sportswear also related to ideals of American identity. The modern sportswear aesthetic used established representational tropes that associated America with both the dynamism and modernity of the city, and the promise of the American landscape. Photographers such as Martin Munkacsi brought avant-garde European documentary techniques to the fashion page, in particular in relation to the representation of New York sportswear. This linked sportswear to a distinct representational style that connected to photo-journalism, for example in Munkacsi's 'snapshot' imagery, and also to modern art, in Louise Dahl-Wolfe's evocations of Edward Weston's studies of natural forms. In terms of sportswear's design, in the hands of women such as Claire McCardell and Mildred Orrick, simplicity could itself seem avant-garde. Ready-to-wear clothes were often decorative, to add a sense of fashion and 'value' to their design. Plainer styles were only gradually accepted into the mainstream, partly influenced by the simple couture styles of Chanel and Vionnet, as well as more practical considerations, as already noted, such as the easier manufacturing of pattern pieces.

As has been shown, sportswear developed between 1929 and 1947, with its balance shifting between conservatism and avant-garde elements. Certain aspects of sportswear remained constant, despite the signifiers of fashion trends, which are incorporated into the designs. While the earlier pictures are often still closely allied to couture sportswear and elite lifestyle, as reinforced in this Slote and Klein advertisement from 1930 (figure 1), the photograph from 1933 (figure 2), for example, already connects sportswear to casual, college life in America. Subsequent photographs show how the modern sportswear aesthetic developed over the years and incorporated environments that evoke city, campus, countryside and holidays. Although there is a unity in the design style of sportswear designs, fashion trends are discernible, for example in the long, narrow line of the suits in the trend for raglan sleeves in 1941 (figure 3) and the nipped in waist and fuller skirt in 1947 (figure 4). These images, alongside with those in the book as a whole, show the wide range of garments that sportswear came to encompass, including neat suits, fluid evening dresses, and smart day dresses. The three key categories of active sportswear, town and country and resort wear blurred during the war, as less active wear was shown, but it had re-emerged by 1947, as wartime concerns were replaced by a wider range of leisure activities. Thus, the photographs of eighteen years of New York sportswear included in this book demonstrate its development into the American Look, which transcended European prototypes, while still retaining evidence of its origins, especially in active and town and country wear.

New York sportswear, the 'sports body' and to an extent the modern sportswear aesthetic were formulated by American women who were, during the 1930s and 1940s, working at executive levels within the fashion industry. Although the ideals they constructed through the clothes, magazines, and promotional and merchandising material they produced expressed the attitudes of a small segment of the population, these women were in themselves role models, with

1.   Slote and Klein advertisement, *Harper's Bazaar*, March 1930

2.   Martin Munkacsi, Tweed Shop, Best & Co., *Harper's Bazaar*, December 1933. © Joan Munkacsi. Courtesy Howard Greenberg Gallery, NYC

3.   Martin Munkacsi, Saks Fifth Avenue, *Harper's Bazaar*, May 1941. © Joan Munkacsi. Courtesy Howard Greenberg Gallery, NYC

4.   Wesley Simpson advertisement, *Vogue*, 15 August 1947

successful careers that were often combined with family life. As has been shown, women still received far lower wages than men, faced prejudice and discrimination in the workplace, and were undervalued even when they were successful in the fashion world, as this was seen as 'only' a women's business. Women who worked in advertising, promotion, forecasting, retail and fashion magazines, such as Carmel Snow, Eleanor Lambert, Tobé Coller Davis, Dorothy Shaver and Estelle Hamburger, worked to promote women's status within the industry both individually and as part of the Fashion Group, an organisation that symbolised women's professional involvement in the industry. Designers such as Carolyn Schnurer, Claire McCardell, Tina Leser, Joset Walker, Vera Maxwell and Clare Potter were equally important in presenting an image of accomplished, creative women, who had active, independent lives. These women rarely, if ever, identified themselves with the feminist movement, but could be said to have 'acted out' the promise of feminism through their careers and promotion of the status of women in the industry. The Fashion Group consolidated and gave focus to this professionalisation of women's role in the fashion industry. The fact that it was still mainly men who ran manufacturers, department stores and magazine publishing houses does not detract from the real progress that these women achieved and the significance of their work. They helped to shape the idea of American fashion that was formed during the 1930s and 1940s and which went on to be so pervasive in the later twentieth century.

Indeed, New York sportswear's influence had already begun to spread in the years immediately after the war, as a fashion story from *Vogue's* 15 June 1947 edition showed. Dagmar's illustrations of Parisian couture sportswear outfits clearly recalled New York styles, in particular Hermès' beach suit, which looked like a version of the McCardell diaper shape, Mme. Grès' shorts and bandage wrap top, which was reminiscent of Tina Leser's mid-1940s Grecian styles, and Piguet's pedal pushers and off the shoulder top, which was similar to Carolyn Schnurer's designs. New York sportswear was itself, however, drawing influence from Paris, as seen in the rounded silhouettes and ladylike accessories of another Dagmar spread for *Vogue* from 1 November 1947.

The American fashion industry was keen to strengthen its position in the international market, and had undertaken various initiatives to ensure its success in the post-war period. In 1943, for example, *Life* published an article about a scheme to send clothes to Europe. While this clearly had humanitarian aims, the title of the piece indicated other potential results: 'Europe's Clothes, The U.S. will dress liberated peoples in outfits that will make them look like Americans'. The accompanying text explained that complete garments, plus pattern pieces, ready to be made-up at their destination, were being sent to Europe. The clothes were made to be 'models of economy', and followed stricter rationing than was already in place under the L–85 scheme in America. They had no zips or other metal fastenings, for example, but had been made to take into consideration hot and cold climates and the differing figures of the nations to which they were being sent. *Life* described the $54,000,000 worth of garments that was to be sent to liberated Europe to dress ten million people as 'designed in American styles … the dresses and pants and coats will clothe Europe in America's image'.[12] The clothes, in their lean silhouettes and plain styling, replicated many of the signature elements of contemporary sportswear design.

Although this example was directly linked to Europeans' needs because of the hardships of the war, America continued to involve itself in other country's fashions after the war's end. Most famously, the Italian fashion industry was built up after the American model, with close ties to the New York fashion industry growing steadily from 1945 onwards.[13] Alongside such long-term involvements with international fashion industries, the New York fashion industry continued to produce publicity-seeking schemes and promotions to increase its profile in other countries. In 1947, for example, a trousseau of American fashions was sent to Britain's Princess Elizabeth. It was reported to be 'representative of American taste and workmanship but conforming to British [rationing] regulations', and included designs by Claire McCardell, Tina Leser and Clare Potter.[14]

As previous discussions of New York sportswear have described, the middle of the twentieth-century was central to the formation of a distinctive American Look. By close analysis of the 1930s, this book has demonstrated how significant this under-explored (in fashion terms) decade was in the creation of design and promotional techniques that would prove crucial Èto sportswear's rise within the New York fashion industry. The economic constraints of the Depression years, and the fashion industry's response to the depressed financial climate, provided the circumstances for American designers to emerge from their previous anonymity, and for sportswear's mass-produced styles to enter the realm of high fashion magazines. This environment was coupled with the rise of a modern aesthetic within fashion photography, magazine layouts and other forms of design. Sportswear became the most effective exponent of this aesthetic, allied as it was to more dynamic ideals of femininity. Its design and representation were not a simple reaction to the democratic ideals of the United States. It was rather, as has been shown, part of a complex of wider historical and cultural shifts in, for example, women's roles and was also an expression of the contradictory nature of modernity.

By 1947, sportswear had become a significant part of American fashion, while simultaneously rising above ephemeral trends to produce wardrobes of wearable, adaptable clothing that projected ideals of Americanness. Although Dior's New Look popularised a more traditionally feminine silhouette, New York sportswear continued to provide clothes that related to a more active life. Between 1929 and 1947 it had evolved to incorporate influences from elite culture, including avant-garde dance and aristocratic lifestyles, and mass culture, such as consumerism and suburban lifestyles. The economic situation in the Depression years, and the sense of uncertainty that this generated, had influenced its growth within the American fashion industry. The war had furthered its integration into high fashion, as it was marketed as a patriotic response to the lack of Parisian influence and a reflection of the greater number of roles women needed to take on over the period. Its lean aesthetic already fitted into the L–85 regulations' demands, and it could easily be promoted as morale-boosting for women, who needed easy to care for and stylish clothes for their new lives. Despite the anxieties surrounding ideals of femininity and women's role within American culture once the war ended, sportswear retained the traces of its avant-garde past, and continued to suggest women's potential to live active lives outside the domestic sphere. However, New York sportswear's simplicity created an ambiguous image that could be shaped to fit with a number of different lifestyles. It was thus a clothing type that had been created by designers and manufacturers to be worn in various situations. Its very adaptability meant that it could integrate into many different kinds of women's wardrobes. As America entered a period of post-war affluence, New York sportswear, which had been shaped by the austerity of the Great Depression and the Second World War, was also marketed to fit into the suburbs.

By the 1940s, New York sportswear had become an important element of the domestic fashion industry and its profile was also building internationally. It had become an important symbol of America's fashion identity, which itself expressed a diverse range of ideals that related to, for example, femininity, taste, cleanliness and athleticism. These meanings were apparent in New York sportswear's pared-down design, and enhanced by myriad advertisements, editorial photographs and promotions. It had evolved from its European roots to include not just specialist active-wear, travel and holiday wear, but clothing that embodied American leisure and work ethics. As New York's mayor, Fiorello LaGuardia, told the Fashion Group in 1940: 'you must remember that you're designing for two million people in New York City and they travel on buses and subways and they must walk and they can't walk with dainty steps'.[15] This practical ideal was evident in the sensible suiting produced by manufacturers such as Davidow. It was amplified by, for example, Munkacsi's photographs of women striding through New York in sportswear, which made their bodies seem more efficient and ready for the city's streets. While New York sportswear was developing its international significance, it continued to clothe women for the city in which it was created. Sportswear's ability to incorporate seemingly contradictory elements, in this case conformity and individuality, were part of its inherent modernity. Sportswear appeared to be simple, with its clean, modern design aesthetic, yet it masked the ambiguities and complexities of contemporary gender, ethnicity and class. Thus, both the clothing's design and its representation enabled the American woman, to stand above the exigencies of fashion and the chaos of the city, and to become an embodiment of New York sportswear's modern, rational and efficient identity.

1   Osborn Elliott, 'Cover Story: Fashion Designer Claire McCardell', *Time*, 2 May 1955, 85.

2   'Dress Trade More Attentive to Resort Wear', *Women's Wear Daily, Section 1,* 11 November 1938, 9.

3   'Dress Trade More Attentive', 86.

4   Jessie Stuart, *The American Fashion Industry* (Boston: Simmons College, 1951), 74.

5   Cross, *An All-Consuming Century,* 38.

6   '*Vogue's* Eye View of the 10th Americana Issue February 1 1947', *Vogue*, 1 February 1945, 149.

7   'American Fashion Marvels', *Vogue*, 1 February 1945, 188.

8   'American Fashion Marvels', 188.

9   'American Fashion Marvels', 188.

10 Helen Augur, 'It's All America', *Mademoiselle*, May 1946, 150.

11 Augur, 'It's All America', 151.

12 'Europe's Clothes, The U.S. will dress liberated peoples in outfits that will make them look like Americans', *Life*, 18 October 1943, 49.

13 See Nicola White, *Reconstructing Italian Fashion: America and the Development of the Italian Fashion Industry* (Oxford and New York: Berg, 2000).

14 'Style Industry Sends a Gift to Elizabeth', *The New York Times,* 14 November 1947, 30.

15 Fiorello H. LaGuardia speaking to The Fashion Group, 20 March 1940, The Fashion Group Archives, File 8, Box 73, New York Public Library.

BIBLIOGRAPHY

PRIMARY MATERIAL

ARCHIVES USED

United Kingdom

Bath: Costume Collection, Museum of Costume and Research Centre; London: Costume and Textiles Department, Victoria and Albert Museum.

United States

Frederick, Maryland: Frederick Historical Society; New York: Costume Collection and Irene Lewisohn Costume Reference Library, Costume Institute, Metropolitan Museum of Art; Fashion Group International Archives; Fashion Group Archives, New York Public Library; Gladys Marcus Library, Special Collections, Fashion Institute of Technology; Costume Collection, The Museum at Fashion Institute of Technology; Costume Collection and Prints and Photographs Collection, Museum of the City of New York; The Anna-Maria and Stephen Kellen Archives Center of Parsons The New School of Design; Philadelphia: Department of Costume, Museum of Art; Washington, D.C: Prints and Photographs Department, Library of Congress; United States National Archives and Records; Archives Center, Division of Home and Community Life: Clothing and Accessories, Division of Music, Sports and Entertainment: Sports and Leisure, Division of Information Technology and Communications: Photography, National Museum of American History, Smithsonian Institution; Department of Photography, National Portrait Gallery; National Museum of Women in the Arts.

BOOKS

Abbott, Berenice. *New York in the Thirties: As Photographed by Berenice Abbott* (New York: Dover Press, 1973, first published 1939).

Allen, Frederick Lewis. *Only Yesterday: An Informal History of the 1920s* (New York and London: Harper and Brothers, 1931).

Since Yesterday: the 1930s in America (New York: Harper and Row, 1986).

Armitage, Merle, ed., *Martha Graham* (California: Lynton R. Kistler, 1937).

Ballard, Bettina. *In My Fashion* (London: Secker and Warburg, 1960).

Beaton, Cecil. *The Glass of Fashion* (London: Cassell, 1989, first published 1954).

Beauvoir, Simone de. *The Second Sex* (London: Vintage, 1997, first published 1949).

Bennet, Margaret Elaine and Lewis Madison Terman. *College and Life: Problems of Self-discovery and Self-direction* (New York and London: McGraw Hill Book Co.,1933).

Bishop, Edna Bryte. *The Bishop Method of Clothing Construction* (Chicago: Lippincott, 1959).

Burbank, Emily. *Woman as Decoration* (New York: Dodd, Mead and Co., 1920).

The Smartly Dressed Woman: How She Does It (New York: Dodd, Mead and Co., 1925).

Byers, Margaretta. *Designing Women: The Art, Technique and Cost of Being Beautiful* (New York: Simon and Schuster, 1938).

Cantwell, Mary. *Manhattan Memoir: American Girl; Manhattan; When I was Young; Speaking with Strangers* (New York: Penguin, 1998).

Centers, Richard. *The Psychology of Social Classes: A Study of Class-Consciousness* (Princeton, New Jersey: Princeton University Press, 1949).

Chambers, Bernice Gertrude. *Color and Design in Apparel* (New York: Prentice-Hall, 1942).

A Fashion Manual (Ann Arbor, Michigan: Edwards Brothers Inc., 1946).

Keys to a Fashion Career (New York and London: McGraw Hill, 1946).

Fashion Fundamentals (New York: Prentice-Hall, 1947).

Chase, Edna Woolman and Ilka Chase. *Always in Vogue* (London: Gollancz, 1954).

Cheever, John. *The Stories of John Cheever* (London: Vintage, 1990).

Clymer, Eleanor and Lillian Erlich. *Modern American Career Women* (New York: Dodd, Mead and Co., 1959).

Crawford, Morris de Camp. *One World of Fashion* (New York: Fairchild, 1946).

The Ways of Fashion (New York: Fairchild, 1948).

Philosophy in Clothing: Written for the Clothing Exhibition, 15 March–5 May 1940 at the Brooklyn Museum, Brooklyn Institute of Arts and Science (New York: Brooklyn Museum, 1940).

Curle, Richard. *Women: An Analytical Study* (London: Watts and Co., 1949).

Dahl-Wolfe, Louise. *A Photographer's Scrapbook* (London: Quintet, 1984).

Daves, Jessica. *Ready-Made Miracle: The Story of American Fashion for the Millions* (New York: G. P. Putnam's Sons, 1967).

Dessner, Clyde Matthew. *So You Want To Be A Model!* (Garden City, New York: Halcyon House, 1944).

Dingwall, Eric John. *The American Woman: A Historical Study* (London: Gerald Duckworth and Co., 1956).

Dior, Christian. *Dior by Dior* (Harmondsworth: Penguin, 1958).

Dooley, William H. *Economics of Clothing and Textiles: The Science of the Clothing and Textile Business* (Boston: D. C. Heath, 1934).

Ellis, Albert. *The American Sexual Tragedy* (New York: Twayne, 1954).

Fashion Group. *The Fashion Group Presents New York's Fashion Futures with the Collaboration of the Fashion Originator's Guild, the Dressmaking Departments of the Uptown Retail Guild Shops, Creators of Fur, Hats, Shoes and Accessories* (New York: Advertising Compositions Incorporated, 1940).

Fitz-Gibbon, Bernice. *Macy's, Gimbels, and Me: How to Earn $90,000 a Year in Retail Advertising* (New York: Simon and Schuster, 1967).

Friedan, Betty. *The Feminine Mystique* (London: Penguin, 1993, first published 1963).

Golden Anniversary of Fashion, 1898, 1948: Official Publication of the Mayor's Committee for the Commemoration of the Golden Anniversary of the City of New York (New York, 1947).

Haire, Frances H. *The American Costume Book* (New York: A. S. Barnes, 1934).

Hamburger, Estelle. *It's a Woman's Business* (New York: The Vanguard Press, 1939).

Fashion Business: It's All Yours (San Francisco: Hearndon, 1976).

Hardy, Jack. *The Clothing Workers* (London: Martin Lawrence, c.1935).

Hardy, Kay. *Costume Design* (New York: McGraw Hill, 1948).

Harrison, Margaret Case. *And the Price is Right* (Cleveland and New York: The World Publishing Company, 1958).

Hawes, Elizabeth. *But Say It Politely* (Boston: Little, Brown, 1951).

Anything But Love: A Complete Digest of the Rules for Feminine Behavior…Given Out In Print, On Film and Over the Air etc (New York and Toronto: Rinehart and Co, 1948).

Fashion is Spinach (New York: Random House, 1938).

Good Grooming (Boston: Little, Brown, 1942).

Hurry Up Please, It's Time (New York: Reynal and Hitchcock, 1946).

It's Still Spinach (Boston: Little, Brown, 1954).

Men Can Take It (New York: Random House, 1939).

Why Is a Dress? (New York: Viking Press, 1942).

Why Women Cry, or, Wenches With Wrenches (New York: Reynal and Hitchcock, 1943).

Heal, Edith. *The Young Executive's Wife: You and Your Husband's Job* (New York: Dodd, Mead and Co., 1958).

Herndon, Booton. *Bergdorf's on the Plaza: The Story of Bergdorf Goodman and a Half-Century of American Fashion,* (New York: Knopf, 1956).

Hower, Robert, M. *History of Macy's of New York, 1858–1919* (Cambridge,Massachusetts: Harvard University Press, 1946).

Hurlock, Elizabeth B. *The Psychology of Dress: An Analysis of Fashion and Its Motive* (New York: The Ronald Press Company, 1929).

Kahl, Joseph A. *The American Class Structure* (New York and London: Holt, Rinehart and Winston, 1965, first published 1953).

Kempton, Murray. *Part of Our Time: Some Ruins and Monuments of the Thirties* (New York: New York Review Books, 1998, first published 1955).

Kinsey, Alfred, et al. *Sexual Behavior in the Human Female* (Philidelphia and London: W.B. Saunders and Co., 1953).

Larrabee, Eric and Rolf Meyersohn, eds., *Mass Leisure* (Glencoe, Illinois: The Free Press, 1960).

Lundberg, Ferdinand and Marynia F. Farnham. *Modern Woman; The Lost Sex* (New York: Harper and Brothers, 1947).

Lundberg, George A., Mirra Komarovsky and Mary Alice McInerney, eds., *Leisure: A Suburban Study* (Morningside Heights, New York: Columbia University Press, 1934).

Lynd, Robert S. and Helen Merrell. *Middletown: A Study in Contemporary American Culture* (New York: Harcourt Brace and Co., 1929).

Magriel, Paul. *Isadora Duncan* (New York: Henry Holt and Co., 1947).

Mark, Edwina, pseudonym i.e. Edwin J Fadiman. *The Odd Ones* (London: Neville Spearmen, 1960, first published 1959).

McCardell, Claire. *What Shall I Wear? The What, When, Where and How Much of Fashion* (New York: Simon and Schuster, 1956).

McCarthy, Mary. *Memories of a Catholic Girlhood* (London, Melbourne, Toronto: Heinnemann, 1957).

Sights and Spectacles, 1937–58 (London: Heinneman, 1959).

The Company She Keeps (Weidenfeld and Nicholson, 1982, first published 1942).

The Group (New York: Harcourt and Brace, 1963).

McClellan, Elizabeth. *History of American Costume, Book One and Two* (New York: Tudor, 1937).

Metropolitan Museum of Art. *A Woman of Fashion 1947, Spring/Summer: The Bloomingdale Collection* (New York: Metropolitan Museum of Art, 1947).

Metropolitan Museum of Art. *Renaissance in Fashion 1942: Special Opening April 22, 1942* (New York: Metropolitan Museum of Art, 1942).

Meyer, Elizabeth Burris. *This is Fashion* (New York: Harper and Brothers, 1943).

Mikes, George. *How to Scrape Skies: the United States Explored, Rediscovered and Explained* (Harmondsworth: Penguin, 1966, first published 1948).

Munkacsi, Martin. *Fool's Apprentice* (New York: The Reader's Press, 1945).

Munkacsi, Martin. *Nudes* (New York: Greenberg, 1951).

National Retail Dry Goods Association. *Twenty-Five Years of Retailing* (New York: National Retail Dry Goods Association, 1936).

National American Women's Suffrage Association, *Victory: How Women Won It, A Centennial Symposium, 1840–1940* (New York: The H. W. Wilson Co., 1940).

Neather, Carl Albert. *Advertising to Women* (New York: Prentice-Hall, 1928).

Nystrom, Paul H. *Economics of Fashion* (New York: The Ronald Press, 1928).

Fashion Merchandising (New York: The Ronald Press, 1932).

Oglesby, Catharine. *Business Opportunities for Women* (New York: Harper and Brothers, 1932).

Fashion Careers American Style (New York and London: Funk and Wagnalls, 1937).

Ovesey, Regina. *Exploring Careers in Contemporary Communication by the Fashion Group Foundation, Inc.* (New York: Rosen, 1983).

Page, Betty. *On Fair Vanity* (London: Convoy, 1954).

Parker, Dorothy. *The Portable Dorothy Parker* (New York and London: Penguin Books, 1976, first published 1944).

Parsons, Frank Alvah. *The Art of Dress* (Garden City, New York: Doubleday, 1928).

The Psychology of Dress (Garden City, New York: Doubleday,1923).

Parsons School of Art, *Parsons: New York School of Fine and Applied Art, 1939– 40 Prospectus* (New York: Tri-Arts Press, 1986).

Passos, John Dos. *Manhattan Transfer* (New York and London: Penguin, 2000, first published 1925).

Plath, Sylvia. *The Bell Jar* (London: William Heinneman, 1964, first published 1953).

Pruette, Lorine, ed., *Women Workers through the Depression: A Study of White Collar Employment Made by the American Woman's Association* (New York: The Macmillan Company, 1934).

Rauschenpush, Winifred. *How to Dress in Wartime* (Los Angeles: Coward McCann Ltd., 1942).

Roshco, Bernard. *The Rag Race: How New York and Paris run the Breakneck Business of Dressing American Women* (New York: Funk and Wagnells,1963).

Rudofsky, Bernard. *Are Clothes Modern?* (Chicago: Paul Theobold, 1947).

Schilder, Paul. *The Image and Appearance of the Human Body: Studies in Constructive Energies of the Psyche* (New York: International Universities Press Inc., 1970).

Seidman, Joel. *Labor in Twentieth Century America: The Needle Trades* (New York and Toronto: Farrar and Rinehart, 1942).

Sellner, Eudora. *American Costume:, 150 Years of Style in America, 1775–1925* (Worcester, Massachusetts: The School Arts Magazine, c.1925).

Sices, Murray. *Seventh Avenue* (New York: Fairchild, 1953).

Smith, Henry Nash. *Virgin Land: The American West as Symbol and Myth,* (Cambridge, Massachusetts: Harvard University Press, 1950).

Snow, Carmel, with Mary Louise Aswell. *The World of Carmel Snow* (New York, Toronto and London: McGraw Hill, 1962).

Stevenson, Margaretta, ed., *How the Fashion World Works: Fit Yourself for a Fashion Future, Addresses Given at the Fashion Group's Training Courses by Fashion and Merchandising Experts* (New York and London: Harper and Brothers, 1938).

Stuart, Jessie. *The American Fashion Industry* (Boston: Prince School Publications, 1951).

Swinney, John B. *Merchandising of Fashions: Policies and Methods of Successful Speciality Stores* (NewYork: Ronald Publishers, 1942).

Taylor, Frederick W. *The Principles of Scientific Management* (New York and London: Harper and Brothers, 1913, first published in 1911).

The History of Lord & Taylor, 1826–1926 (New York: Guinn, n.d.).

Valentine, Helen and Thompson, Alice. *Better than Beauty: A Guide to Charm* (New York: Modern Age Books, 1938).

W.P.A. *New York: City Guide Series* (New York: Random House, 1939).

Walton, Frank L. *Thread of Victory* (New York: Fairchild, 1945).

Warshow, Robert. *The Immediate Experience: Movies, Comics, Theatre and Other Aspects of Popular Culture* (Cambridge, Massachusetts and London: Harvard University Press, 2001, first published 1948).

Weidman, Jerome. *I Can Get that for You Wholesale* (New York: Avon, 1951, first published 1937).

Wilcox, R., Turner. *Five Centuries of American Costume* (NewYork: Scribner,1963).

Williams, Beryl. *Fashon is Our Business* (London: John Gifford Ltd, 1948).

Young Faces in Fashion (Philidelphia: J.B. Lippincott Company, 1956).

Young, Agnes Brooks. *Recurring Cycles of Fashion, 1760–1937* (New York and London: Harper and Bros., 1937).

Zaharis, Babe Didrikson, as told to Harry Paxton, *This Life I've Led: My Autobiography* (London: Robert Hale Ltd., 1956).

JOURNAL ARTICLES

Barber, Bernard and Lyle S. Lobel. ' "Fashion" in Women's Clothes and the American Social System', *Social Forces, vol. 31, no.2* (December 1952): 124–131.

Hurlock, Elizabeth B., 'Motivation in Fashion', *Archives of Psychology, no.111* (1929): 71.

Jack, Nancy Koplin and Betty Schiffer. 'The Limits of Fashion Control', *American Sociological Review, vol. 13, no. 6* (December 1948): 730–738.

Rhoda, E. McCulloch. 'A Challenge to American Women', *Journal of Educational Sociology, vol. 15, no. 5* (January 1942): 301–5.

Wilder, Harris Hawthorne and Margaret Washington Pfeiffer 'The Bodily Proportions of Women in the United States, Based upon Measurements Taken from One Hundred Smith College Students', *Proceedings of the American Academy of Arts and Sciences, vol. 59, no. 16* (Boston, 1924).

Young, Estelle de. 'A Psychological Analysis of Fashion Motivation', *Archives of Psychology, no. 171* (1934): 100.

MAGAZINES AND NEWSPAPERS

Charm (January 1942–November 1946 and September 1947).

Department Store Buyer (August 1939).

Glamour (January–June 1942, January–December 1944, January–June 1945 and January–December 1947).

Harper's Bazaar (January 1929–December 1947).

Harper's Bazaar (British), Folio of Fashion and Beauty, October 1948.

Junior Bazaar (1946).

Life (1936–47).

Mademoiselle (August–September 1937, March–August and December 1938, May–December 1940, January 1941–December 1947).

The Christian Science Monitor (January 1929–December 1947).

The Los Angeles Times (January 1929–December 1947).

The New York Times (January 1929–December 1947).

The Washington Post (January 1929–December 1947).

Vogue (January 1929–December 1949).

Women's Wear Daily

SECONDARY MATERIAL

BOOKS

Aaron, Daniel and Robert Bendiner, eds., *The Strenuous Decade: A Social and Intellectual Record of the 1930s* (Garden City, New York: Anchor Books, Doubleday and Co., 1970).

Adie, Kate. *Corsets to Camouflage: Women and War* (London: Hodder and Stoughton, published in association with the Imperial War Museum, 2003).

Albers, Patricia. *Shadows, Fire, Snow: The Life of Tina Modotti* (New York: Clarkson Potter, 1999).

Andrews, Maggie and Mary M. Talbot, eds., *All the World and Her Husband: Women in Twentieth Century Consumer Culture* (London and New York: Cassell, 2000).

Anspach, Karlyne. *The Why of Fashion* (Ames: Iowa State University Press, 1967).

Armstrong, Timothy, ed., *American Bodies: Cultural Histories of the Physique* (New York: New York University Press, 1996).

Armstrong, Tim. *Modernism, Technology and the Body: A Cultural Study* (Cambridge and New York: Cambridge University Press, 1998).

Arnold, Rebecca. *Fashion, Desire and Anxiety: Image and Morality in the Twentieth Century* (London: I. B. Tauris, 2001).

Atkins, Jacqueline M. *Wearing Propaganda: Textiles on the Home Front in Japan, Britain, and the United States, 1931–45* (New Haven and London: Yale University Press, 2005).

Badger, Anthony J. *The New Deal: The Depression Years, 1933–40* (New York: Hill and Wang, 1993).

Banner, Lois. *American Beauty: A Social History through Two Centuries of the American Idea, Ideal, and Image of the Beautiful Woman* (New York: Alfred A. Knopf, 1983).

Banta, Martha. *Imaging American Women: Ideas and Ideals in Cultural History* (New York: Columbia University Press, 1987).

Barthel, Diane. *Putting On Appearances: Gender and Advertising* (Philadelphia: Temple University Press, 1988).

Basinger, Jeanine. *A Woman's View: How Hollywood Spoke to Women, 1930–1960* (London: Chatto and Windus, 1993).

Baskerville, Stephen W. and Ralph Willett, eds., *Nothing Else to Fear: New Perspectives on America in the Thirties* (Dekalb: Northern Illinois University Press, 1988).

Bauman, John F. and Thomas H.Coode. *In the Eye of the Depression: New Deal Reporters and the Agony of the American People* (Dekalb: Northern Illinois Press, 1992).

Bauret, Gabriel. *Alexey Brodovitch* (New York: Assouline, 2005).

Belfrage, Sally. *Un-American Activities: A Memoir of the 1950s* (New York: Harper Collins, 1994).

Bender, Thomas and Michael Peter Smith, eds., *City and Nation: Rethinking Place and Identity* (New Brunswick, New Jersey: Transaction Publications, 2001).

Bender, Thomas. The *Unfinished City: New York and the Metropolitan Idea* (New York: New Press, 2002).

Benfield, G.J. Barker and Catherine Clinton. *Portraits of American Women: From Settlement to the Present* (New York: St Martins Press, 1991).

Benson, Susan Porter. *Counter Cultures: Saleswomen, Managers and Customers in American Department Stores, 1890–1940* (Urbana and Chicago: University of Illinois Press, 1986).

Benstock, Shari and Suzanne Ferriss, eds., *On Fashion* (New Brunswick, New Jersey: Rutgers University Press, 1994).

Benton, Charlotte, Tim Benton and Ghislaine Wood, eds., *Art Deco, 1910–1939* London: V&A, 2003).

Berch, Bettina. *Radical by Design: The Life and Style of Elizabeth Hawes, Fashion Designer, Union Organizer, Best-selling Author* (New York: E.P. Dutton, 1988).

Berman, Marshall. *All that is Solid Melts into Air: The Experience of Modernity* (London: Verso, 1983).

Birmingham, Nan Tillson. *Store* (New York: Putnam's Sons, 1978).

Bjelajac, David. *American Art: A Cultural History* (London: Laurence King, 2000).

Bledstein, Burton J. and Robert D. Johnson, eds., *The Middling Sorts: Explorations in the History of the American Middle Class* (New York and London: Routledge, 2001).

Bluttal, Steven, ed., *Halston* (New York: Phaidon, 2001).

Bocock, Robert and Kenneth Thompson, eds., *Social and Cultural Forms of Modernity* (Oxford and Cambridge: Polity Press in Association with Open University, 1992).

Bolt, Christine. *Feminist Ferment: The Women Question in the USA and England, 1870–1940* (London: University College London Press, 1995).

Bolton, Andrew. *The Supermodern Wardrobe* (London: Victoria and Albert Museum, 2002).

Bordo, Susan, *Unbearable Weight: Feminism, Western Culture and the Body* (California: University of California Press, 1995).

Bourdieu, Pierre, *Distinction: A Social Critique of the Judgement of Taste* (London: Routledge, 1996).

Brady, Maxine. *Bloomingdales* (New York and London: Harcourt Brace and Johanovich, 1980).

Braybon, Gail and Penny Summerfield. *Out of the Cage: Women's Experiences of the Two World Wars* (London: Pandora, 1987).

Breines, W. Young, *White and Miserable: Growing Up Female in the Fifties* (Boston: Beacon Press, 1992).

Brennan, Marcia. *Painting Gender, Constructing Theory: The Alfred Stieglitz Circle and American Formalist Aesthetics* (Cambridge, Massachusetts: M.I.T., 2001).

Bridge, Gary and Sophie Watson. *The Blackwell City Guide* (Oxford: Blackwell, 2002).

Broby-Johanson, Rudolf. *Body and Clothes: An Illustrated History of Costume* (New York: Reinhold Book Corporation, 1968).

Brown, Dorothy M. *Setting a Course: American Women in the 1920s* (Boston, Massachusetts: Twayne Publishers, 1987).

Bunch, Lonnie, Ellen Roney Hughes, Steven Lubar and Jeff Brodie. *Smithsonian's America: An Exhibition on American History and Culture* (Tokyo: American Festival, 1994).

Bunker, George R. et al. *Alexey Brodovitch and his Influence* (Philadelphia: Philadelphia College of Art with the Smithsonian Institute, April 1972).

Burke, Peter. *What is Cultural History?* (Cambridge: Polity, 2005).

Calvocoressi, Richard and David Hare. *Lee Miller: Portraits* (London: National Portrait Gallery, 2005).

Cahn, Susan K. *Coming On Strong: Gender and Sexuality in Twentieth Century Women's Sport* (Cambridge, Massachusetts and London: Harvard University Press, 1994).

Cameron, Ardis. *Looking for America: The Visual Production of Nation and People* (Malden, Massachusetts and Oxford: Blackwell, 2005).

Campbell, Neil and Alasdair Kean. *American Cultural Studies: An Introduction to American Culture* (London: Routledge, 1997).

Cannadine, David, ed., *What is History Now?* (London: Palgrave Macmillan, 2002).

Carson, Fiona and Claire Pajaczkowska, eds., *Feminist Visual Culture* (Edinburgh: Edinburgh University Press, 2000).

Carter, Ernestine. *Twentieth Century Fashion: A Scrapbook 1910 to Today* (London: Eyre Methuen, 1975).

The Changing World of Fashion, 1900 to the Present (London: Weidenfeld and Nicholson, 1977).

With Tongue in Chic (London: Joseph, 1974).

Cassara, Beverley Beuner and Ethel Josephine Alpenfels, eds., *American Women: The Changing Image* (Boston: Beacon, 1962).

Castelbajac, Kate de. *The Face of the Century: 100 Years of Make-up and Style* (New York: Rizzoli, 1995).

Certeau, Michel de. *The Practice of Everyday Life* (Berkeley, Los Angeles, London: University of California Press, 1988).

Chafe, William H. *The American Woman: Her Changing Social, Economic and Political Roles, 1920–70* (New York: Oxford University Press, 1972).

The Paradox of Change: American Women in the Twentieth Century (New York: Oxford University Press, 1991).

Chapsal, Madeleine. *La Chair de la Robe* (Paris: Fanard, 1989).

Chatwin, Bruce. *What am I Doing Here* (London: Picador, 1990).

Cheekwood Botanical Gardens and Fine Arts Center. *The Fashion Photography of Louise Dahl-Wolfe, 7 June–27 July, 1980* (Nashville: Cheekwood Botanical Gardens and Fine Arts Center,1980).

Chermayeff, Catherine. et al., eds., *Lillian Bassman: Photographs by Lillian Bassman* (Boston, New York, Toronto and London: Little, Brown and Company, 1997).

Conor, Liz. *The Spectacular Modern Woman: Feminine Visibility in the 1920s* (Bloomington and Indianapolis: Indiana University Press, 2004).

Coote, Jack H. *Illustrated History of Colour Photography* (Surbiton, Surrey: Fountain Press, 1993).

Corn, Wanda M. *The Great American Thing: Modern Art and National Identity, 1915–1935* (Berkeley, Los Angeles and London: University of California Press, 1999).

Craik, Jennifer. *The Face of Fashion: Cultural Studies in Fashion* (London and New York: Routledge, 1994).

Cross, Gary. *An All-consuming Century: Why Commercialism Won in Modern America* (New York: Columbia University Press, 2000).

Time and Money: The Making of Consumer Culture (New York: Routledge, 1993).

Cummins, Duane D., and William Gee White. *Contrasting Decades: The 1920s and 1930s* (Encino, California: Glencoe Publishing Co. Inc., 1980).

Cunningham, Patricia A. and Susan Voso Lab, eds., *Dress In American Culture* (Bowling Green, Ohio: Bowling Green State University, 1993).

Curtis, Joshua James. *Sunkissed: Sunwear and the Hollywood Beauty, 1930–1950* (Portland, Oregon: Collector's Press, 2003).

Daly, Ann. *Done Into Dance: Isadora Duncan in America* (Indianapolis: Indiana University Press, 1995).

Daniel, Robert L. *American Women in the Twentieth Century: The Festival of Life* (Harcourt Brace Janovich, 1987).

Daria, Irene. *The Fashion Cycle* (New York: Simon and Schuster, 1990).

Davis, Fred. *Fashion, Culture and Identity* (Chicago and London: Chicago University Press, 1992).

De Grazia, Victoria and Ellen Furlough. *The Sex of Things: Gender and Consumption in Historical Perspective* (Berkeley and London: University of California Press, 1996).

Denning, Michael. *The Cultural Front* (London and New York: Verso, 1996).

Diedrich, Maria and Dorothea Fischer-Hornung, eds., *Women and War: The Changing Status of American Women from the 1930s to the 1950s* (New York and London: Berg, 1990).

Dodd, Nigel. *Social Theory and Modernity* (Cambridge: Polity Press, 1999).

Donald, James. *Imagining the Modern City* (London: The Athlone Press, 1999).

Douglas, Ann. *The Feminization of American Culture* (London: Papermac, 1996).

Downs, Anthony. *Opening Up the Suburbs: An Urban Strategy for America* (New Haven and London: Yale University Press, 1973).

Dubofsky, Melvyn, ed., *The New Deal: Conflicting Interpretations and Shifting Perspectives* (New York and London: Garland Publishing, 1992).

Dyer, Glenda and Martha Reed, eds., *The Consumer Culture and the American Home, 1890–1930: The Proceedings of McFaddin-Ward House Museum Conference, 27–29 October 1988, Beaumont, Texas* (Beaumont, Texas: McFaddin-Ward House, 1989).

Dyer, Richard. *White* (London and New York: Routledge, 1997).

Eauclaire, Sally and Louise Dahl-Wolfe. *Louise Dahl-Wolfe: A Retrospective Exhibition* (Washington D.C.: National Museum of Women in the Arts, 1987).

Eisen, George and David K. Wiggins, eds., *Sport in North American History and Culture* (Westport, Connecticut: Greenwood, 1994).

Eisler, Benita. *Private Lives: Men and Women of the Fifties* (New York: Franklin Watts, 1986).

Ellis, Edward Robb. *A Nation in Torment: The Great Depression, 1929–39* (New York, Tokyo and London: Kodansha International, 1995).

Emmet, Jake. *Fashion for America! Designs in the Fashion Institute of Technology* (New York: Emmet Publishing, 1992).

Esten, John. *Diana Vreeland: Bazaar Years, Why Don't You* (New York: Universe, 2001).

Evans, Caroline and Minna Thornton. *Women and Fashion: A New Look* (London: Quartet, 1989).

Evenberg, Lewis A. *Steppin' Out: New York Nightlife and the Transformations of American Culture, 1890–1930* (Chicago: Chicago University Press, 1984).

Ewen, Stuart and Elizabeth. *Channels of Desire: Mass Images and the Shaping of American Consciousness* (New York: McGraw Hill Book Company, 1982).

Ewing, Elizabeth. *History of Twentieth Century Fashion* (London: B. T. Batsford, 1993).

Ewing, William A. *Blumenfeld: A Fetish for Beauty* (London: Barbican Art Gallery and Thames and Hudson, 1996).

Fashion Institute of Technology. *All-American: A Sportswear Tradition* (New York: Fashion Institute of Technology, 1985).

Fausch, Deborah, Paulette Singley and Rodolphe El Khoury, eds., *Architecture In Fashion* (New York: Princeton Architectural Press, 1994).

Featherstone, Mike, Mike Hepworth and Bryan S.Turner, eds., *The Body as Social Process and Cultural Theory* (London, Newbury Park and New Dehli: Sage, 1991).

Ferry, John William. *A History of the Department Store* (New York: Macmillan, 1960).

Festle, Mary Jo. *Playing Nice: Politics and Apologies in Women's Sports* (New York: Columbia University, 1996).

Finkelstein, Joanne. *After a Fashion* (Victoria: Melbourne University Press, 1996).

Fischer, Lucy. *Designing Women: Cinema, Art Deco, and the Female Form* (New York: Columbia University Press, 2003).

Fisher, Andrea. *Let Us Now Praise Famous Women: Women Photographers for the United States Government, 1935–1944* (London and New York: Pandora, 1987).

Fleischhauer, Carl and Beverley W. Brannan. *Documenting America, 1935–45* (Berkeley, Los Angeles and London: University of California, 1988).

Folly, Martin. *The United States and World War II: The Awakening Giant* (Edinburgh: Edinburgh University Press, 2002).

Folmar, Wilson. *American Fashion Designs, Montgomery Museum of Fine Arts, Montgomery Alabama, 16 September–29 October 1978* (Montgomery, Alabama: Montgomery Museum of Fine Arts, 1978).

Foucault, Michel. *The History of Sexuality: Volume Three, Care of the Self* (London: Penguin, 1990).

Foulkes, Julia L. *Modern Bodies: Dance and American Modernism from Martha Graham to Alvin Ailey* (Chapel Hill and London: North Carolina University Press, 2002).

Franko, Mark. *Dancing Modernism/Performing Politics* (Bloomington and Indianapolis: Indiana University Press, 1995).

Friedel, Frank, ed., *Intercity Differences in Costs of Living in March 1935 – 59 Cities* (New York: Da Capo Press, 1971).

Frissell, Toni. *Photographs 1933–1967* (London: Andre Deutsch, 1994).

Gaines, Jane and Charlotte Herzog, eds., *Fabrications: Costume and the Female Body* (New York and London: Routledge, 1990).

Gaines, Steven. *Simply Halston* (New York: G. P. Putnam's Sons, 1991).

Galassi, Peter. *American Photography, 1890–1965: From the Museum of Modern Art New York* (New York: Museum of Modern Art, 1995).

Gamber, Wendy. *The Female Economy: The Millinery and Dressmaking Trades, 1860–1930* (Urbana and Chicago: University of Illinois Press, 2000).

Garland, Madge. *The Indecisive Decade: The World of Fashion and Entertainment in the Thirties* (London: MacDonald, 1968).

Gatlin, Rochelle. *American Women Since 1945* (Hampshire and London: Macmillan, 1987).

Gidley, Mick, ed., *Modern American Culture* (London: Longman, 1993).

Glaab, Charles Nelson and Andrew Theodore Brown. *A History of Urban America* (New York: Macmillan, 1976).

Glaab, Charles, ed., *The American City: A Documentary History* (Homewood, Illinois: Dorsey Press,1963).

Globus, Dorothy Twining, ed., *Louise Dahl-Wolfe* (New York: Abrams, 2000).

Gluck, Sherna Berger, ed., *Rosie the Riveter Revisited: Women, the War and Social Change* (Longbeach, California: School of Social and Behavioral Sciences, Oral History Resource Center, California State University, 1987).

Goodman, Paul and Frank O. Gatell. *America in the Twenties: The Beginnings of Contemporary America* (New York, London and Sydney: Holt, Rinehart and Winston, 1972).

Gould, Lois. *Mommy Dressing: A Love Story, After a Fashion* (New York: Doubleday, 1998).

Graham, Martha. *Blood Memory* (New York: Doubleday, 1992).

Grand Palais Paris. *Alexey Brodovitch, 27 October – 29 November 1982* (Paris: Grand Palais,1982).

Green, Nancy L. *Ready-to-Wear, Ready-to-Work: A Century of Industry and Immigrants in Paris and New York* (Durham and London: Duke University Press, 1997).

Gregory, Alexis. *The Golden Age of Travel, 1880–1939* (London: Cassell, 1998).

Griffiths, Ian and Nicola White, eds., *The Fashion Business: Theory, Practice, Image* (New York and Oxford: Berg, 2000).

Gronberg, Tag. *Designs on Modernity: Exhibiting the City in 1920s Paris* (Manchester and New York: Manchester University Press, 1998).

Gross, Elaine and Fred Rottman. *Halston: An American Original* (London: Harper Collins, 1999).

Grover, Kathryn, ed., *Hard at Play: Leisure in America, 1840–1940* (Amherst: University of Massacusetts Press, 1992).

Grundberg, Andy. Brodovitch, *Masters of American Design: Documents of American Design* (New York: Abrams, 1989).

Guttmann, Allen. *The Games Must Go On: Avery Brundage and the Olympic Movement* (New York: Columbia University Press, 1984).

Hall, Lee. *Common Threads: A Parade of American Clothing* (Boston, Toronto and London: Bulfinch Press Book, Little, Brown and Co., 1992).

Hall, Stuart and Bram Gieben, eds. *Formations of Modernity* (Cambridge and Oxford: Polity Press in association with the Open University, 1993).

Hall-Duncan, Nancy. *The History of Fashion Photography* (New York: Alpine Book Company Inc., 1979).

Hamburger, Estelle. *Fashion Business: It's All Yours* (San Francisco: Hearndon, 1976).

Harrison, Martin. *Appearances* (London: Jonathan Cape, 1991).

Beauty Photography in Vogue (New York: Stewart, Tabori and Chang, 1987).

Hartman, Rose. *Birds of Paradise: An Intimate View of the New York Fashion World* (New York: Dell Pub. Co., 1980).

Hartmann, Susan M. *The Home Front and Beyond: American Women in the 1940s* (Boston: Twayne, 1982).

Harvey, Brett. *The Fifties: A Woman's Oral History* (New York: Harper Collins, 1993).

Harvey, John and Roberta E. Pearson, eds., *American Cultural Studies: A Reader* (Oxford: Oxford University Press, 2000).

Harvey, Sheridan, ed., *American Women: A Library of Congress Guide for the Study of Women's History and Culture in the United States* (Washington: Library of Congress, 2001).

Hearst Corporation. *125 Great Moments of Harper's Bazaar: A Commemorative Collection of Outstanding Photographs, Illustrations and Texts that have Appeared in Harper's Bazaar, in Celebration of the Magazine's 125th Anniversary* (New York: Hearst Corporation, 1993).

Hendrickson, Robert. *The Grand Emporiums: The Illustrated History of America's Great Department Stores* (New York: Stein and Day, 1979).

Heron, Liz and Val Williams, eds., *Illuminations: Women Writing on Photography from the 1850s to the Present* (London: I. B. Tauris, 1996).

Heuer, Otto. *Martin Munkacsi* (Photofind Gallery, Woodstock, New York: 1985).

Higonnet, Margaret Randolph. *Behind the Lines: Gender and the Two World Wars* (New Haven: Yale University Press, 1987).

Hillhouse, Marion Strong. *Dress Design and Selection* (New York: Macmillan, 1963).

Hogeland, Ronald W., ed., *Women and Womanhood in America* (London and Lexington, Massachusetts: D. C. Heath, 1973).

Hollander, Anne. *Seeing Through Clothes* (Berkeley, Los Angeles and London: University of California Press, 1993).

Sex and Suits: The Eroticism of Modern Dress (New York: Kodansha, 1994).

Feeding the Eye: Essays (Berkeley, Los Angeles and London: University of California Press, 1999).

Hoobler, Dorothy and Thomas. *Vanity Rules: A History of American Fashion and Beauty* (Brookfield: Millbrook Press, 2000).

Hooks, Margaret. *Tina Modotti: Photographer and Revolutionary* (London: Pandora, 1993).

Horney, Karen. *Feminine Psychology* (London: Routledge and Kegan Paul, 1967).

Hoy, Suellen. *Chasing Dirt: the American Pursuit of Cleanliness* (New York and Oxford: Oxford University Press, 1995).

Humphreys, Nancy K. *American Women's Magazines: An Annotated Historical Guide* (New York: Garland, 1989).

Jacobson, Matthew Frye. *Whiteness of a Different Color: European Immigrants and the Alchemy of Race* (Cambridge, Massachusetts and London: Harvard University Press, 2000).

James, Edward T., Janet Wilson James and Paul Boyer, eds., *Notable American Women, 1607-1950: A Biographical Dictionary* (Belknap Press, 1974).

Jarrow, Jeanette and Beatrice Judell. *Inside the Fashion Business* (New York: Wiley, 1965).

Johnson, Jill. *Jasper Johns: Privileged Information* (New York and London: Thames and Hudson, 1996).

Johnson, Joyce. *Minor Characters* (New York: Houghton Mifflin, 1983).

Johnson, Patricia. *Real Fantasies: Edward Steichen's Advertising Photography* (Berkeley, Los Angeles, London: University of California Press, 1997).

Joselit, Jenna Weissman. *A Perfect Fit: Clothes, Character and the Promises of America* (New York: Henry Holt and Company, 2001).

Kalaidjian, Walter, ed., *The Cambridge Companion to American Modernism* (Cambridge and New York: Cambridge University Press, 2005).

Kamitsis, Lydia. *Vionnet* (London: Thames and Hudson, 1996).

Kammen, Michael. *American Culture, American Tastes: Social Change in the Twentieth Century* (New York: Knopf, 1999).

Kanin, Ruth. *The Manufacture of Beauty* (Boston: Brandon Publishing, 1990).

Kelly, Kate. *The Wonderful World of Women's Wear Daily* (New York: Saturday Review Press, 1972).

Kennedy, David M. *The American People in the Great Depression: Freedom from Fear: Part I* (Oxford and New York: Oxford University Press, 1999).

Kidwell, Claudia Brush and Margaret C. Christman. *Suiting Everyone: The Democratization of Clothing in America* (Washington D.C: Smithsonian Institution Press, 1974).

Kidwell, Claudia Brush, and Valerie Steele, eds., *Men and Women: Dressing the Part* (Washington: Smithsonian Institution Press, 1989).

Kirke, Betty. *Madeleine Vionnet* (San Fransisco: Chronicle Books, 1998).

Kirkham, Pat and David Thoms. *War Culture: Social Change and Changing Experience in World War Two Britain* (London: Lawrence and Wishart, 1995).

Kirkham, Pat, ed., *Women Designers in the USA, 1900–2000* (New York: BCG and Yale, 2001).

Kitch, Carolyn. *The Girl on the Magazine Cover: The Origins of Visual Stereotypes in American Mass Media* (Chapel Hill and London: University of Carolina Press, 2001).

Kitses, Jim. *Horizons West* (London: Thames and Hudson/BFI, 1970).

Kobal, John. *People Will Talk* (London: Aurum Press, 1986).

Koda, Harold and Richard Martin. *Three Women:* Madeleine Vionnet, Claire McCardell and Rei Kawakubo (New York: Fashion Institute of Technology, 1987).

Komarovsky, Mirra. *Women in College: Shaping New Feminine Identities* (New York: Basie, 1985).

Kreisel, Martha. *American Women Photographers: A Selected and Annotated Bibliography* (Connecticut and London: Westport Press, 1999).

Kurth, Peter. *Isadora: A Sensational Life* (Boston: Little, Brown and Co., 2001).

Kwolek-Folland, Angel. *Incorporating Women: A History of Women and Business in the United States* (New York: Palgrave, 1998).

Kyvig, David E. *Daily Life in the United States, 1920–1940: How Americans Lived Through the 'Roaring Twenties' and the Great Depression* (Chicago: Ivan R. Dee, 2004).

Laird, Pamela Walker. *Advertising Progress: American Business and the Rise of Consumer Marketing* (Baltimore, Maryland and London: Johns Hopkins University Press, 1998).

Lambert, Eleanor. *World of Fashion: People, Places, Resources* (New York and London: R. R. Bowker, 1976).

Lant, Antonia. *Blackout: Reinventing Women For Wartime British Cinema* (Princeton, New Jersey: Princeton University Press, 1991).

Latham, Anglea J. *Posing a Threat: Flappers, Chorus Girls, and Other Brazen Performers of the American 1920s* (Hanover: University Press of New England, 2000).

Leach, William. *Land of Desire: Merchants, Power and the Rise of a New American Culture* (New York: Vintage, 1994).

Country of Exiles: The Destruction of Place in American Life (New York: Vintage, 1999).

Lee Levin, Phyllis. *The Wheels of Fashion* (Garden City, New York: Doubleday, 1965).

Lee Potter, Charlie. *Sportswear in Vogue since 1910* (London: Thames and Hudson, 1984).

LeGates, Richard T. and Frederic Stout. *The City Reader* (London and New York: Routledge, 1997).

Levenson, Michael, ed., *The Cambridge Companion to Modernism* (Cambridge: Cambridge University Press, 2003).

Levine, David O. *The American College and the Culture of Aspiration, 1915–1940* (Ithaca and London: Cornell University Press, 1986).

Levine, Donald, ed., *On Individuality and Social Forms* (London: University of Chicago Press, 1971).

Lewis, Adam. *Van Day Truex: The Man Who Defined Twentieth Century Taste and Style* (New York, London: Viking: 2001).

Ley, Sandra. F*ashion for Everyone: The Story of Ready-to-Wear, 1870–1970* (New York: Charles Scribner's Sons, 1975).

Lharmon, W.T. *Deliberate Speed: The Origins of Cultural Style in the American 1950s* (Washington D.C: Smithsonian Institution, 1990).

Since You Went Away: World War Two Letters from American Women on the Home Front (New York and Oxford: Oxford University Press, 1991).

Litoff, Judy Barrett and David C. Smith, eds., *American Women in a World at War: Contemporary Accounts from World War Two* (Wilmington, Delaware: Scholarly Resources, 1997).

Livingston, Jane. *The New York School: Photographs 1936–63* (New York: Stewart Tabori and Chang, 1992).

Löfgren, Orvar. *On Holiday: A History of Vacationing* (Berkeley, Los Angeles and London: University of California Press, 1999).

Lowe, Margaret A. *Looking Good: College Women and Body Image, 1875–1930* (Baltimore, Maryland and London: Johns Hopkins University Press, 2003).

Lubar, Steve and W. David Kingery, eds., *History From Things: Essays On Material Culture* (Washington D. C. and London: Smithsonian Institution Press, 1993).

Lupton, Ellen. *Mechanical Brides: Women and Machines From Home to Office* (New York: Cooper Hewitt National Museum of Design, Smithsonian Institution and Princeton Architectural Press, 1993).

Maidment, Richard A., ed., *The United States in the Twentieth Century: Key Documents* (London: Hodder and Stoughton, 1994).

Marchalonis, Shirley. *College Girls: A Century in Fiction* (New Brunswick, New Jersey: Rutgers University Press, 1995).

Marcus, Stanley. *Minding the Store, A Memoir* (London: Elm Tree Books and Hamish Hamilton, 1975).

Marks, Robert W. and Peter E. Palmquist. Robert W. Marks: *Writings in Celebration of Photography's Centennial 1938–41* (Arcata, California: Peter E. Palmquist, 1998).

Martin, Richard. *American Ingenuity: Sportswear 1930s–1970s* (New York: Metropolitan Museum of Art, 1998).

Martin Munkacsi (Bielefeld and Dusseldorf: Edition Marzona, 1980).

Massey, Doreen, John Allen and Steve Pile, eds., *City Worlds* (London and New York: Routledge and Open University, 1999).

Masotti, Louis H. and Jeffrey K. Hadden, eds., *Suburbia in Transition* (New York: A New York Times Book, 1974).

McDowell, Colin. *Forties Fashion and the New Look* (London: Bloomsbury, 1997).

McElvaine, Robert S. *The Great Depression: America, 1929–41* (New York: Times Books, 1984).

McEwan, Melissa A. *Seeing America: Women Photographers between the Wars* (Kentucky: Kentucky University Press, 2000).

Mejerowitz, Joanne, ed., *Not June Cleaver: Women and Gender in Postwar America, 1945–1960* (Philadelphia: Temple University Press, 1994).

Melosh, Barbara, ed., *Gender and American History since 1890* (London and New York: Routledge, 1993).

Melosh, Barbara. *Engendering Culture: Manhood and Womanhood in New Deal Public Art and Theater* (Washington D.C. and London: Smithsonian Institution Press, 1991).

Melzer, Arthur M., Jerry Weinberger and Richard Zinman, eds., *Democracy and the Arts* (Ithaca and London: Cornell University Press, 1999).

Milbank, Caroline Rennolds. *Couture* (London: Thames and Hudson, 1985).

New York Fashion: The Evolution of the American Look (New York: Harry N. Abrams, 1996).

The Couture Accessory (New York: Harry N. Abrams, 2002).

Miller, Daniel, ed., *Material Cultures: Why Some Things Matter* (London: University College Press, 1998).

Miller, Tyrus. *Late Modernism: Politics, Fiction and the Arts Between the World Wars* (Berkeley, Los Angeles and London: University of California Press, 1999).

Milkman, Ruth. *Gender at Work: The Dynamics of Segregation by Sex during World War II* (Urbana and Chicago: University of Illinois Press, 1987).

Mirabella, Grace with Judith Warner. *In and Out of Vogue: A Memoir* (New York: Doubleday, 1995).

Mizejewski, Linda. *Ziegfeld Girl: Image and Icon in Culture and Cinema* (Durham and London: Duke University Press, 1999).

Mollenkopf, John Hull, ed., *Power, Culture and Place: Essays on New York City* (New York: Russell Sage Foundation, 1988).

Monti, Daniel J. Jr. *The American City: A Social and Cultural History* (Malden, Massachusetts and Oxford: Blackwell, 1999).

Morris, Jan. *Manhattan '45* (Baltimore, Maryland: Johns Hopkins University Press, 1998).

Motz, Marilyn Ferris and Pat Browne. *Making the American Home: Middle Class Women and Domestic Material Culture, 1840–1940* (Bowling Green, Ohio: Bowling Green State University Popular Press, 1988).

Mowry, George E. and Blaine A. Brownell. *The Urban Nation 1920 – 1980* (New York: Hill and Wang, 1981).

Mulvagh, Jane. *Vogue History of Twentieth Century Fashion* (London: Viking, 1988).

Munkacsi, Martin. *Spontaneity and Style: A Retrospective, 22 March to 30 April 1978* (New York: International Center of Photography, 1978).

Musée de la Mode et du Textile. *Garde-robes: Intimitiés Dévoilées, de Cléo de Mérode à …* (Paris: Union Centrale des Arts Décoratifs, Musée de la Mode et du Textile, 1999).

Nelson, Daniel. *Frederick W. Taylor and the Rise of Scientific Management* (Wisconsin: University of Wisconsin Press, 1980).

O'Brien, Kenneth Paul and Lynn Hudson Parsons, eds., *The Home Front: World War Two and the American Society* (Westport, Connecticut: Greenwood Press, 1995).

O'Donnol, Shirley Miles. *American Costume, 1915–1970: A Source Book for the Stage Costumer* (Bloomington: Indiana University Press, 1982).

O'Neill, William L. *Everyone Was Brave: The Rise and Fall of Feminism in America* (Chicago: Quadrangle Books, 1969).

The Woman Movement: Feminism in the United States and England (London: George Allen and Unwin,1969).

Olian, Joanne, ed., *Everyday Fashions of the Forties: As Pictured in Sears Catalogue* (New York: Dover, 1992).

Oliver, Valerie, Burnham. *Fashion and Costume in American Popular Culture: A Reference Guide* (Westport, Connecticut: Greenwood Publishing Group, 1996).

Palmer, Phyllis. *Domesticity and Dirt: Housewives and Domestic Servants in the United States, 1920–1945* (Philidelphia: Temple University Press, 1989).

Peiss, Kathy and Christina Simmons, eds., *Passion and Power: Sexuality in History* (Philadelphia: Temple University Press,1989).

Peiss, Kathy. *Cheap Amusements: Working Women and Leisure at the Turn of the Century* (Philadelphia: Temple University Press, 1986).

Hope in a Jar: The Making of America's Beauty Culture (New York: Metropolitan Books, 1998).

Per Una Storia della Moda Pronta, Problemi e Ricerche, Atti del V Convergo Internazionale del CISST Milano, 26–28 febbraio 1990 (Firenze: Pitti Imagine, 1991).

Phillips, *New York. The Forties, Fifties and Fashion: to be sold by Auction, April 8th, 1981* (New York, 1981).

Pope, Daniel. *Making of Modern Advertising* (New York: Basic Books,1983).

Probert, Christina. *Vogue Covers, 1900–1970* (New York: Harmony, 1976).

Purcell, Kerry William. *Alexey Brodovitch* (London: Phaidon Press, 2002).

Quant, Mary. *Quant by Quant* (New York: Putnam, 1966).

Reynolds, Nancy and Malcolm McCormick. *No Fixed Points: Dance in the Twentieth Century* (New Haven: Yale University Press, 2003).

Riegel, Robert Edgar. *American Women: A Story of Social Change* (Rutherford: Fairleigh Dickinson University Press, 1970).

Riley, Glenda. *Inventing the American Woman: A Perspective on Women's History* (Arlington Heights, Illinois: Harlan Davidson, 1986).

Roberts, Mary Louise. *Civilization Without Sexes: Reconstructing Gender in Postwar France, 1917–1927* (Chicago and London: Chicago University Press, 1994).

Rosenberg, Caroll Smith. *Disorderly Conduct: Visions of Gender in Victorian America* (New York and Oxford: Oxford University Press, 1985).

Rosenberg, Rosalind. *Divided Lives: American Women in the Twentieth Century* (London: Penguin, 1993).

Roshco, Bernard. *The Rag Race: How New York and Paris Run the Breakneck Business of Dressing American Women* (New York: Funk and Wagnalls, 1963).

Ross, Ishbel. *Crusades and Crinolines* (New York: Harper and Row, 1963).

Rowbotham, Sheila. *A Century of Women: The History of Women in Britain and the United States in the Twentieth Century* (New York: Penguin, 1999).

Rubinstein, Ruth P. *Dress Codes: Meanings and Messages in American Culture* (Boulder, San Francisco and Oxford: Westview Press, 1995).

Sage, George H. *Sport and American Society: Selected Readings* (Reading, Massachusetts, London and Sydney: Addison-Wesley Publishing Company, 1980).

Savignon, Jeromine. *L'Esprit Vionnet et ses Influences de Fin des Annees Vingt a nos Jours* (Lyon: L'Association pour l'Université de la Mode, 1991).

Scanlon, Jennifer. *Inarticulate Longings: The Ladies Home Journal, Gender and the Promises of Consumer Culture* (New York, London: Routledge, 1995).

Schneider, Sara K. *Vital Mummies: Performance Design for the Show-Window Mannequin* (New Haven and London: Yale University Press, 1995).

Schoeser, Mary and Celia Rufey. *English and American Textiles, from 1790 to the Present* (London: Thames and Hudson, 1989).

Schorman, Rob. *Selling Style: Clothing and Social Change at the Turn of the Century* (Philadelphia: University of Pennsylvania Press, 2003).

Schreier, Barbara A. *Fitting In: Four Generations of College Life* (Chicago:Chicago Historical Society, 1991).

Becoming American Women: Clothing and the Jewish Immigrant Experience, 1880–1920 (Chicago: Chicago Historical Society, 1994).

Scranton, Philip, ed., *Beauty and Business: Commerce, Gender, and Culture in Modern America* (New York, London: Routledge, 2001).

Scull, Penrose. *From Peddlers to Merchant Princes: A History of Selling in America* (Chicago and New York: Follett Publishing Company, 1967).

Seebohm, Caroline. *The Man Who Was Vogue: The Life and Times of Condé Nast* (New York: Viking Press, 1982).

Seeling, Charlotte. *Fashion: The Century of the Designer, 1900–1999* (Cologne: Koneman, 1999).

Seltzer, Mark. *Bodies and Machines* (New York and London: Routledge, 1992).

Sennett, Richard, ed., *Classic Essays on the Culture of Cities* (New York: Appleton-Century-Crofts, 1969).

Sennett, Richard. *Flesh and Stone: The Body and the City in Western Civilization* (New York: Norton 1994).

Severa, Joan. *Meet Bonnie Cashin, Clothes in the Twentieth Century: A Gallery Guide* (Madison Wisconsin: State Historical Society of Wisconsin, 1984).

Shannon, David A. *Between the Wars: America 1919–1941* (Boston: Houghton Mifflin Company, 1979).

Shi, David E. *Facing Facts: Realism in American Thought and Culture, 1850–1920* (New York and Oxford: Oxford University Press, 1995).

Shorter, Edward. *A History of Psychiatry: From the Era of the Asylum to the Age of Prozac* (New York, Brisbane and Toronto: John Wiley and Sons, 1997).

Smith, Catherine and Cynthia Grieg. *Women In Pants: Manly Maidens, Cowgirls and Other Renegades* (New York: Harry N. Abrams, 2003).

Snowman, Daniel. *America Since 1920* (London: Hiennemann, 1980).

Sochen, June. *Movers and Shakers: American Women Thinkers and Activists, 1900–1970* (New York: Quadrangle, 1973).

Solnit, Rebecca. *River of Shadows: Eadweard Muybridge and the Technology of the Wild West* (London: Penguin, 2003).

Sparhawk, Ruth M., *American Women in Sport, 1887–1987: A 100-Year Chronology* (Metuchen, New Jersey: Scarecrow Press, 1989).

Sparke, Penny. *As Long as It's Pink: The Sexual Politics of Taste* (London and San Francisco: Harper Collins, 1995).

Spivey, Donald, ed. *Sport in America: New Historical Perspective* (Westport, Connecticut and London: Greenwood Press, 1985).

Squiers, Carole, ed., *The Critical Image: Essays on Contemporary Photography* (Seattle: Bay Press, 1990).

Stange, Maren. *Symbols of Ideal Life: Social Documentary Photography in America 1890–1950* (Cambridge: CambridgeUniversity Press, 1990).

Starr, Roger. *The Rise and Fall of New York City* (New York: Basic Books, 1986).

Stearns, Peter N. *Fat History: Bodies and Beauty in the Modern West* (New York: New York University Press, 2002).

Steele, H. Thomas. *The Hawaiian Shirt* (London: Thames and Hudson, 1984).

Steele, Valerie. *Fifty Years of Fashion: New Look to Now* (New Haven and London: Yale, 1997).

Women of Fashion: Twentieth Century Designers (New York: Rizzoli, 1991).

Stern, Radu. *Against Fashion: Clothing As Art, 1850–1930* (Cambridge, Massachusetts and London: MIT Press, 2004).

Stevens, Mark. *Like No Other Store in the World: The Inside Story of Bloomingdales,* (New York: Crown, 1996).

Stewart, Mary Lynn. *For Health and Beauty: Physical Culture for Frenchwomen, 1880s–1930s* (Baltimore, Maryland and London: Johns Hopkins University Press, 2001).

Stimpson, Catharine R. *Women and the American City* (Chicago and London: University of Chicago Press, 1981).

Stoler, Mark A. and Melanie S. Gustafson, eds., *Major Problems in the History of World War II* (Boston and New York: Houghton Mifflin Company, 2003).

Stoneley, Peter. *Consumerism and American Girl's Literature, 1860–1940* (Cambridge and New York: Cambridge University Press, 2002).

Strom, Sharon Hartman. *Beyond the Typewriter: Gender, Class and the Origins of the Modern American Office Worker, 1900–1930* (Urbana and Chicago: University of Illinois Press, 1992).

Sullivan, Charles, ed., *American Beauties, Women in Art and Literature: Paintings, Sculptures, Drawings, Photographs and Other Works of Art from the National Museum of American Art, Smithsonian Institution* (New York: Harry N. Abrams in association with the National Museum of American Art, Smithsonian Institution, 1993).

Sussman, Warren I. *Culture as History: The Transformation of American Society in the Twentieth Century* (Washington D.C: Smithsonian Institution Press,1984).

Taylor, Lou. *The Study of Dress History* (Manchester: Manchester University Press, 2002).

Taylor, William R. *In Pursuit of Gotham: Culture and Commerce in New York* (New York and Oxford: Oxford University Press, 1992).

Teaford, Jon C. *The Twentieth Century American City* (Baltimore, Maryland and London: Johns Hopkins University Press, 1993).

Thesander, Marianne. *The Feminine Ideal* (London: Reaktion, 1997).

Thrahey, Jane, ed., *Harper's Bazaar: 100 Years of the American Female* (New York: Random House, 1967).

Tomerlin Lee, Sarah, ed., *American Fashion: The Life and Lines of Adrian, Mainbocher, McCardell, Norell, Trigere* (New York: Andre Deutsch, 1975).

Trachtenberg, Alan, Peter Neill and Peter C. Bunnell, eds., *The City: American Experience* (New York: Oxford University Press, 1971).

Reading American Photographs: Images as History, Mathew Brady to Walker Evans (New York: Hill and Wang, 1989).

The Incorporation of America: Culture and Society in the Gilded Age (New York: Hill and Wang, 1982).

Traub, Marrin and Tom Leicholz. *Like No Other Store...The Bloomingdales' Legend and the Revolution in American Marketing* (New York: Random House, 1993).

Turner, Peter, ed., *American Images: Photography 1945–1980* (London: Barbican Art Gallery and Penguin, 1985).

Vassiliev Aleksandere. *Beauty in Exile: The Artists, Models and Nobility who Fled the Russian Revolution and Influenced the World of Fashion* (New York and London: Harry N. Abrams, 2000).

Veillon, Dominique. *Fashion under the Occupation* (New York and Oxford: Berg, 2002).

Von Furstenberg, Diane. *Diane: A Signature Life* (New York: Simon and Schuster, 1998).

Vreeland, Diana. *American Women of Style: An Exhibition* (New York: Metropolitan Museum of Art, 1975).

D.V. (New York: Da Capo Press, 1997).

Dance (New York: Metropolitan Museum of Art, 1981).

The 10s, the 20s, the 30s: Inventive Clothes, 1909–1939 (New York: Metropolitan Museum of Art, 1973).

Wagner, Peter. *A Sociology of Modernity: Liberty and Discipline* (London and New York: Routledge, 1994).

Walker, Nancy A., ed., *Women's Magazines, 1940–1960: Gender Roles and the Popular Press* (Boston: Bedford and St. Martin's, 1998).

Wallach Scott, Joan. *Gender and the Politics of History* (New York: Columbia University Press, 1999).

Wandersee, Winifred D. *Women's Work and Family Values, 1920–40* (Cambridge, Massachusetts and London: Harvard University Press).

Ward, David and Olivier Zunz. *The Landscape of Modernity: Essays on New York City, 1900–1940* (New York: Russell Sage Foundation, 1992).

Ward, Graham, ed., *The Certeau Reader* (Oxford and Massachusetts: Blackwell, 2000).

Ware, Susan. *Beyond Suffrage: Women in the New Deal* (Cambridge, Massachusetts and London: Harvard University Press, 1981).

Holding Their Own: American Women in the 1930s (Boston: Twayne, 1982).

Modern American Women: A Documentary History (Chicago : Dorsey Press, 1989).

Letter to the World: Seven Women Who Shaped the American Century (Cambridge, Massachusetts and London: Harvard University Press, 2000).

Warner, Marina. *Monuments and Maidens: The Allegory of the Female Form* (London: Vintage, 1996).

Weatherfield, Doris. *American Women and World War Two* (New York: Facts on File, 1990).

Weegee's New York: Photographs 1935–1960 (Munich: Schirmer Art Books, 1996).

Welters, Linda and Patricia A. Cunningham, eds., *Twentieth Century American Fashion* (Oxford and New York: Berg, 2005).

Wexner Center for the Arts. *In Black and White: Dress from the 1920s to Today,* Wexner Center for the Arts, The Ohio State University, 12 April–9 August, 1992(Columbus, Ohio: Wexner Center for the Arts, 1992).

White, Nancy A., ed., *Women's Magazine's 1940 – 1960: Gender Roles and the Popular Press* (Boston: Bedford and St Martins, 1998).

White, Nancy and John Esten. *Style in Motion: Munkacsi Photography '20s, '30s, '40s* (New York: Clarkson N. Potter Inc, 1979).

White, Nicola. *Reconstructing Italian Fashion: America and the Development of the Italian Fashion Industry* (Oxford and New York: Berg, 2000).

Wigley, Mark. *White Walls, Designer Dresses: The Fashioning of Modern Architecture* (Cambridge Massachusetts and London: M.I.T. Press, 1995).

Williams, Esther, with Digby Diehl. *The Million Dollar Mermaid* (London: Pocket Books, 1999).

Williams, Raymond. *The Politics of Modernism: Against the New Conformity* (London and New York: Verso, 1994).

Williamson, Judith. *Consuming Passions: the Dynamics of Popular Culture* (London and New York: Marion Boyars, 1986).

Wilson, Richard Guy, Dianne H. Pilgrim and Dickran Tashjian. *The Machine Age in America, 1918–1941* (New York: Brooklyn Museum in association with Abrams, 1986).

Winkler, Mary G. and Letha B.Cole, eds., *The Good Body: Ascetism in Contemporary Culture* (New Haven and London: Yale, 1994).

Wolff, Janet. *Feminine Sentences: Essays on Women and Culture* (Oxford: Polity Press, 1990).

Woloch, Nancy. *Women and the American Experience* (New York: McGraw Hill, 1994).

Wood, Paul, Francis Frascina, Jonathan Harris and Charles Harrison, eds., *Modernism In Dispute: Art Since the Forties* (New Haven and London: Yale University Press in association with the Open University, 1993).

Woodham, Jonathan. *Twentieth Century Design* (Oxford: Oxford University Press, 1997).

Woodhead, Lindy. *War Paint: Helena Rubinstein and Elizabeth Arden, Their Lives, Their Times, Their Rivalry* (London: Virago, 2003).

Wosk, Julie. *Women and the Machine: Representations from the Spinning Wheel to the Electronic Age* (Baltimore, Maryland and London: Johns Hopkins University Press, 2001).

Yohannon, Kohle and Nancy Nolf. *Claire McCardell: Redefining Modernism* (New York: Harry N. Abrams, 1998).

Yohannon, Kohle. *John Rawlings: 30 Years in Vogue* (Santa Fe, New Mexico: Arena Editions, 2001).

Zingg, Paul L., ed., *The Sporting Image: Readings in American Sport History* (Lanham, New York and London: University Press of America, 1988).

Zunz, Olivier. *Why the American Century?* (Chicago and London: University of Chicago Press, 1998).

DISSERTATIONS

Donahue, Mary. 'Design and the Industrial Arts in America, 1894–1940: An Inquiry into Fashion Design and Art and Industry', PhD Dissertation (The City University of New York, 2001).

Johnson, S.A. 'The Consumption of Middle Class American Women's Clothing Through Mail Order Catalogs, 1850–1900', PhD Dissertation (University of Brighton, 2003).

Recordan, Susanne. 'The Birth of a New Art Form: A Study of Modern Dance of Ruth St Denis and Isadora Duncan as Expressions of American Culture in the Years, 1900–1939', M.A. Dissertation (University of Oregon, 1980).

White, Nicola. 'The Role of America in the Development of the Italian Fashion Industry, 1945–65' M.Phil. Dissertation (Kingston University, 1997).

JOURNAL ARTICLES

Adams, Samuel Hopkins. 'The Dishonest Paris Label', *Dress*, vol. 4 (1978): 17–23.

Albrecht, Juliana, Jane Farrell-Beck and Geitel Winakor. 'Function, Fashion and Convention in American Women's Riding Costume, 1880–1930', *Dress*, vol.15 (1988): 57–67.

Arnold, Rebecca. 'Looking American: Louise Dahl-Wolfe's Fashion Photographs in the 1930s and 1940s', *Fashion Theory, The Journal of Dress, Culture and Body*, vol. 6, issue 1 (2002): 45–60.

Martin Harrison and Lillian Bassman. 'Capturing the Intimate Gesture', *Graphis*, vol. 51, no. 298 (July–August 1995): 30–39.

Bill, Katina. 'Attitudes Towards Women's Trousers: Britain in the 1930s', *Journal of Design History*, vol. 6, no. 1 (1993): 45–54.

Boardman, Michelle. 'Shoulder to Shoulder: Women's Patriotic Scarves of World War Two', *Dress*, vol. 25 (1998): 3–16.

Boehlke, Heidi L. Ruth M. Kapinas, 'Munsingwear's Forgotten "Foundettes" Designer', *Dress*, vol. 20 (1993): 45–52.

Bryant, Nancy O. 'The Interrelationship between Decorative and Structural Design in Madeleine Vionnet's Work', *Costume*, no. 25 (1991): 73–88.

Buckland, Sandra Stansbery and Gwendolyn S. O'Neal. '"We Publish Fashions Because They Are News": The New York Times 1940 through 1945', *Dress*, vol. 25 (1998): 33–41.

Cooper, Arlene. 'Casual but Not that Casual, Fashion in the Fifties', *Dress*, vol. 11 (1985): 47–56.

Cunningham, Patricia. 'Swimwear in the 1930s: The B.V.D. Company in a Decade of Innovation', *Dress*, vol. 12 (1986): 11–27.

Fischer, Lucy. 'The Image of Woman as Image: The Optical Politics of Dames', in *Film Quarterly*, vol. XXX, no. 1 (Fall 1976): 2–11.

Gustafson, Robert. 'The Power of the Screen: The Influence of Edith Head's Film Design on the Retail Fashion Market', *The Velvet Light Trap*, no. 19 (1982): 8–15.

Hatchett, Tiffany Webber. 'Dorothy Shaver: Promoter of the "American Look",' in *Dress*, vol. 30 (2003): 80–90.

Haye, Amy de la. 'The Dissemination of Design from Haute Couture to Fashionable Ready-to-Wear Dress during the 1920s', *Textile History*, vol. 24 (1993): 39–48.

Jarvis, Anthea. (ed.). 'Methodology Issue', *Fashion Theory, The Journal of Dress, Body and Culture*, vol. 2, issue 4 (1998).

Kirkham, Pat. (ed.). 'Women Designers in the USA, 1900–2000', *Studies in the Decorative Arts* vol.VIII, no. I (Fall-Winter, 2000–2001).

Martin, Richard. 'The New Soft Look: Pollock, Beaton, American Fashion, 1951', *Dress*, vol. 7 (1981): 1–8.

Peiss, Kathy. 'Making Faces: The Cosmetics industry and the Cultural Construction of Gender, 1890–1930', *Genders*, no. 7 (Spring 1990): 143–169.

Pumphrey, Martin. 'The Flapper, the Housewife and the Making of Modernity', *Cultural Studies*, vol. 1, no. 2 (1987): 79–194.

Samek, Susan M. 'Uniformly Feminine: The "Working Chic" of Mainbocher', *Dress*, vol. 20 (1993): 33–44.

Sims, Joseph S. 'Adrian', *Costume*, vol.8 (1974): 13–17.

Stewart, Mary Lynn and Nancy Janovicek. 'Slimming the Female Body?: Re-evaluating Dress, Corsets, and Physical Culture in France, 1890s–1930s', *Fashion Theory, The Journal of Dress, Body and Culture*, vol. 5, issue 2 (2001): 173 –194.

Warner, Patricia Campbell. 'Clothing as Barrier: American Women in the Olympics, 1900–1920', *Dress*, vol. 12 (1997): 55–69.

'Public and Private: Men's Influence on American Women's Dress for Sport and Physical Education', *Dress*, vol. 14 (1988): 48–55.

Wass, Ann Bauermann and Clarita Anderson. 'What did Women Wear to Run?' *Dress*, vol. 17 (1990): 169–85.

MAGAZINES AND NEWSPAPERS

Anon. 'A Great Age', *Life*, Fall 1988.

Anon. 'Are You Cut Out for 7th Avenue?' *Mademoiselle*, March 1962.

Anon. 'Bonnie Cashin Obituary', *The Economist*, 12 February 2000.

Anon. 'Bonnie Cashin', *Harper's Bazaar*, July 2000.

Anon. 'Fashion's Grande Dame', *Harper's Bazaar*, February 1993.

Anon. 'In the Industry – Forum News', *Interior Design*, vol. 71, no. 8, 2000.

Anon. 'Louise Dahl – Wolfe: A Photographer's Scrapbook', *Vogue*, August 1984.

Anon. 'Social Study', *Vanity Fair*, January 1994.

Anon. 'Toni Frissell, Obituary', *Current Biography,* June 1988.

Anon. Vionnet', *Sunday Times Magazine,* 4 March 1973.

Astor, Josef and Nancy Franklin. 'Showcase: Refashioning Diana Vreeland', *The New Yorker,* 16 September 1996.

Kirkland, Sally. 'Arthur Penn's Open Door', *American Theatre,* 1 January, 1992.

Lambert, Eleanor. '1930s Fashion Publicist Eleanor Lambert recalls Era of Scandalous Elegance', *Vogue,* November 1999.

Nemy, Enid. 'Eleanor Lambert, Empress of Fashion, Dies at 100', *The New York Times,* 8 October 2003.

Pressler, Margaret Webb. 'Giving Us a Fit: 2,4,6,8, Some Consistent Sizing We'd Appreciate', *Washington Post,* 2 May 2004.

Scherman, Rowland and Hilton Als. 'Showcase: Diana Vreeland', *The New Yorker,* 22 September 1997.

Schiro, AnneMarie. 'Clare Potter, Who Set Trends In Women's Clothes, Dies at 95', *The New York Times,* 11 January 1999.

Scully, James. 'Cashin In', *Elle,* October 2000.

Spindler, Amy M. 'Critic's Notebook: Tracing the Look of Alienation', *The New York Times,* 24 March 1998.

Design For Living: Her Clothes Weren't Just Beautiful They Were Sophisticated Tools For Freedom And Fun' Bonnie Cashin Obituary, *The New York Times Magazine,* 7 January 2001.

Tapert, Annette. 'The American Comfort Class', *Harper's Bazaar,* September 1998.

Tomkins, Calvin. 'The World of Carmel Snow', *The New Yorker,* 7 November 1994.

White, Constance C. R. 'Fashion: Real to Bold and Vice Versa', *The New York Times,* 22 September 1998.

White, Constance, C. R. 'Celebrating Claire McCardell', *The New York Times,* 17 November 1998.

Wilson, Mary Louise. 'Where Are the Witty Bitches? How I fell for Diana Vreeland', *American Theatre,* October 1987.

Wulbern, Helen. 'Claire McCardell: A Discourse on Designing for Oneself', *WWD* 13 September 1999.

INDEX